FOLLOW THE MONEY

FOLLOW THE MONEY

Who Controls New York City Mayors?

LYNNE A. WEIKART

STATE UNIVERSITY OF NEW YORK PRESS

Published by
STATE UNIVERSITY OF NEW YORK PRESS, ALBANY

© 2009 State University of New York

For information, contact State University of New York Press, Albany, NY
www.sunypress.edu

Production and book design, Laurie Searl
Marketing, Anne M. Valentine

Library of Congress Cataloging-in-Publication Data

Weikart, Lynne A., 1943–
    Follow the money : who controls New York City mayors? / Lynne A. Weikart.
        p. cm.
    Includes bibliographical references and index.
    ISBN 978-1-4384-2531-3 (hardcover : alk. paper)
    ISBN 978-1-4384-2532-0 (pbk. : alk. paper)
    1. Mayors—New York (State)—New York. 2. Corporate power—New York (State)—
New York. 3. New York (N.Y.)—Politics and government. I. Title.

JS1234.A1W45 2009
974.7'10430922—dc22   2008027669

10 9 8 7 6 5 4 3 2 1

This book is dedicated to the next generation,

Eric and Jeanne.

CONTENTS

ILLUSTRATIONS

ACKNOWLEDGMENTS

This study has drawn upon primary source materials in New York City's Municipal Archives and the New York Public Library's collections in municipal history; I am indebted to both library staffs for their time and efforts in finding documents for me. I am also grateful to staff members from the Independent Budget Office and the New York State Financial Control Board for their research assistance. I benefited from the Archive on Municipal Finance and Leadership in the Newman Library at Baruch College. I would like to thank Professors Dall Forsythe, Dennis Judd, and Wilbur Rich for reading parts or all of this manuscript. Their readings were accompanied by many suggestions, for which I am grateful. At SUNY Press, my editor, Michael Rinella, was incredibly helpful as was Laurie Searl, Rosemary Wellner, and Anne Valentine. I am also grateful to Erin Niumata, a terrific editor. I am indebted to others who edited and offered advice—Barbara Buoncristiano and Sylvia Friedman—and to David Gentile for rescuing me whenever my knowledge of computers faltered. Most of all, I thank Laura Gentile for her never-ending encouragement, editing, and wisdom.

ONE

INTRODUCTION

"... control over capital flows allows the banking community to socially construct economic reality for governments and corporations alike."

—David Glasberg[1]

There were three revolutions in America: the overthrow of the British empire in 1776, the New Deal in the midst of the Great Depression of 1929, and Ronald Reagan's New Federalism. In the first American Revolution, American colonists revolted against their king in response to severe taxation and brutal economic conditions. In the second American Revolution, voters swept into office Franklin Delano Roosevelt who led Americans out of the collapse of capitalism by spending government money and fundamentally changing the role of government in the United States. Finally, in the third American Revolution, voters dissatisfied with deep inflation and an oil crisis voted in Ronald Reagan who, in 1980, ran on the slogan "Government was the problem, not the solution" and proceeded to "starve the beast" of tax revenue that had secured the New Deal safety net, largely revising the relationship between government and the governed.

The signs of the third American Revolution began earlier, in 1975, during the oil crisis, when New York City experienced its worst fiscal crisis since the Great Depression. Our focus is on this third revolution—the ways in which New York City presaged other municipal crises and was burdened by the national economy and new political regime in order to answer the question: who controls urban mayors?

New York has been a city of progressive thought and a provider of generous social services for its citizens beginning with the Great Depression of 1929. The Great Depression offered the opportunity for progressive elected officials to construct a safety net of social services for citizens. New York City did so by embracing redistributive policies. During the Depression, Mayor

1

Fiorello LaGuardia, with financial support from President Franklin Roosevelt, established extensive governmental services for city residents—public housing, new public schools, rent control, expansion of public health services, and public hospitals, to name just some of the most important actions. The Great Depression brought substantial progressive services for the city's citizens for over forty years until the fiscal crises of the 1970s unraveled the safety net of that earlier period.[2]

Today, the city retains a semblance of rent control, to the consternation of the powerful real estate lobby, and is one of the few remaining cities that does so. It supports eleven public hospitals, the only city in the nation to provide this service. It also has the largest public housing authority in the country. And it runs the country's third largest public university, which, until 1975, charged no tuition.[3]

Nevertheless, the city has also lost a great deal. The 1975 fiscal crisis sparked the end of an era in the history of New York City and in the history of America. In 1975, the city had a $1.5 billion deficit out of a $12 billion budget as well as $11.3 billion in debt of which $4.5 billion was in short-term notes maturing within a year.[4] Certainly, the city needed rescuing. The city, in effect, would run out of cash unless the banks bought its bonds, and this, in 1975, was what the banks refused to do. They declined to buy any more city bonds. "The terms of the financial rescue put the city in a budgetary straitjacket that made it impossible to sustain the high level of social activism and income redistribution that had characterized the Lindsay and Beame mayoral years."[5] In secret meetings with Mayor Abraham Beame, the Financial Community Liaison Group (FCLG), consisting of officials from the largest New York banks, insisted that the mayor slash services and end free tuition at the City University system.[6] Faced with the worst fiscal crisis since the Depression and under enormous pressure from the combined forces of Governor Carey and the FCLG, Mayor Beame agreed to charge tuition at the City University system (CUNY) and to lay off 40,000 workers, disrupting vital city services.

The cutbacks were devastating. The schools were in chaos as over 10,000 teachers were laid off; park maintenance was abandoned; crime increased as the police force was reduced; fire stations and health clinics were closed, and a third of CUNY's faculty was terminated. Tuition was established at CUNY that has now increased dramatically to $2,000 a semester.

The schools were beleaguered. Over a two-year period, from 1975 to 1977, over 5,700 classroom teachers in the elementary schools, over 2,000 in the junior high schools, and over 1,800 in the high schools were terminated. The impact of these layoffs was a loss of one in five teachers in elementary schools and about one in six on the upper levels.[7] And it was not simply teachers who were let go—assistant principals, guidance counselors (one out of every two at the elementary school level), school secretaries, thousands of paraprofessionals, school crossing guards, and security guards. The schools were in chaos from the loss of staff resources and from teacher transfers as seniority rights took precedent; teachers were transferred all over the city.

Public health was compromised for years to come. In 1977, the city's Department of Health (DOH) cut 1,700 staff members, 28 percent of its 1974 workforce.[8] The agency lost seven of its district health centers, dramatically curtailed its methadone program, terminated the employment of fourteen of nineteen health educators, and closed twenty of seventy-five child health centers (responsible for tuberculosis screening and diagnosis). At the city's Health and Hospitals Corporation (HHC), the city payroll was cut by 17 percent between 1975 and 1978. In 1975, HHC eliminated all of its fifty community-based clinics. John Holloman, president of HHC from 1974 to 1976, fought the cuts and was fired. These budget cuts played an important role in the resurgence of tuberculosis in the 1980s and the city's lack of preparation for dealing with the AIDS crisis.[9]

The Parks Department lost 1,440 employees in those two years. The green lawn in Sheeps Meadow became a dust bowl. The Parks Department has never recovered from the drastic cutbacks between 1975 and 1977. The city now spends the least on its parks of all high-density cities. Chicago, with only one-third of New York City's population, spends more on its parks. Among high-density cities, New York City ranks last in the number of swimming pools and recreation centers. Philadelphia has twice the number of pools and four times as many recreation centers for a population one-fifth New York City's size.[10]

The housing stock was equally devastated. Before the fiscal crisis, the city had one of the first programs in the United States that changed ownership of privately held buildings to low-income tenants. The program expanded rapidly so that "by 1973 there were 136 properties, which included a total of 286 buildings, at various stages of the process. However, only forty-two of these properties had completed rehabilitation and conversion when the program was aborted as a result of the New York City fiscal crisis in 1975."[11]

The subway system underwent radical reduction in services and a rapid increase in crime. The subway fare was increased 43 percent. Ridership dropped 27 percent between 1965 and 1982. Unmanageable graffiti, track fires, and frequent train breakdowns became nationally recognized symbols of the degradation of a once-great transit system, and the Second Avenue subway dig was stopped.[12]

Public safety suffered due to the devastating loss by the Police Department of 20 percent of its workforce. In 1972, the city's police force numbered 31,000; by 1980, it had shrunk to 22,000. Robberies had increased by 15 percent by 1983; murders saw a slight rise of 2 percent. The Fire Department had previously undergone cuts that were exacerbated during the fiscal crisis. Ladder companies were reduced from six to five people, and engine staffs were reduced from five to four people in 1975. "By 1976, and in rapid succession, some thirty-five fire companies had been removed from primarily high fire-incidence areas and fire department personnel had decreased from about 14,700 in 1970 to about 10,200 in 1976."[13] The "burning of the Bronx" was found to be closely related to the reduction in fire protection in the 1970s.

Another disappointing trend was the migration out of the city. Whites fled the city—almost two million left between 1975 and 1983. Although the methodology used for counting ethnicity changed somewhat between 1970 and 1980, the drop in the white population was still quite serious. Both the African American and Hispanic communities saw slight increases, but New York City's population was in serious decline, dropping from 7.9 million to 7.1 million by 1983.[14] In addition, the median family income fell from $43,952 in 1969 to $38,593 in 1979 as the more educated populace left for the suburbs. The percentage of households with low income increased by almost 10 percent while medium- and high-income households decreased 3.3 percent and 5.4 percent, respectively.[15] New York City was no longer perceived as an attractive place to live.

City residents were infuriated at the ravaging of city services. Abe Beame, a former city comptroller who had won his job on a platform of financial responsibility, lost all credibility with the voters and became a one-term mayor. No one denies that the city spent more than its revenues. What is open for interpretation was why the only solution involved drastic cutbacks that created miserable living conditions in the city, resulting in a mass exodus to the suburbs for those who could afford it. Why did conservative forces demand cutbacks before helping the city regain its financial stability? Could Mayor Beame have adopted different strategies to avoid this devastation? Could anyone?

The fiscal crisis did not end with Mayor Beame's tenure. The Municipal Assistance Corporation (MAC), Emergency Financial Control Board (EFCB), and the New York State Special Deputy Comptroller for New York City—all institutions created by the combined forces of New York State officials and bankers during the fiscal crisis—have constrained the fiscal policy choices of subsequent mayors to this day, more than thirty years after the fiscal crisis.

Municipal creditors were commercial banks and are now investment banks that buy and sell bonds to individual American and foreign investors, pension funds, mutual funds, insurance companies, and overseas governments. Bankers are financial intermediaries who provide financial services to all levels of government—they buy and sell government bonds. These financial leaders profit from the need for all levels of government to borrow funds for long-term capital improvements (bonds) or short-term revenue needs (revenue anticipation notes or tax anticipation notes). Government bonds represent a promise by government to pay back lenders both the principal and interest of the amount borrowed. The borrowed funds are used for a vast array of projects.

Although there are several bond sectors—corporate, U.S. Treasury, agency, asset-backed securities, mortgage, and municipal—we are focused on the municipal bond market in which state and local governments and their authorities raise funds. The municipal bond market is made up of many kinds of professionals. Principally, there are the sellers (state and local government officials) and the buyers (bank corporations, mutual funds, insurance firms, individual investors, etc.). For New York City, Wall Street banks often become the underwriters, buying the city's bonds and reselling them to investors of all kinds. The underwriters, in effect, manage the sale of the bonds. These banks often form underwriting syndicates and work together to sell billions of bonds for the city.

Each subsequent mayor experienced sizeable fiscal crises. From 1975 to the present, New York City has undergone cycles of economic strength and decline—fat surpluses followed by huge deficits. These cycles are closely related to national and regional economic trends.[16] In each of these subsequent crises, the financial structures established during the 1975 fiscal crisis have dominated New York City fiscal policy. These institutions call upon the city to reduce taxes and cut back government services based on the theory that private business will be stimulated by the tax reductions and that less government spending means more capital for the private sector. However, at some point, having fewer government services works against the city's ability to be attractive enough for business.

The financial elites use their power to control the city's access to the bond market to pressure city officials to keep taxes low and spending lower. All mayors have felt this pressure. During the 1975 fiscal crisis, Ellmore (Pat) C. Patterson, chief executive officer of JP Morgan; Walter Wriston, chief executive officer of Citibank; David Rockefeller of Chase; and Chairman Gabriel Hauge of Manufacturer's Hanover Trust formed the FCLG to put pressure on the mayor to cut his proposed budget. In 1979, Mayor Koch faced extreme fiscal pressure from Comer S. Coppie, executive director of FCB, when he sought to rehire sanitation workers.[17] In 1993, Felix G. Rohatyn, a partner at Lazard Freres, and chairman of MAC, demanded and got Mayor Dinkins' financial team to meet in Rohatyn's office to make last-minute changes to the budget. When Mayor Giuliani put together his first budget, the FCB warned him that hiring was out of bounds. Only Mayor Bloomberg, a highly successful business executive, who filled his first budget with one-shots, was treated with deference by financiers.[18]

Through this case study of New York City's fiscal crises, we consider the strength of the financial elites in their relationships with elected officials. Is it possible for mayors to oppose business interests or is the influence of the financial elites indomitable? If states are in close alliance with financial elites, what kinds of options do urban mayors have in developing local fiscal policy? Elkin maintains that "political leaders have choices in how to respond to this economic context."[19] As the world center of financial services, New

York City is an informative case study of the power that financial elites exert over the political leadership and how mayors can push back to assert their own political agendas. In the final analysis, although some mayors do achieve their own policy initiatives, their choices are significantly limited by these powers of the financial interests.

TWO

THEORIES ABOUT URBAN POLITICAL

POWER AND FINANCIAL ELITES

They (real estate and oil interests) committed a sin against the family of
New York. They cost us our investment rating. They did it cynically and
they did it arrogantly.

—Governor Mario Cuomo, 1983[1]

The history of the United States can be examined through several lenses.
It is the history of the power of ideas centering on the natural rights of
the individual. It is a history of our military power, from a fledging state at
first in Concord and Lexington to the later supreme military power in the
world displayed in the destruction of Hiroshima. It is also a history of the
power of creditors over debtors as recession after recession demonstrated
the struggle between the two. The following are some examples of these
financial power struggles.

When Americans declared their freedom from Britain, they did so
in part because of the struggle between British creditors and American
debtors. In 1777, the Virginia legislature passed an act to sequester British
property. Virginia citizens could nullify their debts to the British by paying
the amount they owed to Virginia's treasury.[2] Of course, payments could be
made in Virginia's paper currency, rather than British pounds, which was far
cheaper. Paper currency was worth only a tenth of the British pound. Hence,
plantation owners in Virginia were eager to cut ties with the British.

Shay's Rebellion (named after Daniel Shay, a revolutionary war
hero) is another example of creditors and debtors at war with one another.
And this time they were all Americans. After the Revolutionary War, in
1786, Massachusetts farmers protested the seizing of their farms for debts.
The farmers, retired revolutionary soldiers who had returned home with

7

government certificates found to be worthless, discovered their land taxes to be horribly burdensome and were unable to pay their debts. Farms were then seized by creditors (merchants and government officials). Over 4,000 farmers organized and marched on debtors' courts to stop the foreclosures.[3] The rebellion was over by 1787 when the governor of Massachusetts, James Bowdoin, organized a militia that fired on the farmers and routed them. Shay's Rebellion convinced the merchant class that a stronger national government was a must.

In 1819, the nation's economic expansion ended as the Second Bank of the United States tightened credit due to western land speculation. The bank called in its loans, meaning that state banks that had taken out loans from the Second Bank became the debtors and felt the squeeze. Quickly, the state banks in their role as creditors tightened credit on those who had borrowed from them—the land speculators, the new debtors, who could not repay their debts. When these speculators defaulted, the state banks failed, and farmers and merchants lost needed credit. State banks foreclosed on farms and the nation's prosperity was curtailed.[4] Struggles between creditors and debtors continued throughout the nineteenth century.[5] The struggle between creditors and debtors also takes place between bankers and cities (the debtors).

Until the 1840s, the states issued far more debt than municipalities, with the states issuing over $175 million as compared to the $25 million for municipalities. The 1837 depression brought on numerous defaults on state debt issues. As a result, the states passed stricter regulation on state issuance of debt. Only five states currently have no constitutional limitations on government obligation bonds.[6] Municipalities began issuing debt, filling the void of state bonds. By 1870, state debt had doubled to $353 million, yet local debt had grown to $516 million.[7] Following the financial collapse of 1873, states moved to some regulation of municipal debt financing. Restrictions were usually some combination of "prohibitions against lending to private individuals or corporations, requirements to hold referenda before issuing bonds, and caps on the ratio of outstanding debt to assessed valuation."[8]

In 1913, Congress succeeded in passing a federal income tax. Interest earned from municipal bonds, unlike corporate bonds, was exempted from the 1913 income tax law. Interest earned from municipal bonds is usually exempt from state and local taxes as well. The consequence of this tax exemption is that the bonds provide a reasonable rate of return and become a very attractive and stable investment for many Americans.

During the Great Depression, more than 11,000 banks failed. As a result, federal officials passed new laws and tightened regulations separating commercial banks in which deposits were kept and investment banks in which the selling of securities was permitted. The centerpieces of this regulation were the Glass-Steagall Act of 1932 and the Bank Act of 1933 that provided deposit insurance and separated commercial and investment banking. Under these new laws, commercial banks were not permitted to underwrite corporate stocks or bonds, although they were allowed to underwrite state and municipal government obligation bonds. Corporate stocks and bonds were considered too risky; from now on, investment banks would become the providers of Wall Street while commercial banks would maintain the less lucrative functions—taking individual deposits, clearing checks, and making loans.[9] Subsequently, the state and municipal bond markets became an important profit center for commercial banks.

The state and local bond market grew enormously after World War II from $5.3 billion in 1950 to $60 billion in 1975. Currently, there are over $1.5 trillion in municipal bonds (munis) outstanding in the country. There is also an exchange by which bonds can be resold to institutional and individual investors throughout the life of the bond.

For many years, bonds were government obligation bonds (GOs), backed by the full faith and credit of the government issuing the bonds. The GOs are quite secure because, in case of bankruptcy, the government issuing the bonds guarantees payment. Yet state constitutional debt limitations were circumvented. Beginning in the 1970s, a shift occurred; financial interests created many different types of debt instruments that were not GOs and did not require voter approval. Revenue bonds, backed by a specific state or city asset, became popular.

Revenue bonds were not backed by the state but instead by the revenue flow that ensued from the project generated by the bonds—tolls for bridges and fees for utilities. This type of debt was called nonguaranteed debt. Courts have ruled that constitutional limitations on debt do not apply to revenue bonds because taxpayers are not directly liable.[10] Of course, the changes from GOs to nonguaranteed debt resulted in significantly higher borrowing costs.

Another type of borrowing is lease-purchase agreements or lease-payment agreements. In lease-purchase agreements, a state or local government sells an asset to a state corporation (authority) that then leases the building back to the state or local government. The prime example of lease-purchase occurred when New York State sold Attica Prison to a New York State–created authority, the Urban Development Corporation (UDC), for $200 million, which helped meet the state's budget gap. The UDC then issued thirty-year bonds to pay for the cost of the prison. Unfortunately, with interest, the UDC will pay out far more than $200 million. Usually, lease-payment agreements are more common; that is, a public authority will issue nonguaranteed lease-payment bonds to build a facility and then the state will lease the facility from the public authority.

There are also short-term securities called notes, lasting less than a year, that come in many different kinds—tax anticipation notes (TANs), revenue anticipation notes (RANs), and bond anticipation notes (BANs). These types of notes are issued in anticipation of taxes, revenue, or bond offerings. If they are issued in the investor's home state, they are usually exempt from state and city taxes. In New York State, school districts often issue revenue anticipation notes while awaiting receipt of state aid.

Another type of bond was industrial revenue bonds (IRBs), tax-exempt bonds that state and local governments issue to finance endeavors by private firms. In effect, the bond was a loan to a private company. The backing for such bonds was the revenue from the financed projects. The reason for such bonds was to promote private industries by lowering their borrowing costs. This was done in two ways. First, often the private company benefited from a property tax exemption for the life of the bond. Second, an IRB offered tax exemptions to the private companies. These IRBs became particularly popular in the 1960s onward as the northeastern and midwestern states sought to compete with the southern and western regions of the country as jobs and populations moved. Concerned with the loss of revenue, by 1968, Congress had limited the federal tax exemption for IRBs with some exceptions such as airports and convention centers. But IRBs still offer property tax exemptions and sometimes federal tax exemptions.

Until the 1975 fiscal crisis, the major buyers of general obligation municipal bonds were commercial banks. In the 1975 fiscal crisis, it was usually the heads of commercial banks, such as Chase, Citibank, and JP Morgan, who led the fight to resolve the city's fiscal crisis. Commercial banks began to disengage from the municipal bond market for more lucrative pastures during the 1970s fiscal crises in U.S. cities. Bonds purchased by commercial banks were replaced by financial intermediaries, mutual funds, insurance companies, and individual investors. See Table 2.1.[11]

Of course, the institution of banking has changed dramatically since the 1975 fiscal crisis. As a result of that crisis, Congress passed the Securities Acts Amendments of 1975 which created the Municipal Securities Rulemaking Board (MSRB) to regulate the buying and selling of municipal bonds. Its authority extended only to the municipal securities activities of banks; the MSRB had no authority over cities or states that issue municipal bonds.

Table 2.1 Holdings of municipal bonds by category of investor, 1980–1999

Category	1970	1980	1989	1999
Commercial banks	48.6%	37.3%	11.8%	7.2%
Households	31.6	26.2	48.2	35.0
Property and casualty insurance companies	12.3	20.2	11.9	13.7
Financial intermediaries (mutual funds)	3.1	1.6	15.9	33.7
Other	4.5%	14.8%	12.2%	10.4%

Source: Westalotemel; Lamb and Rappaport.

During the 1980s, the nation lost the "hometown banker" and, in his place, national and international bankers bought up regional banks. These national bankers were far removed from the parochial concerns of a town and more concerned with the inner workings of the national or international banking system. In 1986, the Federal Reserve Board, using its power under the Bank Holdings Act, permitted commercial banks to obtain up to 5 percent of their gross revenues from investment banking business. In the next year, the Federal Reserve Board allowed investment banks to handle municipal revenue bonds. The Federal Reserve Board permitted the partial integration of commercial and investment banking until the Glass-Steagall Act was repealed. The merging of commercial and investment banking was not complete until the Financial Services Modernization Act of 1999 when Congress repealed the Glass-Steagall Act.

The financial services establishment organizes itself into organizations to lobby government officials and influence public decision-making. Two nonprofits were organized to represent their points of view. The Citizens Budget Commission (CBC) is a nonprofit, nonpartisan organization begun in 1932 in the midst of the Great Depression to examine and report on the finances of New York City and State governments. Its 130 members are a who's who of financial and real estate leadership in New York City. The CBC members see themselves as both a research organization and a monitoring organization making recommendations to city and state leaders about financial and management issues. When the CBC issues a report, the mayor, governor, city council members, and state legislators listen. The CBC's staff is highly skilled, knowledgeable, and experienced.

Businesspeople have organized themselves in associations to protect their interests since the beginning of our country's history. The New York Chamber of Commerce was founded in 1768 by "a group of merchants whose purpose was to encourage business and industry . . . and encourage the development of growing industries."[12] It merged with the New York City Partnership, which was also a nonprofit organization that consisted of two hundred CEOs from top corporate, financial, and entrepreneurial firms and was founded by David Rockefeller in 1979 after the 1975 fiscal crisis. The two organizations merged to become the Partnership for New York City.

New York City expects to have about $48.4 billion of general obligation bond debt by 2010. Much of this debt is for its capital plan—new school construction, bridge reconstruction, highways, sewage systems, and a water filtration plant. In 2006, the city issued $6.78 billion of long-term bonds to finance its capital needs and refinance certain outstanding bonds to capture a lower interest rate.

In 2002, the city paid underwriting fees of about $7,380 per $1 million of bonds.[13] Thus, when the city sells $1 billion worth of bonds in one issue, the city pays the underwriters a great deal of money. In 2006, the largest Wall Street banks that manage the offerings of New York City's municipal bonds are investment banking institutions such as Merrill Lynch, Citigroup, Bear Stearns, and Morgan Stanley.[14] As of 2007, there were four Wall Street banks chosen through competition to be the underwriters of planned debt sales for the city: Merrill Lynch, Citigroup, Bear Stearns, and Morgan Stanley will lead banks in managing offerings of governmental obligation bonds. The underwriting fees will average $5.46 per $1,000 bond. In addition, Goldman Sachs Group Inc., Lehman Brothers Holdings Inc., JPMorgan Chase & Co., and Morgan Stanley will be the underwriters for the New York City Transitional Finance Authority (TFA), which permits the city to borrow beyond its constitutional debt limit.

Across the country, state and local governments have created government corporations (authorities) that are given authority to sell bonds in order to construct and operate facilities for the public or to coordinate work in the public sphere. Perhaps the best known are the Port Authority of New York and New Jersey and the Metropolitan Transit Authority. Usually governed by boards and appointed by governors, such authorities do not need approval from state and local officials or voters to sell their bonds. Special districts with authority to sell bonds are usually created for water, sewer, and utility services. For example, over the years, officials in New York have created over seven hundred public authorities, many of them operated by independent boards appointed by the governor and other state officials. These public authorities control the capital budget of the state and wield tremendous power through massive resources and sizeable tracts of land within the major cities, including New York City. Governor Nelson Rockefeller prided himself on the creation of numerous public authorities to finance and meet the capital needs of the state. Total authority debt in New York State in 2005 was $124 billion. Of this, $45 billion was state-funded debt, which means that New York State pays the debt service (interest payments and principal for a fiscal year) on that debt out of its expense budget.

The bond market is not apolitical. These financial institutions and the people who run them wield enormous power over municipalities because of the sheer amount of money that cities need to borrow from these financial institutions to finance capital construction or to borrow in anticipation of future revenues. If investors lose confidence in the city's financial management, then they may not buy the bonds necessary for a city to maintain its infrastructure or its spending plans.

It is, however, a two-way street. There is a governing motto—"pay to play"—even after regulations were put into effect (G-37) by the Municipal Securities Rulemaking Board to prevent underwriters from making large political contributions to politicians. *The Bond Buyer* is the daily trade publication for the public finance industry. In October 2002, *The Bond Buyer* "surveyed political races in Massachusetts, New York, and Pennsylvania and found that wives of municipal finance professionals covered by G-37 were actively making campaign contributions to those running for office.

If elected, these officials could influence the selection of municipal bond underwriters."[15] Nothing prohibits firms from donating to political parties rather than politicians, which is what Governor Pataki announced in his 1997 fund-raiser—"the invitations stated that anyone covered by G-37 should make a donation to the New York Republican Party's housekeeping account rather than to his campaign."[16]

Closely related to banking institutions are the credit rating agencies. Credit ratings are provided by several private companies. The three most prominent credit rating agencies are Standard & Poor's, Fitch Ratings, and Moody's. Private credit rating agencies issued publicly available bond ratings beginning in 1909 and, in 1918, began rating municipal bonds. In 1936, federal regulators required banks to invest in bonds that were at least "investment grade" (BBB or above). In 1975, the Securities & Exchange Commission (SEC) created the category "Nationally recognized statistical rating organizations" (NRSRO), and included the three largest rating companies in this category. In 2006, Congress passed the Credit Rating Agency Reform Act—which sought to improve credit rating quality—after the Enron and WorldCom scandals.

Beginning in the 1980s, the credit rating agencies became more prominent as the watchdogs of fiscal concerns in municipalities. These agencies were part of the financial structures created to ensure financial security for those involved. States and municipalities depend on the credit ratings and risk assessments of credit rating agencies in order to sell their bonds to finance city services, including schools, highways, hospitals, bridges, and tunnels. With the financial services crisis of 2008, the credit rating agencies became even more important as fiscal watchdogs of municipal finances.

Urban power theorists have seldom studied financial elites at the local level, yet Mollenkopf conducted a useful analysis of urban theories that have an impact on urban fiscal policy.[17] Mollenkopf separated theorists into two camps: pluralists and structuralists. Pluralists emphasized bargaining among a multiplicity of interests that defined the urban power structure and de-emphasized economic power. Structuralists emphasized the relationship between the state and the underlying socioeconomic system that shapes the political agenda. Pluralists, such as Sayre and Kaufman, divided the city between resource providers and service demanders, and concluded that no one group dominated decision making.[18] Other pluralists, such as Ester Fuchs, examined weak mayors and strong interest groups in New York City and concluded that such a combination led to New York City's fiscal crisis.[19] The structuralists are in several camps: regime theory (Stone), public choice critiques (Peterson), and neo-Marxist critiques (Glasberg). Mollenkopf then sought to create a theoretical synthesis among these camps by emphasizing that urban government must interact in two environments—the political and electoral one, and the economic one. In so doing, he sought to broaden the pluralist camp to include private market interests and improve the structuralist approach by "according the political/electoral arena an influence equal to that of economic forces."[20] His synthesis concluded that the political/electoral arena was an influence equal to the market. Mollenkopf's synthesis is important because pluralism has much to offer for understanding the urban political arena. Pluralists correctly delineated the multiple interest groups that influence a city's public policies. Yet pluralists remain blind to the incredible powers of financial interests as compared to other interests.

Mollenkopf is hopeful, but there are limits to his thesis. Time and time again, during the fiscal crises in New York City, mayors attempted to construct political coalitions that would support public policies that were not necessarily in agreement with the private market interests. However, rarely were the mayors successful. The most successful was Mayor LaGuardia in a time before the postindustrial revolution and before the structural changes in New York State law that dictated fiscal policies to New York City. Can it be that the structural changes made to our public institutions during fiscal crises so altered the political landscape in favor of market interests as articulated by financial elites that it became even more difficult for political coalitions to exert any significant influence?

REGIME THEORY

To explore this question, we will examine the role of financial elites in the management of the city's fiscal crises with a focus on the close relationship between financial elites and state officials during fiscal crises. Both regime theory and growth machine theories are useful in locating the role of financial elites. Much has been written about regimes, the combination of formal organizations and informal networks. Regimes are networks, a result of local coalition building among economic and political elites, designed to protect and improve the economic health of their city.[21] The model posits that a "consensus emerges from the interaction between political and economic interests, a confluence of public and private power."[22]

While regime theorists recognize the centrality of economics in urban affairs, they maintain that there are other considerations and that economic strategies are only part of the picture. Stone maintains that, despite pressures from globalization, the interaction between mayor and citizenry need not follow financial dictates.[23] Stone is as hopeful as Mollenkopf. In reality, however, Stone could only name a few alternative examples—San Francisco, Cleveland, and Chicago—all three of which adopted an alternative form for a very short period. Stone, the leader of regime theorists, seeks to establish that politics matter in urban affairs and that economic determinism is too restrictive to explain decision making at the local level. Stone observes, "The imperatives to respond to economic competition are not so all-encompassing or even so clear on many occasions as to dictate a mayor's actions."[24] He concludes that local officials have some degree of control over their financial goals. Other authors concur, such as Ferman, who examines mayors in Boston and San Francisco and finds that mayoral policies can "modify what appear to be structural imperatives."[25]

Then how do we reconcile the role of financial elites and democracy? Elkin carries regime theory further into the pluralist camp, describing a commercial republic linking democracy and capitalism, while acknowledging certain contradictions. The struggle becomes how to promote greater political equality and popular control, and how to ameliorate the business privilege in politics. Reich addresses this question of balance in his book, *In Reconstructing Times Square*, in which he recognizes the dominance of the economic elites but emphasizes the "importance of pursuing democracy and authenticity in urban development."[26]

What are the limitations of regime theory? First, regime theory credits political coalitions with the ability to establish alternative forms to a political/economic coalition, although regime theorists can offer only a few examples. Second, regime theory does not give enough weight to the contribution of the larger environment within which city officials must make decisions, particularly when the economic cycle is at its nadir.

This larger environment consists of specific arenas, one of which is the state and its officials. State governors bring a great deal of power to bear on choices that city officials make. Cities are generally treated in American law as creatures of the state. Frug pointed out that even after home rule "cities are free of state control under home rule only on matters purely local in nature."[27] Turner observes that governors retain the authority and resources to participate as partners in urban development regimes.[28] Consider the 1975 fiscal crisis when Mayor Beame sought to increase taxes. Like most cities, New York City cannot raise taxes, except for the property tax, unless the state legislature agrees, and, in this case, the state legislature initially refused to authorize tax increases. Counties, within which cities exist, can have enormous influence on public policy within a city, although New York City does not have this issue due to coterminous boundaries. These external actors command resources and influence state law. Regime theorists often ignore these other governments and the consequent straitjacket in which elected officials find themselves when dealing with financial elites who invariably have a great influence on state officials during hard times.

PUBLIC CHOICE THEORISTS

Early on, Paul Peterson, advocating an economic development agenda, clearly defined the policy limits of American cities through his analysis of the limited choices facing city officials. The "primary interest of cities [is] the maintenance and enhancement of their economic activity."[29] Building on Musgrave's resource allocation categories, Peterson examined three resource allocation arenas—developmental, allocational, and redistributive—and concluded that a city's focus had to be on economic development. Peterson's form of economic determinism had a profound effect on the study of cities. Scholars moved toward a gloomier and more dire prediction of the future of American cities as caught in a web of economic forces. Mollenkopf responded to Peterson's economic determinism with his book, *The Contested City*, making the case that political factors, not economic ones, are central to urban policy.[30] He traced the web of federal urban development programs and established that initiatives for policy developments came from the political system and were not driven solely by economics. Mollenkopf succeeded in integrating economic variables within a political analysis with this book. However, his analysis did not focus on times of recession, only those of growth.

GROWTH MACHINE THEORISTS

Growth machine theorists define cities as engines of economic development led by business interests. Growth machine theorists give little support to the idea that mayors can exert some control over the allocation of resources. Most of the major growth machine theorists concentrate on land-based economic power. Logan and Molotch, critics of regime theorists, are major growth machine theorists. They posit that too little attention is paid to financial and business interests. Logan and Molotch reach the heart of the relationship between economic interests and mayors when they focus on "land-based" economic elites interested in attracting investment, concentrating on economic development, and pressuring mayors to invest in development functions.[31] Logan and Molotch's work has been endorsed by many, including Vojnovic, who points out that growth "is not viewed as inevitable or a rational fiscal response, but rather, as a policy outcome potentially resulting from effective politicking by the city's elites."[32] Vojnovic maintained that the benefits to a member of the financial elite could also mean heavy burdens for others. At one point, Molotch anticipated the development of a countercoalition "organized around environmental and redistributional concerns." Such a coalition could become a powerful adversary to economic elites.[33] Domhoff, famous for his analysis of power elites at the national level, endorsed the concept of land-based growth coalitions.[34]

    Another major growth machine theorist is Andrew Glasberg, one of the few political scientists to closely examine the power of financial institutions in the fiscal crises of Cleveland, among other entities. Glasberg concluded that banks had enormous power to declare a crisis; Glasberg saw banks as having enormous power to construct the social and economic environment of cities and countries.[35] Indeed, during hard times, residents were often asked to sacrifice in different ways, such as accepting lower wages to convince a company to relocate to their city or agreeing to a smaller tax base, reducing school funding to keep a corporation from moving away. Renney described the limited choices available to Mayor Harold Washington in Chicago when confronting steelworkers seeking to keep their plant open: "Broadening the base of support for the mayor meant accommodating those interests—land developers, lawyers, big organized labor, and others—that in an earlier period had formed the backbone of the pro-growth alliance."[36]

Robert Fitch's book, The Assassination of New York, demonstrates the incredible power held by real estate and financial elites in New York City. "Comprehensive planning south of Canal Street begins in 1958 with David Rockefeller's Downtown Lower Manhattan Plan . . . which featured a complete post-industrial makeover for the downtown office district."[37] Like other growth machine theorists, Fitch understands the power of controlling land use. In addition, he combined these insights with the financial acumen of the Rockefeller family, clearly demonstrating the broad reach the Rockefellers held over New York City.

The growth machine theorists recognized the inequities residents can suffer at the hands of economic development. Lichten sees this period as the austerity period—a time of class conflict caused by fiscal crises. Glasberg, who focused on banking institutions, painted a bleak story and was the only growth machine theorist who emphasized financial rather than land economic power.

GLOBALIZATION THEORISTS

Other theorists examine the "dual city," a city with a growing inequality of income. This polarization is a result of the dualism of a global economy that promotes the rise of a wealthy class tied to the new financial services economy and leaves behind a growing number of people who cannot find a niche in the new urban economy.[38] William Robinson has created a theory of global capitalism that examines a range of classes: industrial capital, commercial capital, and financial capital.[39] He goes further and describes a transnational class that is splitting from the traditional national classes. Sassen depicts the economic restructuring affecting cities in several ways: the loss of manufacturing jobs and the growth of services, the geographic redistribution of those jobs both within the United States and outside it, a shift in the wage structure with a greater incidence of low-wage, low-skill jobs and high-wage professional jobs in service industries at the same time, and the feminization of the job supply.[40] Such theories of globalization challenge the idea that mayors can prevail when up against financial elites.

Globalization and the resultant intense economic competition place enormous stress on American cities to protect their economic bases.[41] The relocation of corporations to other countries throughout the world threatens localities with job losses, and, therefore, losses in their local tax base: "there is a new hyper mobility of capital that is placing local jobs and local tax bases at risk. The relocation of major employers threatens local economies and hence the jobs of not just those employed by them but also of those working in the local service sector, and in local government."[42]

To deal with these threats, elected urban officials organize their constituents to promote their city as a climate in which corporations can flourish. They champion their city as the ideal place for further investment with no need for businesses to leave and every reason for new businesses to relocate to their city. Elected officials are often persuaded that their only option is to create a good business climate by minimizing government, taxes, and regulation.[43] As the new international economy of globalization grows, cities place economic development as their highest priority. Fainstein explained this "entrepreneurship" in the cities: "Whereas city governments once restricted their activities to building infrastructure and providing services, virtually all now take an active role in promoting economic growth."[44] Such a priority requires the partnership, and perhaps even the domination, of corporate and financial elites in policy setting.[45] This power that corporate and financial elites wield by threatening to leave a city or negotiating tax breaks to come to a city is not new; what is new is the intensity of that power. The urban globalization urban literature predicts diminishing local autonomy in local decision making.

Sinclair (2005) examines the role of the credit rating agencies in the era of globalization.[46] Rating agencies operate between government and the market and, as such, play a crucial role in legitimizing local governments' strategies. These rating agencies have a professional expertise needed by all the players to set standards so that the market can function confidently. Yet there is no institution that holds these private agencies accountable. They avoid financial responsibility for "bad calls" because they are only issuing an opinion; no investor needs to follow their opinion. Sinclair describes the actions of the rating agencies as the "private making of public policy" because these agencies by definition set limits as to what elected officials can choose to do.[47]

STATE CONTROL

Some legal theorists are in agreement with public choice theorists that cities have city limits. Cities have limited autonomy because of state authority. Gerald Frug, a legal scholar, explains: "A city is the only collective body in America that cannot do something simply because it decides to do it. Instead, under American law, cities have power only if state governments authorize them to act."[48] When a city experiences fiscal stress, state officials have the authority to take any number of actions such as raising or lowering taxes in that city, creating institutions to monitor that city's finances, or forcing the city into bankruptcy. Cities are extremely limited in how they can approach a fiscal problem without turning to the state: "city government is itself a weak player in a larger system of power."[49]

New York State's control of its municipalities lies in its constitution in which several articles dictate the limits of local autonomy. Article VIII, Finance Law, and Article IX, Home Rule, set limits on local control. The state legislature adopts laws to enforce the state constitution. The finance law sets limits on the power of local governments to tax themselves and incur debt. Home rule is an affirmative grant of power, but has restrictions in that debt ceilings are in place. In addition, a municipality cannot raise taxes except for the property tax without the consent of the state legislature. Under home rule, municipalities must not adopt any local law that is inconsistent with the state law or constitution.[50]

In the 1800s, New York's limiting municipal autonomy duplicated state efforts across the nation. States sought to limit the amount of debt municipalities could incur after the Civil War when, at one point, one-fifth of all municipal bonds were in some form of default.[51] In 1853, New York passed a law restricting the amount of municipal debt. Later, in 1884, the New York State Constitution was amended to tie the debt amount to the assessed value of taxable property within a municipality. However, the state legislature had authority to write in exceptions to this requirement. In her book, *Class, Tax, and Power*, Irene Rubin explored the control of the states over municipalities and found great variation among the states.[52] Regardless of the variation, most states had a great deal of involvement in local finance.

To further municipal limitations, the courts, basing their decisions on English law, ruled that state control of municipal governments was essential to minimizing the mingling of public and private functions. Federal Judge Dillon in his *Treatise on the Law of Municipal Corporations of 1872* made clear that municipalities had been irresponsible in their investments in private enterprises and that the states needed to set limits.[53] Dillon's rule, which stated that cities are creatures of the states, had a widespread influence in courts around the country. States were encouraged by his decision to rein in municipalities' enthusiasm for debt.

Although Ester Fuchs heaped blame for the city's fiscal crisis on strong interest groups, she did examine a state-oriented perspective.[54] The legal arrangement between the state and the city meant that New York City, unlike Chicago, could not share its enormously expensive redistributive programs with counties. This legal arrangement meant that Albany's many mandates affected the city's budget directly without any cushion that would be obtained from sharing mandates with counties.

Savitch and Kantor examine cities as creatures of state and national government.[55] They conclude that theories of economic determinism are not enough to explain urban public policymaking; rather there are other considerations. "Cities have a stake in promoting their bargaining position to realize their own objectives."[56] Savitch and Kantor conclude that bargaining is central to city officials achieving their own goals. Bargaining can be shaped by economics but, just as important, bargaining can be shaped by intergovernmental support, systems of popular control, and local political traditions or culture. This type of framework can prove useful as we examine New York City over an eighty-year period.

CORPORATE ELITE THEORISTS

Corporate elite theory focuses on national policy changes and how these changes are often dominated by corporations.[57] These theorists do not focus on urban mayors but do examine the making of fiscal and monetary policy. Their contribution lies in documenting the way in which boards of business policy organizations (BPOs) are dominated by both liberal and conservative corporate elites. Although there are differences among financial and corporate elites, as Domhoff has demonstrated, just as there are at the local level, both camps have a central voice in fiscal and monetary policy at the national level. Within these corporate elite theorists there is little analysis of the influence of corporate elites on the local level; instead the emphasis is national.

TYPOLOGIES

This book uses typologies that have been created by previous writers. The first is Stone's regime types. Stone defines four different regime types, only one of which includes financial elites:

- Maintenance or caretaker regimes focusing on service delivery.

- Development regimes focusing on pro-growth strategies and a combination of business, financial institutions, and elected officials.

- Middle-class progressive regimes that aim to protect the environment and preserve the historical nature of the town.

- Lower-class opportunity expansion regimes that emphasize human investment policy.[58]

There is also another regime type:

- Public order regimes—regimes that focus on restoring and enlarging the policing functions of a city that may sometimes, although not always, relate to a development regime.

The second typology incorporates typologies designed by Musgrave and Peterson to define allocation arenas. Three arenas have been expanded to five to represent the changing allocation patterns since Peterson's time:

1. Economic development

2. Maintenance of public order

3. Quality of life

4. Investment in human capital (education)

5. Redistributive functions

Stone advocated a human investment category rather than a redistributive one, but it is possible to distinguish between the two.[59] See Appendix A for a list of city departments in each of these categories. The two additional arenas are the maintenance of public order and the investment in human capital. The maintenance of public order began in the 1980s with the sizeable increase in the prison population concurrent with a definitive call for law and order in American cities. Another arena, quality of life, increasingly appears in urban literature.[60] The investment in human capital, as a function of urban government, focuses on the investment in local educational systems and programs dedicated to educating the populace.

There has been too little research on the extent to which financial institutions, through the mechanisms of municipal borrowing, can have a major impact on decision making. In addition, there is little in regime theory or growth machine theory that focuses on the state government's role. Instead, the focus is on issues internal to the city. Mollenkopf maintains that politics is as important as economic forces in determining public policy. But we cannot wish this and make it true. We need to examine the external forces on the city as well as the internal political and economic forces to determine who influences municipal decision making. This book describes the significant role, expanding on the theories of Mollenkopf and Stone, that financial elites and state officials play in determining a city's public policies around resource allocation.

THREE

LAGUARDIA AND THE GREAT DEPRESSION

The real fight today is against inhuman, relentless exercise of capitalistic power. . . . The present struggle in which we are engaged is for social and industrial justice.

—U.S. Supreme Court Justice Louis Brandeis[1]

Mayor Fiorello LaGuardia, a Republican, was driven to improve the living conditions of the city's residents. Speaking seven languages and beginning his New York career as a clerk at the Ellis Island Immigration Center, LaGuardia can best be described as an "Italian-Jewish American Episcopalian mayor with a Lutheran wife of German descent."[2] Once accused by his opponent of being anti-Jewish, LaGuardia went to the Lower East Side and delivered a stinging rebuke in Yiddish, challenging his opponent to a debate in that language. His chief characteristics were a hyperenergy that surpassed any of his staff, an uncanny political intelligence that defeated Tammany, and an enormous passion to do good.

When LaGuardia entered City Hall in January 1934, he faced a city in a deep economic depression that was embedded with corruption after decades of Tammany rule. His energy and commitment to deal with the fiscal crisis and end the corruption were enormous and infectious. Pulling together a talented and energetic staff, LaGuardia set new standards for government service. He staged unannounced inspections of city agencies to ensure that employees were present, working, and treating citizens with respect. His commissioners spent a full day and often evenings in the office, to the surprise of the city's reporters who had become accustomed to the more leisurely work pace of Tammany patronage appointees.

In the fall of 1932, before LaGuardia's term, the previous mayor, John L. O'Brien, signed on to a "Bankers' Agreement," created by the governor and bankers, in which the banks would agree to loan the city $70 million for relief funds; in return, the city would not raise real estate taxes but would make drastic cuts in the city's payroll.[3] Unfortunately, the "Bankers' Agreement" was not enough to balance the budget. When Mayor LaGuardia entered office, he was faced with a budget deficit of $30 million and more than $500 million in debt obligations due. His response was quite aggressive. He asked Governor Herbert Lehman to support the "Economy Act," legislation that LaGuardia sent to the New York State legislature. This act would give LaGuardia power to reorganize the agencies to save money, fix salaries for the officers and employees of the city, and declare a month-long furlough for city employees.

The governor was furious. He deeply resented LaGuardia's charges that the city did not have enough relief funds in return for a tax freeze and cutbacks in government service. He called LaGuardia's proposal "dictatorial," saying that the bill completely scrapped "the present City Charter and gives you the authority, single-handed and with full dictatorial powers, to set up another and different (city) charter."[4] The governor had put together the "Bankers' Agreement" with great care and time. He was furious at the mayor's claiming constantly that New York City was bordering on fiscal chaos. Governor Lehman, "on his personal insistence," had worked out a four-year deal with the financial community for the banks to provide sufficient funds to the city for relief. The response from LaGuardia was startling in its directness and accusatory tone:

> It is ... absolutely necessary to relieve the City of New York from a presently existing dictatorship, which you shared in creating. Namely, the citizens of New York and their elected officials are not now masters of their own finances. Because of the city's needs, you found it necessary last summer to call the bankers to your home and to direct a negotiation, which pledged virtually all its revenues to prevent the city from defaulting on its commitments. . . . The very terms of the agreement itself impact upon the city an additional annual item of about $57,000,000, to be added in our budget to the $164,000,000 already required for interest and sinking fund charges on debts of previous administrations. . . . It is our purpose to end the financial dictatorship by courageous, drastic and effective action, made possible by the Economy Bill.[5]

Mayor LaGuardia went on to state that using borrowed money to run the city had brought it close to ruin. Mayor LaGuardia wanted very much to stop borrowing funds for the city's operating expenses because he feared the loss of control to the banks. His solution was to create a plan to cut expenses and raise taxes. But raising taxes was not a part of Governor Lehman's agreement with the bankers.

Mayor LaGuardia also had to contend with the Democratic Party, dominated by Tammany, which opposed his Economy Bill because of pressure from city employees, such as teachers, firemen, and policemen, who did not want layoffs, as well as opposition from the vast patronage machine. Negotiations commenced and the governor supported a watered-down version of the bill, giving powers to the Board of Estimate rather than the mayor, but the Democrats were not so easily moved. The Democrats wanted to protect jobs and, in the end, managed to retain control of the five county (borough) offices from the mayor's grasp. After intervention from the White House, the Democrats supported the bill, and a modifed version of the Economy Bill was passed in April 1934. The Board of Estimate was given the power to implement payless furloughs, salary reductions, and reorganization of city government; however, LaGuardia could not touch county government (five borough offices), which the Democratic Party kept intact.

President Franklin Roosevelt was an enormous help to LaGuardia, who turned consistently to him. LaGuardia made numerous trips to Washington, and benefited from the number of New Yorkers surrounding the president, who had previously served as the governor of New York. "I listen to Fiorello," FDR said with a chuckle, "and then I give him what he wants."[6] LaGuardia's financial successes were directly related to the immense amount of federal aid flowing into the city during his four terms of office; his willingness to embrace taxes rather than create more debt helped him keep his independence from the bankers. During later fiscal crises, New York mayors could not duplicate LaGuardia's strategies or his success.

With the passage of the Economy Act, Mayor LaGuardia immediately sought to restructure government. He cut salaries, adopted furloughs, and merged departments, such as the Works Division and the Home Relief Bureau, which were combined into a new Emergency Relief Bureau. The strong functioning of the Emergency Relief Bureau was essential because one in five New Yorkers was on relief. LaGuardia divided the city into thirty health districts, each with a health care center. With the help of Harold Ickes, Roosevelt's Secretary of the Interior, Mayor LaGuardia established the New York City Housing Authority within a month of taking office. In his first term, Mayor LaGuardia spent 24.4 percent of his budget on welfare and unemployment relief.[7]

LaGuardia forced new taxes on corporations—one-twentieth of 1 percent on the gross income of most corporations, industries, and professions—and renewed a 1.5 percent tax on the gross monthly receipts of utilities.[8] The protests of businessmen did not discourage him. LaGuardia was able to balance the budget, and the comptroller could sell revenue bonds at the lowest interest rate (3.5 percent) since 1931.

At that time, the relief budget was separate from the city's budget. In the summer of 1934, LaGuardia asked the governor and state legislature for

new taxes to fund relief; he did not wish to continue borrowing funds to provide for it. "You can't have relief on a four percent interest basis . . . I repeat
that the municipalities cannot absorb more debt."[9] LaGuardia's proposals to
raise general taxes on business caused an immediate protest—a thousand
businessmen marched on City Hall. A few days later, at a Labor Day speech
at the World's Fair in Chicago, LaGuardia called for a "new order" that
would end unemployment, and blamed the Depression on those in control
of finance. LaGuardia went so far as to suspend payments for home relief
for three days to dramatize the fact that the city had to borrow in order to
pay for it, but the governor would not relent. Finally, in November, another
loan was arranged. Eventually LaGuardia won—via an increase in the sales
tax—an increase he had fought against while in Congress because the sales
tax was a regressive one—but better a sales tax than expensive debt.

Bankers were far too overextended with bad investments. If one act can
be said to have had an enormous negative impact on the economic stability
of investment, it is the Federal Reserve Act of 1913, which, for the first time,
allowed national banks to establish banks on foreign soil. American bankers
became the premier bond salesmen in Latin America after the passage of
that act, pushing bond issues to Latin American governments with dubious
opportunity to pay back such debts.[10] That is why Mayor LaGuardia was
widely applauded when he commented: "The bankers of this country are
more to blame than any other group for the present depression."[11]

CONCLUSION

Mayor Fiorello LaGuardia represented a lower-class opportunity expansion
regime that emphasized human investment policy. At the same time, he was
extremely successful as a mayor leading an economic development regime.
With support from the president and his aides, along with his own incredible
tenacity, Mayor LaGuardia succeeded in passing needed tax reform, building much needed public housing, and establishing public hospitals. He used
federal dollars to create jobs for hundreds of thousands of New Yorkers, while
other cities still had their work relief programs on the drawing boards.[12] He
defeated the governor and the financial elites in their attempts to control
the city's spending. But Mayor LaGuardia would not have succeeded without
the support of a higher level of government to realize his goals—namely,
the U.S. president and his staff. Mayor LaGuardia also benefited from the
national view of bankers as "vultures," a uniform class of elites who helped
cause the Great Depression. He was at the beginning of the "Fordist class
compromise" in which capitalists were forced to settle with workers and
agree on some constraints of the power of capital by recognizing workers'
rights in exchange for labor peace.[13] This is the intergovernmental support
that Savitch and Kantor talked about that could and did provide a balance

to market forces.[14] This period of class compromise began breaking down in the 1970s when the capitalist system came under enormous stress, and the allocation of resources from the federal government to the cities was drastically reduced.

FOUR

THE PRELUDE TO THE 1975 FISCAL CRISIS

Of course, the banks played a role in what happened in New York. You know, redlining is bad, and greenlining is bad. That's what you are talking about.

—Tom Clausen, Bank of America[1]

POST WORLD WAR II

President Roosevelt was in office at the beginning of the Keynesian era in which an alliance was built among labor, capital, and the state.[2] The Keynesian era ushered in a time when unions flourished and the economy boomed. After World War II, America's economy took off and grew at unprecedented rates. Europe and Asia were reeling from the devastation of the war. Economic competitors were nonexistent; America maintained this supremacy until the Vietnam War in the 1960s.

Signs of changing times were clearly recognizable by the 1960s when "guns and butter" were the beginning of what became known as the "great inflation." The Federal Reserve had sought to deter inflation by putting a ceiling on interest rates that commercial banks could pay, thereby eliminating interest rate competition among commercial banks. Banks turned to the overseas market that had no interest rate ceilings. Rather than investing in the United States, money began moving overseas.

In the spring of 1970, several financial collapses produced a worrying trend. First, Penn Central Railroad could not roll over its loans. This was followed by the near collapses of Commercial Credit and Chrysler Financial. Next came the collapse of Franklin National Bank, which had aggressively issued negotiable certificates of deposit and was a "large borrower in the Eurodollar interbank market."[3] With the collapse of Franklin came the failure of Herstatt, a private bank in West Germany. Such events

29

indicated a general instability and a growing recognition that banks were overextended in liabilities. The 1975 fiscal crisis in New York City took place during this larger economic instability of the 1970s—the globalization of American banking, the oil crisis, major inflation, and the collapse of real estate prices.

In addition, innovative technology facilitated the electronic transfer of money to anywhere in the world. The New York Clearing House Interbank Payments System (CHIPS) resulted in a considerable increase in Eurodollar transactions. This encouraged the internationalization of banking.

THE EARLY 1970S

The year 1973 was significant. Egypt attacked Israel, an American ally. The United States quickly came to the support of Israel and Egypt was defeated. In reaction to the loss, Arab nations strengthened the Organization of Petroleum Exporting Countries (OPEC) into an aggressive cartel, and oil prices shot up. The Middle East was awash in money, and American banks found far greater profitability there than in the United States.[4] As one Senate report described it, "[w]hile the oil price was something close to a disaster for the world economy, it created a bonanza for the banks."[5]

The petrodollars sitting in U.S. banks were recycled into third world countries. "Eight American banks had foreign branches in 1960; by 1980, there were 150 American banks with foreign branches, spread across most of the globe."[6] Citibank led the way. By 1974, Citibank earned 40 percent of its profits from developing countries using only 7 percent of its assets.[7] With this increased liquidity, banks invested in third world countries, and bankers could gain far higher interest rates than could be found domestically. The fiscal crisis precipitated in New York City represented the collapse of this Bretton Woods postwar order "when the balance shifted to a preponderance of global market integration and the subordination of domestic economics."[8] The 1970s were the beginning of capital deregulation, an incredible growth in the flow of capital out of America to more lucrative markets in the Middle East and South America. Throughout the 1970s, American banks increased their loans overseas; consequently, their share of third world debt increased dramatically, from 13 percent to 60 percent.[9] From 1970 to 1981, Latin American countries in particular borrowed nearly $200 billion from transnational banks eager to expand credit.[10] The result was that, by 1975, New York banks were not interested in investing in New York City bonds when the developing world was paying far more for American dollars. Overall, banks in New York and across the country sold roughly $2.3 billion in New York securities between the summer of 1974 and March 1975, when the market collapsed.[11] "The market glut created a scarcity of capital for New York City debt, which in turn allowed the very banks that had provoked the collapse of the city bond market to gain in a twofold manner. First, it allowed them to receive high interest rates for the money they eventually did loan the city. . . . Second, it gave them a crucial degree of control over the city's budget and spending priorities."[12]

In 1975, America was in recession—with an unemployment rate of 9 percent and an inflation rate of 12 percent. "Inflation had a corrosive effect on both the domestic and international marketplace." Massive loans to less developed countries that were keyed to the U.S. prime rate meant that any increase in America's domestic inflation rate forced up interest rates in the less developed countries.[13] As long as the countries paid, the banks benefited from collecting higher interest from third world countries.[14] Meanwhile, increasing inflation in the 1970s played havoc with long-term municipal bonds. "A long-term bond loses roughly half its value when interest rates double, and as interest rates trailed inflation rates skyward, the value of portfolio holdings dropped like a stone."[15] Traders soon found it difficult to find buyers for highly rated quality municipal bonds, let alone New York City bonds.

To add to the turmoil, American banks were overexposed in another arena. New laws in the 1960s had allowed them to create Real Estate Investment Trusts (REITs), which enabled small investors to buy shares in property. Some of the largest trusts were subsidiaries of banks, and when the stock market and real estate markets dropped, the trusts could not be sustained because they were so highly leveraged. Chase and other big banks were left with bad debts, which provided all the more reason to seek out more lucrative markets than municipal bonds because of their need for greater liquidity.[16] There is no question that the banks helped bring about the city's 1975 fiscal crisis by shifting their investments from New York City to less highly taxed areas where they were less vulnerable.[17]

New York banks had loaned the city a great deal of money. Before the fiscal crisis, the banks, led by Chase, profited from the city's financing needs by making a great deal of money from city bonds. "New York City bonds offered higher, tax-free interest rates than other equally rated municipal bonds and notes."[18] Felix Rohatyn warned that some banks had 20 percent of their paper in the city. "Morgan Guaranty alone had an estimated $300 million of city notes and bonds in its portfolio."[19] Chase admitted to having lent $400 million to the city, followed by Chemical Bank with $379 million and Citibank with $340 million.[20] Thus, the banks were interested in getting out of the city's unstable municipal bond market in which so much was invested. The banks headed overseas—where profits were, at the time, plentiful. The banks could not leave New York City fast enough.

THE STATE ROLE

American cities are creatures of the state; New York City, even with home rule, is limited by state law and regulation. "Cities have only those powers delegated to them by state governments, and traditionally these powers have been rigorously limited by judicial interpretation."[21] New York State has tight control of local governments. Although New York cities gained the power to draft and amend city charters in 1923, the cities had little control over financial decisions. The state controlled the tax structure, except for the property tax. The state legislature possessed the authority to enact general laws, imposing mandates and restraints on political subdivisions.

The city's fiscal crisis originated within the financial and political environment of New York State. Between 1960 and 1970, the state's employment grew only 8.7 percent as compared to 16.4 percent in the country; before the 1975 fiscal crisis, the state's employment declined by 1 percent, even though employment grew in the nation by 11 percent.[22] And while the population and median family income grew, they did not grow as fast as the country on the whole, 8 percent compared to 13 percent and 33 percent compared to 36 percent, respectively.[23] Except for a brief period in 1985, the nation's gross domestic product grew at a faster rate than New York State's did.[24]

A large part of this decline lay in aging industries—textile mills were moving south and steel plants were shutting down. What caused this economic downturn? The loss of jobs was both regional and global. It was the rise of the sun belts; the Northeast and Midwest lost to the South and West. The population in the metropolitan areas of the Northeast and Midwest grew in much smaller increments than in the South and West. The same was true for employment.[25] The country was moving South and West and the entire Northeast was at risk. In addition, jobs started to flow overseas.

The governor of New York, Nelson Rockefeller, who served from 1959 to his resignation in 1973 to become President Gerald Ford's vice president, was not successful in remediating this dismal economic picture. In 1962, he created the Job Development Authority to provide long-term, low-interest fixed asset loans to manufacturers.[26] He offered tax incentives and other tax preferences as part of an economic development plan to save manufacturing, but to no avail. The country was moving South and West; New York was bleeding jobs. It is unclear that Governor Rockefeller could have turned the trend around to the state's advantage. Perhaps if he had been more successful in addressing the loss of jobs rather than embracing debt to build immense construction projects, the state might not have undergone such a steep economic decline. His strategy to strengthen the economy through construction jobs failed. In any event, he left a dubious legacy, which included extensive construction, substantial debt, and questionable yet innovative financing arrangements.

New York State spent more than any other state during Governor Nelson Rockefeller's era in which he increased the budget from $2.04 billion in Fiscal Year 1960 to $8.8 billion in Fiscal Year 1974. His massive construction programs, including the State University of New York and the

Empire State Plaza, resulted in the largest debt of any state in the nation, growing from $1.97 billion in 1961 to $13.37 billion in 1973.[27]

The Rockefellers created postindustrial New York City. Through comprehensive planning and close cooperation with real estate interests, the Rockefeller family, led by David, head of Chase, and Nelson, governor of New York, managed to put in place an incredible scenario for the city—phasing out manufacturing and establishing the city as the financial capital of the world. In the process, the Rockefellers were at the center of massive building projects: the United Nations, Rockefeller Center, Lincoln Center, the World Trade Center, the IND Sixth Avenue subway line, Battery Park City, the World Financial Center, and South Street Seaport.

The state constitution requires the governor to seek permission from voters to borrow using general obligation bonds. Governor Rockefeller was not about to wait for permission from voters who were known to be cautious about embracing debt. To aid in his borrowing to fund construction, Governor Rockefeller created 230 public authorities that could borrow money without permission from voters or the state legislature.[28] These authorities are public benefit corporations created by New York State law with full authority to borrow by issuing bonds. These are moral obligation bonds and do not carry the full faith and credit pledge of the state; instead, the state legislature is morally obligated to support these bonds. Moral obligation bonds were designed by John Mitchell, later to become infamous as the U.S. attorney general in the Watergate scandal of the Nixon administration. It was the role of these authorities to act to force the capital budget for the State of New York and act they did. The most famous example was the Urban Development Corporation (UDC), established in 1967 by Governor Rockefeller and headed by Ed Logue, who invented creative financing. Instead of issuing twenty bond issues for twenty projects, he issued nonspecific, nonproject bonds starting twenty projects using 10 percent of the bonds revenues as a fast start-up. The trouble arose when the UDC ran out of money and defaulted in 1974.[29]

Rockefeller's borrowing through the backdoor of public authorities became a disaster as it set a path for New York City officials to follow: "the State invented bond anticipation financing (BAN), but it was the City (with legislative authorization) that carried the device to the extreme, in perpetual BAN financing of the city Mitchell-Lama Program. . . . Hindsight shows that the Legislature should not have been so incautious. But in reality, it would have been difficult, in the expansive climate, for the state to have been conservative in regard to the City when it was being apparently, so daring in regard to its own practices."[30]

As long as Nelson Rockefeller remained governor, his brother, David, as head of Chase, would be careful to maintain stability among the financial elites. In addition, the banks were comforted by knowing that Governor Rockefeller had control of the legislature "which would have to be persuaded to vote for appropriations if the authorities encountered financial problems."[31] In late 1973, Nelson Rockefeller left the governorship to become vice president for Gerald Ford, who had assumed the presidency when Richard Nixon resigned in 1974. The vice presidency was as close as Nelson Rockefeller would ever come to his presidential dreams. He left behind a mountain of debt. Governor Rockefeller knew that the UDC was running short of cash and could not redeem its bonds. But there was an election for governor in 1974 and Governor Rockefeller said nothing. His brother came to the rescue. David Rockefeller lent enough money to the UDC to get it through the election.[32] It was left to the next governor, Hugh Carey, to resolve the crisis. According to Carey, the troubles began with the failure to observe financial fundamentals:

> Sort of a preface to the crisis was the largest single (MO) moral obligation agency to default, the Urban Development Corporation (UDC), which was former Gov. Nelson Rockefeller's way to do quick mobilization to build things. They started building, but they didn't build economically and they didn't manage the house. . . . Rockefeller went to Washington to become Gerald Ford's vice president, I took over, and there was no way to meet the obligations for the UDC's debt.[33]

The UDC had the right to borrow money; it offered moral obligation bonds. As Carey said, "You do it by exposing yourself to a moral obligation to pay it back. A future legislature would put the money up. . . . It was important to preserve that, as long as it was there, or the state would be in all credit markets marked as a default."[34] The UDC could no longer redeem its bonds and defaulted. The impact was immediate—out-of-town investors became leery of all New York bonds, including those for New York City. "Why should I buy the moral obligations of immoral politicians?" screamed one Wall Street bond trader.[35] The default of the UDC was the precursor to the city's problems the following year.

Governor Rockefeller also had another major impact on the city, one that resulted from his close relationship to labor unions. In 1967, Governor Rockefeller signed the Public Employees' Fair Employment Act (Taylor Law) which gave public employees in the state the right to collective bargaining. And the public labor unions sought to organize. But the governor interfered with labor negotiations between the mayors and unions. His most infamous intervention came in 1971 when Mayor Lindsay asked the governor to call out the National Guard during the city's sanitation strike. Instead, the governor "had a meeting in his townhouse here on 54th Street. Mayor John Lindsay was there but didn't take part. Union President John Delury was there and did take part, although Delury was supposed to be in jail. . . . we (Governor Rockefeller) worked out a deal, and it was a better deal than Lindsay could have worked out."[36] The governor agreed that union workers could retire at age fifty-five and draw half-pay after twenty years of work. Newspaper editorials severely criticized the governor for his generous agreement with the sanitation workers. Rockefeller's actions portrayed his contempt for Mayor Lindsay with whom he had constant quarrels.

Governor Rockefeller's swift pace won him many supporters, but the next governor would face a different reality as the state entered a major recession. Governor Rockefeller understood what he had left behind as revealed by his comment to Governor Carey: "I had the champagne, you have the hang-over."[37]

NEW YORK CITY BEFORE THE FISCAL CRISIS

The city's economy was particularly problematic—consistently lagging in job growth behind the rest of the state during the 1960s and 1970s. Scholars maintain that if the city's job growth had been close to the national rate rather than below it, the 1975 fiscal crisis would not have occurred.[38] Roy Bahl points out that New York State's deteriorating economic base was particularly problematic because the state had such a strong public sector that was not easily controllable by cutting expenditures in response to declining revenues.[39] Bernard Gifford explained the inequality of tax payments and receipts between New York State and the federal government, noting that New York State has always provided more to the federal government than it has received. This negative income flow has been acknowledged by federal officials.[40]

New York City led the state's struggle for jobs. Employment dropped steadily. From a peak of 3.8 million jobs in 1969, employment in the city fell to 3.4 million in 1975—a drop of 11 percent. The recession continued in the Northeast and Midwest while the rest of the United States was booming. The United States saw thirteen million jobs added despite recessions.[41] From the mid-1970s on, each time the city was in fiscal crisis, the percentage of private jobs as compared to the city's population was quite low. The city could not sustain its level of public service without an adequate number of private sector jobs to support the city's tax revenue base. The search for sufficient private jobs at decent salary levels would prove to be a major issue for each of the subsequent mayors after the 1975 fiscal crisis. See Figure 4.1 for the change in percentage of jobs in the city for each mayor.[42]

At the same time, inflation increased government expenditures. The impact of inflation during 1972 to 1974, the period immediately preceding the 1975 fiscal crisis, was "nearly equal to that which occurred during the entire previous five years, 1967–1972."[43]

Taking a page from Governor Rockefeller's fiscal practices, New York City officials instituted a major period of short-term borrowing from 1965 to 1975. The first instance of debt being used to fund noncapital items

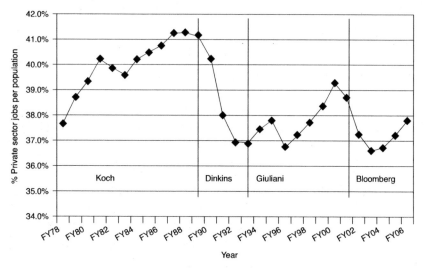

Source: NYC Comptroller's Report, Statistical Section, FY78–FY06.

Figure 4.1 Percentage of private sector jobs per city's population

was during Mayor Robert Wagner's term, when he suggested in 1965 that "the city sell five-year serial bonds to cover a projected gap on the revenue side of the city's operating budget."[44] That year, with the help of Governor Rockefeller, the state legislature passed changes in Section 25 of the Local Finance Law, which, for the first time, "permitted the city to borrow against the Mayor's estimate of federal and state aid applicable to the current year's budget."[45] Thus, the state legislature approved the borrowing of $250 million a year for five years.

The next mayor, John Lindsay, went one step further in 1971 when the city borrowed against total revenues not based on specific sources of revenue. In a congressional investigative report following the 1975 fiscal crisis, the report concluded that, "had sound accounting principles been used, the city would have been unable to show sufficient accrued revenue to support the outstanding RANS."[46] And so it was that Mayor John Lindsay, who pledged fiscal reform, continued the questionable practice of borrowing for expenses. Mayor Lindsay had counted on the 1967 State Constitutional Convention that could have increased the city's home rule powers, particularly in the area of taxation. Governor Rockefeller opposed more home rule for the city as did upstate interests; the result was that the convention did little for the city. Consequently, the mayor had minimal authority to raise taxes without going through the state legislature.

In July 1971, Mayor John Lindsay had to pay the police force more than $200 million in back pay, which he financed through debt approved by the state legislature. As revenues declined during a national recession, this borrowing pattern persisted. "In 1974, the city sold more than $1.58 billion of bonds, three times the $513 million it had sold in 1969 . . . short-term debt of the city increased to more than $5 billion from $747 million in 1969. In 1974, the city sold 17 note issues."[47]

By 1974, it was no wonder that bankers who underwrote the city's bonds were more and more nervous about the city's financial stability. The large amount of short-term debt was the justification the banks needed to leave the city. Hyman C. Grossman, a managing director at Standard & Poor's monitoring the city since 1963, suspended the city's rating in 1975 because "city officials seemed incapable of grasping even the dimensions of the fiscal crisis. Subsequent tax code changes drove commercial banks, widely regarded as heavies who forced city government onto an austerity diet, to invest elsewhere."[48]

In the autumn of 1974, the banks sought to sell New York City bonds, and took a bath. They were left with a $50 million loss. The October sale of $475 million was the largest bond offering in the city's history. And the underwriters were the largest syndicate ever formed—over 148 commercial banks, investment banks, brokerages, and bond houses—in order to spread the risks. Before the City Planning Commission, Roderic O'Connor testified about the difficulty of selling these bonds: "There is a decline in New York's ability to borrow because of the large volume of bonds outstanding and increasing reluctance of financial institutions to buy bonds which are a glut on the market."[49] Part of the problem was the glut—the incredible supply of municipal and state bond offerings on the market from throughout the United States. As these offerings increased, the city had to compete with all the other offerings at a time when banks already were looking overseas for more lucrative investments.

CONCLUSION

The 1975 fiscal crisis in New York City took place during this larger economic instability of the 1970s—the globalization of American banking, the oil crisis, major inflation, and the collapse of real estate prices. The banks helped initiate the city's 1975 fiscal crisis when they shifted many of their investments from New York City to less vulnerable areas. The petrodollars sitting in U.S. banks were no longer used to buy bonds but instead to make loans to third world countries. The city's fiscal problems were compounded by financial practices of the State of New York. Through the state legislature, Governor Rockefeller created many state corporations (authorities) with the right to borrow money. And borrow they did. To build the state university, Empire State Plaza, and countless other projects, the governor created massive state debt. Concurrently, New York City, like New York State and the entire Northeast, was hobbled by severe job loss to the Sun Belt. As revenues declined, Mayor John Lindsay sought to change New York State's constitution to permit the city control over its tax structure. Lindsay did not succeed; hence, he borrowed, and the city's debt became massive. Clearly, Savitch and Kantor's explanatory power of the degree of intergovernmental support is key to understanding the city's fiscal problems.

FIVE

MAYOR ABE BEAME AND THE

1975 FISCAL CRISIS (1974–1978)

Civil government, so far as it is instituted for the security of property, is in reality instituted for the defense of the rich against the poor, or of those who have some property against those who have none at all.

—Adam Smith[1]

Mayor Abraham Beame was elected at a difficult financial time for all of New York. He lasted only one four-year term. He was an accountant by training and a Brooklyn clubhouse politician by inclination. Not a neophyte to the city's fiscal issues, he had been budget director and city comptroller before being elected mayor. Perhaps more than anyone, Mayor Beame understood how much debt the city owed and the burden this created. As city comptroller during Mayor Robert Wagner's last term, Abe Beame had warned against selling bonds to cover current expenses. At that time, he established the Comptroller's Technical Debt Management Committee (CTDMC) made up of the comptroller's staff and underwriters to examine possible public offerings. The voters chose an experienced fiscal expert. And yet he was totally unprepared for what happened within the first year of his mayoralty.

The new mayor quickly appointed a committee to consider the city's fiscal problems—created most notably by a $1.5 billion gap in the $12 billion budget. In addition, the city was saddled with almost $5 billion in short-term debt. Adding to these problems, the city experienced a dramatic change in revenues. During the Beame administration (1974–1978), revenues did increase by 25.5 percent but that was far short of the previous four years in which the city recorded over a 52 percent increase. It must be remembered that the city's financial recordkeeping was limited during the 1975 fiscal year. There was little trust in the expenditure numbers that were provided, even in the comptroller's audited financial statements. See Table 5.1 for revenue growth during this period.[2]

What Mayor Beame did not do was get along with the banking community, many of whom were calling for deep service cuts. Mayor Beame was forced to confront a new paradigm, one in which government was not the solution but the problem, and he could not accept it. Beame faced what Robert Bailey called a financial emergency; that is, an immediate cash flow crisis that had not been seen since 1933.[3] This city's fiscal crisis is distinguished from the subsequent fiscal crises in which mayors confronted large projected deficits, but did not face immediate cash flow issues. Bankers viewed the mayor as someone who would not admit the seriousness of the city's financial problems. In the fall of 1974, bank representatives met secretly with Mayor Beame to communicate quite clearly that New York City needed to get its finances in order. This meant that the city had to reduce spending. Mayor Beame did not comply and threatened to borrow money from the city's pension funds.[4] In January 1975, Mayor Beame called a summit meeting with bankers and union leaders. David Rockefeller recalled the meeting from his point of view:

> To my amazement Mayor Beame began the meeting by accusing the banks of disloyalty to the city. He insisted that it was our duty to go out and sell the city to the rest of the country. If we did so, he assured us, the problem would go away. I was stunned by the Mayor's refusal to accept the gravity of the city's financial situation. I told the Mayor that the bond market was extremely skeptical of the city's financial management and that he had to cut spending

Table 5.1 Comparing revenues before and during the Beame administration from FYs 1970–1974 to FYs 1974–78 (in millions)

Revenues	FY70	FY74	% Change FY70–74	FY78	% Change FY74–78
Total taxes	$3,283	$ 4,650	41.6%	$ 6,356	36.7%
Federal grants	1,074	2,022	88.2%	2,488	23.1%
State grants	1,738	2,535	45.9%	2,303	–9.1%
Unrestricted federal & state	—	—	—	994	—
Charges and fees	439	196	–55.3%	530	170.3%
Other	171	846	395.0%	188	–77.8%
Total revenues	$6,705	$10,249	52.8%	$12,859	25.5%

Note: Columns will not total due to minor revenues being omitted.
Source: NYC Comptroller's Reports, FY1970–FY1978.

and balance the budget if he wanted to regain investor confidence in NYC debt. . . . I recommended that Ellmore (Pat) Patterson, chairman of Morgan Guaranty, head such a working group. The Mayor acquiesced, and a few days later the FCLG, chaired by Patterson, began its last-ditch attempt to enable the city to regain control of its own finances.[5]

Mayor Beame interpreted these meetings differently. He knew the seriousness of the debt. He claimed that the bankers made unreasonable demands. Ultimately, Governor Carey went around the mayor and made a deal directly with the bankers. "Mayor Beame accused the bankers on television of poisoning our wells, and city workers demonstrated outside CityBank's skyscraper."[6] The banks had turned off the spigot, and Mayor Beame was furious. This was very similar to the Great Depression when the governor made a deal with New York City bankers for loans in exchange for reduced taxes. However, Mayor LaGuardia had President Roosevelt as a powerful ally in his fight against these kinds of agreements while Mayor Beame had no higher authority. President Ford, a staunch Republican, was not about to help, resulting in the infamous headline, "Ford to City: Drop Dead." Mayor Beame was isolated. He turned to the labor unions for support, but they were stymied. The very survival of collective bargaining was at stake. If the city went to bankruptcy court, the unions could lose everything.[7] Jack Bigel, consultant to the labor unions, said, "We knew bankruptcy was no good. The editorial page of the Wall Street Journal called for bankruptcy claiming that it would result in the city being able to reopen all labor contracts and pension agreements."[8] All collective bargaining agreements would be gone. The labor union even went so far as to hold secret meetings with the bankers.

Meanwhile, the bankers, led by Ellmore (Pat) C. Patterson, chief executive officer of JP Morgan; Walter Wriston, chief executive officer of Citibank; David Rockefeller of Chase; and Chairman Gabriel Hauge of Manufacturer's Hanover Trust, met regularly to create a solution other than bankruptcy, which no one wanted.[9] Bankruptcy was not welcomed by bondholders since it was unknown if a bankruptcy court would rule in their favor. Victor Gotbaum, union leader of District Council 37 of the American Federation of State, County, and Municipal Employees and chief negotiator for the unions during the fiscal crisis, described the bankers this way:

> We were never going to get real new money from the bankers . . . they were not going to move because they did not have to; they held the cards and the most advantageous position in the negotiations. They didn't have to move, and they didn't. They wanted to avoid default, but it was not important enough for them to risk more money to do it. Default could mean the loss of fifty thousand to

seventy-five thousand union jobs. It could jeopardize pension funds. The loss to our membership could be catastrophic.[10]

Governor Carey created a four-member blue ribbon panel to forge an agreement with Mayor Beame, the banking community, and the unions. They were called "the gang of four" and consisted of Richard Shinn, head of Metropolitan Life; Felix Rohatyn, general partner of the investment banking firm, Lazard Freres; Simon Rifkind, partner in Paul Weiss, Rifkind, Wharton and Garrison; and Donald B. Smiley, CEO of Macy's. On May 26, 1975, Dick Shinn hosted a meeting at his home with the "gang of four" and other New York government officials, including Governor Carey. They worked out a plan to create a new state entity, the Municipal Assistance Corporation (MAC), which would issue, under state auspices, bonds backed by city taxes.[11] MAC would consist of nine members; four appointed by the mayor, five by the governor. In addition, seven representatives of various governmental entities would attend meetings but not vote. The first chairman was William Ellinghaus, quickly replaced by Felix Rohatyn. Other members were Francis Barry, president of Circle Lines Sightseeing Yachts; George M. Brooker, secretary-treasurer of Webb & Brooker, a real estate management and brokerage firm; John A. Coleman, senior partner of Alder, Coleman & Company, a member of the New York Stock Exchange; Thomas D. Flynn, a partner in the international accounting firm, Arthur Young & Company; George D. Gould, president and CEO of the Madison Fund; Dick Netzer, dean of the Graduate School of Public Administration of New York University; Donna Shalala, associate professor of politics at Teachers College, Columbia University, who served as treasurer; and Robert Weaver, distinguished professor of urban affairs at Hunter College. Barry, Brooker, Coleman, and Gould were appointed by the mayor.

Creating the Municipal Assistance Corporation was the first of three strategies developed in 1975 to stabilize the city's fiscal picture. New bonds would be issued by MAC, guaranteed by city taxes (sales tax, stock transfer tax, and per capita aid), and administered by New York State. The stock transfer tax of 1905 was phased out in 1978 by Governor Carey. All payments ended in 1981. If MAC accumulated surplus funds of city tax monies, under state law it could either invest in development it determined to be of long-term benefit to the city or use the money to retire its outstanding debt. The mayor had to negotiate with MAC officials as to how those funds would be used. Until 1990, the MAC surpluses became a negotiating game among Felix Rohatyn, Governor Cuomo, and Mayor Koch. Given that these surpluses were backed by city tax monies, this outside interference from the state and MAC officials made Mayor Koch furious. In 1990, city officials convinced the state legislature to pass a law requiring the surpluses (which at the time of passage were $1.5 billion) to be turned over to the city.

Since New York City was shut out of the market, MAC had to sell bonds for the city. And this was not easy. Donna Shalala, one of the MAC members, describes the selling of MAC bonds:

We traveled around the country visiting investment holders and attempting to convince them to buy MAC bonds. I was a salesperson and I thought a good one. In Texas, I spoke before a large group of investment bankers giving my pitch for New York City. The questions I got were so incredibly hostile, they shook me. "How do you expect me to buy bonds for a city that doesn't even know how many city workers it has?" asked one. What do you say to these guys—"Trust me"?[12]

These complaints were based on the hard truth that New York City's financial systems and procedures were not in order. This was troubling in the investment community and undermined sales efforts.

By July 1975, MAC bonds were no longer being purchased. David Rockefeller described his role:

By mid-July 1975 investors refused to purchase any more of the $3 billion in notes that MAC was selling, and the city again approached default. It became apparent that the market would respond only if the city were persuaded to surrender 'all control' of its financial affairs to a more credible body. . . . On the morning of July 22, I held a press conference at Chase and released a letter that had been sent to the head of MAC. In effect, the letter stated that the bankers would not purchase any more MAC securities unless measures mandating "spartan control on the expenses of the City" were adopted.[13]

When the banks, led by David Rockefeller, insisted that they could not sell MAC bonds unless the city drastically cut its costs and froze wages, the city was forced to drastically reduce its spending. From June 1975 to December 1975, 40,000 municipal employees were laid off, followed by another 7,000 layoffs between January 1, 1976, and April 30, 1976.[14] No one asked New York City residents if they wanted to give up free tuition at the City University of New York. No one asked if they wanted public school class size to increase from twenty-eight to forty.[15] The financial leaders and labor union leaders even arranged to use the unions' pension funds to purchase city securities, but that was not enough.

When MAC failed to sell its bonds, Governor Carey adopted a second strategy—he asked the state legislature to pass the Financial Emergency Act (FEA) to establish the Emergency Financial Control Board (EFCB) that would examine the city's finances and control its spending. This occurred in October 1975. The seven-member board consisted of the governor, state and city comptrollers, the mayor of New York City, and three private members appointed by the governor. They were William M. Ellinghaus, the original Chair of MAC and vice president of ATT and president of New York Telephone Company; Albert V. Casey, chairman of American Airlines; and David I. Margolis, president of Colt Industries, Inc.

The FEA was agreed to by the governor, state legislature, bankers, and, at last, the labor unions, once there was consensus that the integrity of the collective bargaining process would remain. There was another factor in the labor unions' decision. Mayor Beame was furious with the labor unions for "selling out" and agreeing to support the establishment of the EFCB. Labor union leaders—Barry Feinstein, president of Local 237 of the Teamsters Union, and Victor Gotbaum, head of District Council 37, of the American Federation of State, County, and Municipal Employees—described the disagreement with the mayor in an interview: "a hurt Mayor turned to them outside the Governor's office and accused them of having sold out the City. We were stunned at the Mayor's short-sightedness that things were not as bad as they really were."[16] The labor unions witnessed the weakening of the mayor's role as state officials and bankers negotiated the FEA legislation. The unions, backed into a corner by the risk of losing all collective bargaining gains if the city went into bankruptcy, agreed to support the establishment of the EFCB. Mayor Beame was alone.

The FEA was much tougher than the 1933 Bankers' Agreement; the FEA totally controlled the city's spending. The city was required to submit all budgetary actions to the EFCB, including a four-year financial plan. A Special Deputy State Comptroller's office was created to assist the EFCB in its analysis. The EFCB was authorized to review and approve city contracts as well as borrowing by the city. In addition, the FEA mandated that the city adopt a balanced budget, end the fiscal year without a deficit of more than $100 million, conduct an annual audit, and impose strict limits on short-term indebtedness. The creditors were now fully in charge.

As part of the federal loan program, the city was also required to submit regular reports to the U.S. Department of the Treasury. The EFCB required the city to freeze union employees' wages. Cost of living adjustments could only be agreed on if the unions paid for such increases through productivity increases or decreases in fringe benefits. "Between 1976 and 1981, the city's total budgetary outlays have increased only 12%. During the same period, the state's budget has increased 33% and the federal budget has grown 66%."[17] As one observer put it, "The mayor was left with as much power as the mayor of Paris during the Nazis' occupation."[18]

The third strategy was federal loans. The campaign to obtain federal loans went on throughout 1975:

Nearly all the New York bankers, including such champions of free enterprise as Wriston and Patterson, were now appealing to Washington to rescue them with a federal loan: even Tom Clausen from the Bank of America flew to Washington to argue for aid to New York. President Gerald Ford, William E. Simon, former New York investment banker and now United States Secretary of the Treasury, and Arthur Burns, head of the Federal Reserve, were not convinced. Mayor Beame and Governor Carey visited President Ford in September to ask for a loan. His response was, "Are you going to cut down your retirement benefits and your overhead? Are you going to stop giving free tuition to students at the City University?"[19]

This was the constant demand from the federal government and the financial elites. "The city still had not submitted a realistic plan to extend its financial obligations over a longer period of time, persuade trustees of other union pension funds to invest in its securities, freeze pay increases for its workers, readjust retirement benefits, and let go thousands of employees"[20] President Ford made his famous speech on October 31, 1975, when he said that the city was not in fiscal order. He claimed that sanitation workers' salaries were $15,000 and that city employees made no contributions to their pensions. Neither of these statements was true.[21] Mayor Beame gave a point-by-point rebuttal to President Ford's speech, but it made no difference. The city and state needed federal loan guarantees.

President Ford's fear was that other local and state governments would look for a bailout when they ran into fiscal trouble. With a recession at hand, Ford did not wish to risk this. Bill Simon portrayed the story of New York as a terrifying dress rehearsal of the fate that lay ahead of the country if it continued to be guided by the same liberal philosophy of government.[22] President Ford said that New York City officials constantly faced a massive network of pressure groups that prevented elected officials from responsible financial management.[23] Ford thought he could use the city's fiscal crisis to run on a platform of fiscal conservatism for his reelection campaign. "The bankruptcy of New York would be the excuse needed to reverse progressive social thinking from FDR's New Deal through Johnson's Great Society."[24] Nevertheless, the city's bankers wanted federal loans. Simon was furious with New York bankers who made the New York City fiscal crisis a global issue. At the International Monetary Fund meeting, New York City bankers told foreign bankers that a default by the city would damage the world financial system. The bankers' alarm was heightened by their growing dependence on Arab deposits. As Senator Percy put it in Senate hearings in October 1975: "One of the greatest ironies is that the City of New York which is on the precipice of bankruptcy is to a degree dependent upon the Arab countries keeping their money in the New York banks."[25]

This was an election year, and President Ford needed New York votes. The fear of bankruptcy was great, based on the unknown consequences to the banking system and the "possibility that large holders of certificates of deposit at New York banks would withdraw their holdings and seek other sanctuary for them, perhaps abroad . . . [which] could result in a serious contraction of liquidity throughout the country" along with effects throughout the economy that might undermine America's international position.[26] President Ford relented. In December 1975, President Ford announced that he would ask Congress to approve a program of short-term loans to New York, which would be strictly administered by the U.S. Treasury.

There was also another reason President Ford was so reluctant. His chief of staff, Donald Rumsfeld, wanted his home state, Illinois, to benefit from New York City's fiscal meltdown. Governor Carey learned through Melvin Laird that Rumsfeld had convinced President Ford that Chicago could be the financial capital of the world, not New York City.[27] Rumsfeld saw this as a way to damage Nelson Rockefeller's plans for the presidency. Governor Carey called in the help of Mayor Daley to convince the president that London or Paris would take over if New York City imploded, not Chicago.

When a deal was finally made, Governor Carey pointed out that federal demands came with a steep price:

> The federal government put certain restrictions on the state. Until we could qualify, we couldn't get the money. What did we have to do? We had to increase the subway fare, charge tuition to City University. The state had to show its hand and pick up certain responsibilities. We took over the funding of the City University, which the state does today. We took over the Transit Authority, which the state does today. We took over the costs of the courts, which the state does today. We lifted a lot of expenses from the city—nobody realizes that.[28]

Mayor Beame was the one who had to announce the massive layoffs and the end of free tuition at CUNY. He was devastated: "I was a graduate of City College and I had to be the voice to eliminate [the policy of no tuition]."[29]

The New York City Seasonal Financing Act of 1975 permitted the city short-term borrowing of up to $2.3 billion a year for three years. Funds would be repaid within the year. The federal loan gave Congress carte blanche to hold hearings on the city's crisis and closely study its cash flow problem. The federal government also required increased taxes of $200 million on personal income, increases in bank, estate, and cigarette taxes, an increase in the minimum corporate income tax, and an extension of the sales taxes, to which the state legislature agreed.[30] The federal government's harshness toward New York City reflected the conservative ideology of the president and his key appointees, as well as key conservative senators (including Democrat William Proxmire). It did not follow the precedent set by previous presidential administrations that had more freely provided loans to both the public and private sectors. The purpose of the Reconstruction Finance Corporation, created in 1932, was to help local governments and private corporations avoid bankruptcy through guarantees. It financed itself through the sale of capital stock and by borrowing from the Treasury. In 1958, the Interstate Commerce Commission was authorized to guarantee loans to railroads. The Emergency Loan Guarantee Act of 1971 provided direct federal loans to large businesses.[31]

The irony was that New York State bore the bulk of the financing burden. Out of the total $14.4 billion of long-term financing for the city, the state, through MAC and the city, bore almost 89 percent, as compared to 10 percent contributed by the federal government.[32] Senator Daniel Moynihan, in a January 4, 1978, letter to the president, stated that the federal loans to New York City did not cost the U.S. Treasury anything; rather, the loans had earned $30 million in interest for the U.S. Treasury.[33]

CONCLUSION

The elected officials of New York City were powerless. Mayor Beame's administration became a caretaker regime focusing on service delivery, but failed and could not protect the city during its largest fiscal crisis since the Depression. It is unclear if any mayor could have protected the city. Mayor Beame, abandoned by both state and federal officials, was undeniably ineffectual. But was it his failing that he did not respond to the fiscal crisis with his own policy goals when the financial elites banded together and acted forcefully to protect their interests, or was he simply powerless in the face of overwhelming federal, state, and financial interests? National and state officials, labor unions, and bankers were all lined up desperately seeking to avoid bankruptcy, and if the compromise meant cuts, then cuts there would be. The bankers were firm—cuts were required. Carol O'Cleireacain, then working for Victor Gotbaum as his chief economic advisor, said, "the banks are playing real hard ball here. It was like they wanted the ice cream, whipping cream, nuts and the cherry on top."[34] The needs of the people of the City of New York were represented by Mayor Beame and he was alone.

Were there alternative strategies? Of course there were. What would have happened if Mayor Beame had called the bankers' bluff and shut down government—closed the schools, the libraries, all but essential services, and said that the city was out of money? Would the outcry have forced the president to recognize the need for federal loan guarantees earlier? Would Governor Carey and the state legislature have responded differently? Could they? Would the bankers? We don't know because Mayor Beame folded as did the labor unions and other elected officials.

Certainly, New York State officials, alongside the banking establishment, controlled the financial resources of the city. When Governor Carey made a deal for a moratorium on paying the principal on bonds (which was later declared illegal in the courts), Mayor Beame said he was not consulted.[35] When Governor Carey agreed to phase out the stock transfer tax, it was clear to many that he was bowing to pressure from Wall Street regardless of the effect on the city.

New York City continued to struggle for several years after Mayor Beame's solitary term. More federal loans and loan guarantees were agreed to and oversight continued. Fears of bankruptcy were renewed on various occasions. The state's legal and fiscal structures, put in place by the end of 1975 by bankers and state officials, worked toward and set the pattern for similar strategies to be used in other urban fiscal crises in the country for years to come.[36] On a federal level, municipal bankruptcy law was modified for dealing with the possibility of other cities being unable to balance their budgets.[37] New York City served as the dress rehearsal.

SIX

MAYOR KOCH AND THE

UNREMITTING 1975 FISCAL CRISIS

(1978–1990)

We have not come for a handout. We are not asking for a grant. If you want the city to go forward and to live—and I'm sure you want it to live—then give us this package.

—Mayor Ed Koch[1]

We run the risk of turning New York City into a 'guarantee junkie'—coming back, every four years, rather than every three.

—U. S. Senator William Proxmire[2]

In September 1977, Mayor Ed Koch, a congressman and lawyer, won the Democratic primary over law professor Mario Cuomo, later governor of New York State, in a tough election fight. In 1977, New York City was a one-party town; there was no credible Republican challenger in the general election. Mayor Koch promised that his would be an administration that would face reality, and he assured voters that he would support the highest fiscal integrity. Mayor Koch, elected to three four-year terms from 1978 to 1990, was committed in his first term "to regain access to the public credit markets" by presenting balanced and carefully crafted budgets" after the ravages of the 1975 fiscal crisis.[3] He returned the city to fiscally conservative policies, dramatically different from the pre-fiscal crisis days. Mayor Koch maintained that redistributive functions were best left to the national government.

He acted with the "chutzpah" appreciated by New Yorkers when taking on the unions in 1980 and "winning" in a citywide transit strike. He was also contentious and pugnacious—quick to disagree with others and aggressive in defending his positions. Within the first year, he alienated a large portion of African American voters by insisting on closing Sydenham Hospital in Harlem over widespread protests. A year later, he kept open the Public Health Hospital on Staten Island, a borough dominated by the white working class. He further alienated progressive voters and African Americans by implementing harsh policies on welfare benefits in the city's social services agency, the Human Resources Administration (HRA). He supported his commissioner, Blanche Bernstein, who implemented policies to "curb fraud" in welfare payments by closing cases if notices were ignored and requiring face-to-face recertification meetings.[4] His best friend, law partner and corporation counsel Allen Schwartz, described a major meeting between Mayor Koch and the African American leadership when Mayor Koch was abrasive and confrontational with his audience: "I was stunned. Ed Koch was setting a tone that would create problems for him in the future."[5] Deputy Mayor Basil Paterson, the highest ranking African American in the Koch administration, was so upset that he walked out of the meeting. The alienation and anger of African Americans, who constituted 25 percent of the city's population, grew throughout his administration.

EXTERNAL ENVIRONMENT

Mayor Koch, elected on a platform of lower taxes and increased worker productivity, did not enjoy a lengthy honeymoon. During his first term, financial issues continued to plague the city. Neither the state nor federal governments was kind to the city during his first term from Fiscal Year 1978 to Fiscal Year 1982. The federal government dramatically changed its support to cities. First came the push from the growing cities in the West and Southwest and their need for federal dollars for new construction, a need as great as those of the older cities for federal dollars for reconstruction. Then came President Reagan's allocation of federal funds for state and local governments in the form of block grants to the states. The consequences of block grants were twofold. First, the states had the option of how to allocate funds to the cities and counties. Second, the federal government reduced the amount of federal aid in the block grants.[6] Therefore, the city did not get as much as it had previously. The city lost 2.1 percent of its federal funds each year during Koch's first term; he gained only 1.3 percent a year throughout his mayoralty. See Table 6.1. In his first term, as the mayor explained, the city "lost more than $830 million in federal revenues in the last two years. From our own resources, we have provided about $300 million in order to maintain such essential services as day care centers, senior citizen centers, health care and education."[7]

Prior to 1982, commercial banks were allowed to deduct interest paid on deposits used to purchase tax-exempt municipal bonds.[8] This tax preference was reduced in 1982 and eliminated altogether in the federal Tax Reform Act of 1986 (TRA). Such federal action meant that commercial bankers had little reason to remain interested in the financial fortunes of the City of New York—they were out of the municipal bond market.

Governor Carey had his own fiscal troubles, but continued to be financially supportive of the city. Governor Carey was facing the "three R's" (recession, taxpayer revolt, and federal aid reductions).[9] He sought to absorb city Medicaid costs, but was blocked by the Republican Senate during Mayor Koch's first term. Between the state legislature and the governor, state aid to the city was increased by 4.3 percent each year in the mayor's first term. It was the federal government that continued its policy of ignoring the city. Because of a growing economy, Mayor Koch benefited from increased tax revenues to support the budget. As the economy improved and revenues increased in his second and third terms, Mayor Koch increased spending. See Table 6.1.[10]

State Role

Probably the most costly act by the state was the elimination of the stock transfer tax (STT). Such a move demonstrated the power of the financial elites—the State of New York had taxed sales of corporate stocks since 1905. In 1966, the STT was transferred to the city. For a few years, STT revenues were used to back up MAC bonds along with the city's sales tax revenues. But, in 1978, Governor Carey insisted that the STT be phased out. It became a rebated tax—100 percent remitted to the seller of the stock. There is a great sensitivity to any discussion of revisiting this tax. Wall Street firms insisted that if the STT was reconstituted, they would leave New York City.[11] (See section on taxes.)

The state also played a fiscal role in the city's pension systems. The city's five pension systems are the New York City Employees' Retirement System, New York City Teachers' Retirement System, New York City Police Pension Fund, New York City Fire Pension Fund, and the Board of Education Retirement System. Often, labor unions sought state legislative action when mayors blocked increases in their pension benefits. Required contributions by the city are made based on actuarial valuations of assets and liabilities; these contributions may vary from year to year depending on the need. The state legislature determined the level of supplements to pension benefits, even though the city had to pay the bill. Such an action undermined labor negotiations. If unions did not like the city's settlement, they sought supplements in the state legislature. Mayor Koch's frustration was palpable: "Why should the unions negotiate when they know that they can get away with giving us no concessions, since the legislature is already committed to passing the bill and giving them everything they want."[12] Interestingly, as required by law, it is the city council that must ask the

Table 6.1 Revenues during the Koch administration, FY1978–FY1990 (in millions)

Revenues	FY78	% Total	FY90	% Total	% Change	Annual % Change
Total taxes	6,356	49.4%	15,015	57.9%	136.2%	11.4%
Federal grants	2,488	19.3%	2,874	11.1%	15.5%	1.3%
State grants	2,303	17.9%	5,172	19.9%	124.5%	10.4%
Unrestricted federal & state	994	7.7%	687	2.6%	–30.9%	–2.6%
Charges & fees	680	5.3%	1,077	4.2%	58.5%	4.9%
Other	39	0.3%	1,112	4.3%	2758.6%	229.9%
Total revenues	$12,859	100.0%	$25,937	100.0%	101.7%	8.5%

Note: Revenues will not total since minor revenues have been omitted.
Source: NYC Comptroller's Reports, FY1978–FY1990.

state legislature for the action on any supplement to pension benefits. So the city council is part of the problem.

The state also controlled valuable real estate in New York City. State authorities operated within the city's boundaries and were thus exempt from city zoning requirements. Mayor Koch signed a Memorandum of Understanding in 1979 giving Battery Park City Authority, controlled by a three-member board appointed by the governor, the freedom to plan the ninety-two-acre site overlooking the harbor in lower Manhattan.[13] The consequences of having the state own portions of the city meant that the city would not control development and would receive limited financial benefits from the development of that land.

INITIAL SUCCESS

Within six months of taking office in 1978, Mayor Koch immediately faced two crucial issues: renewal of the federal loan guarantees and negotiations over fifty labor union contracts. Fiscally, New York City was still in trouble. The mayor expected help from a Democratic President Carter, but U.S. Treasurer W. Michael Blumenthal, former chairman and CEO of Bendix Corporation, insisted that the city would have to make additional "sacrifices" before the Carter administration would consider an extension. Even though President Carter eventually supported loan guarantees, Congress was not easily persuaded. By March 1978, President Carter presented a plan to Congress to provide federal loan guarantees to New York City of up to fifteen years for up to $15 billion in long-term bonds. The House of Representative's Banking Committee, Koch's colleagues from his congressional days, approved a bill to give the city nearly $2 billion in loan guarantees; however, the Senate was not cooperative.

The lack of a labor agreement made the Senate wary because of the possibility of large settlements. The pressure on Koch to settle the union contracts was enormous—there would be no federal loan guarantees unless labor contracts were resolved. The contract issues were quite difficult since the unions wanted wage increases that had been deferred since 1975. Mayor Koch settled the union contract on June 5, 1978, the day before he was to testify before the Senate Banking Committee. The two-year agreement Mayor Koch struck with the major unions cost the city $757 million in salary increases and was settled without any productivity improvements.[14]

Finally, Congress agreed to the federal loan guarantees for many reasons, not least of which was that both Governor Carey and Mayor Koch were former congressmen and had many friends in Congress. Governor Carey, who had served as deputy whip while in Congress, was instrumental in gaining congressional approval. Carey was adamant that the fiscal health of the entire state was tied to the fiscal health of New York City. He argued that the domino effect of the city's bankruptcy would be disastrous for the state. "I cannot deny that there is a contagion in New York which is about to sweep across the nation. Don't kill us because we are ill."[15]

In his first term, Mayor Koch's strategy was to use the EFCB and MAC to control spending. Since the EFCB was to expire on December 1978, the question became not whether it would be extended but in what form. Mayor Koch called for the extension of the EFCB for thirty years. Felix Rohatyn, chair of the Municipal Assistance Corporation, pushed for a thirty-year extension. Governor Carey agreed and the legislation passed, changing its name to the Financial Control Board and dropping "Emergency" in 1978. The FCB would be phased out in 2008. At another point, Carey urged the FCB to put pressure on the Health and Hospitals Corporation and the Board of Education to act early to prevent deficits by the end of Fiscal Year 1979. Koch attributed "his request to the fact that the Hospital Corporation and Education Board have two of the toughest and smartest lobbies and he needs help in dealing with them."[16] Such a strategy played well in Washington. Mayor Koch was in step with the creditors.

FALLING OUT OF FAVOR

Even though Mayor Koch advocated longevity for the FCB, his relationship with FCB officials was uneasy. Tension between the mayor and the FCB ran high after Mayor Koch settled under what the FCB thought were generous terms with the municipal unions, granting an increase of over 6 percent. Comer S. Coppie, Executive Director of the FCB, sent a letter to Mayor Koch noting more than once the "disturbing trends" in his budget. In June 1979, in the FCB's annual review of the city's budget, he disagreed with Mayor Koch's budget: "The city is not only reluctant to re-establish a program of retrenchment—absent since 1977—but also that given a short-term increase in revenues the city will spend the bulk of these revenues rather than use them to improve its debt position or to ease long-term expenditure problems."[17]

In October 1979, Mayor Koch was scheduled to appear at a meeting of the FCB to submit views of his four-year financial plan. The FCB was to draft the first quarterly report of how the city was progressing under the mayor's plan. The FCB wanted the mayor to correct items before the meeting. Mayor Koch hoped to hire an additional 562 sanitation workers, a step the FCB had criticized. In addition, the FCB wanted to discuss funds due for the municipal labor contracts that might not be forthcoming as well as excessive spending on the part of HHC and the Board of Education.[18] Mayor Koch acquiesced; he did not hire the sanitation workers and met with HHC and Board of Education officials to deal with the deficits.

Mayor Koch chafed against the dictates of the monitors; his quarrels with Felix Rohatyn were legendary. Mayor Koch charged the MAC board with a "moral conflict of interest in awarding" a $250,000 contract to Rohatyn's firm, Lazard Freres, as a financial advisor, after Felix Rohatyn was withdrawing from his role in MAC. Mayor Koch ignored the fact that Rohatyn had dedicated thousands of hours to stabilizing the city's finances without taking a penny in salary. Mayor Koch raised the issue with reporters standing outside of Avery Fisher Hall where Felix Rohatyn was being honored at a dinner given by Governor Carey.[19] Rohatyn was furious as was the governor and George D. Gould, the most recent MAC chair. The firm of Lazard Freres withdrew from the contract.

Squabbles between the New York State special deputy comptroller for the city, Sidney Schwartz, and Mayor Koch and his staff were frequent. Schwartz accused the Koch administration of understating the deficits. He released a report stating that the estimated budget gap for Fiscal Year 1982 would be $2 billion, nearly three times what the city had suggested. Koch, of course, disagreed.[20]

TAXES

Mayor Koch, in cooperation with Governor Carey, participated in tax relief for corporations with the burden switching to individuals. Governor Carey insisted on eliminating the stock transfer tax (STT) in 1978 because of fears that the New York Stock Exchange would leave the city. The governor reimbursed the city for part of that loss until 2001. The reimbursement was called the Stock Transfer Tax Incentive Aid. The STT tax still exists; it is simply immediately rebated to the payer. In 1977, STT collections were $279 million; the rebates in 2003 were $9.3 billion.[21] Corporations receive other tax relief measures. Also in 1977, the general corporation tax rate on net corporate earnings was 10.05 percent, which was lowered to 9.0 percent by 1978; the commercial rent tax (CRT) was reduced by 20 percent over four years from the maximum rate of 7.5 percent to 6.0 percent.[22] And the exemption to the CRT was increased during Mayor Koch's terms of office.

This is not to say that other taxes were not increased during his tenure. Concurrently, ordinary New Yorkers witnessed increases in taxes. During the recession of 1982, there was a temporary surcharge imposed on the personal income tax, which had an annual increase of 21.9 percent in revenues, as well as a surcharge added to parking. In 1986, in a controversial move, Mayor Koch imposed an additional 5 percent on the hotel tax. The Citizens Budget Commission believed that such increases drove away business conventions and tourists in general. The proportion of tax revenue in income taxes increased as Mayor Koch imposed higher income tax rates. See Table 6.2.[23]

Tax revenues increased as the economy improved. Sales tax revenue had an annual increase of 9.0 percent. As the real estate market heated up, mortgage taxes increased by 45.1 percent a year as did the conveyance of real property, which increased by 75.1 percent. See Table 6.2.

Table 6.2 Tax revenues during the Koch administration, FY1978–FY1990 (in millions)

Tax Revenues	FY1978	% of Total	FY1990	% of Total	% Change FY78–90	Annual % Change FY78–90
Property	$3,230	50.8%	$ 6,543	43.6%	102.6%	8.5%
Sales & use	1,342	21.1%	2,796	18.6%	108.3%	9.0%
Mortgage recording	24	0.4%	154	1.0%	540.7%	45.1%
Personal income	700	11.0%	2,538	16.9%	262.6%	21.9%
Corporate & utility income	809	12.6%	1,880	12.5%	134.4%	11.2%
Unincorporated business income	89	1.4%	357	2.4%	300.1%	25.0%
Other taxes	240	3.8%	1,151	7.7%	379.4%	31.6%
Conveyance of real property	22	0.3%	215	1.4%	900.9%	75.1%
Total taxes	$6,356.3	100.0%	$15,014.8	100.0%	136.2%	11.4%

Note: Revenues will not total since minor revenues have been omitted.
Source: NYC Comptroller's Reports FY1978 to FY1990.

SPENDING PATTERNS

Mayor Koch's spending differed dramatically over his three terms as mayor. During his first term, he increased spending in economic development annually by 16.8 percent as well as quality of life areas, such as cultural affairs and environmental programs, by 17.8 percent annually. However, he kept spending to 5.6 percent during his first-term annual increases. He increased redistributive services, such as the public hospitals and social services, only 2.4 percent annually. Mayor Koch became a pro-growth mayor in his second and third terms. As revenues grew in those terms, he increased total spending by 9 percent a year. In human investment, namely, elementary and secondary education and libraries, he increased annual spending by 14.0 percent and spending in public safety by 15.8 percent. In his three terms, he increased spending in economic development areas by 207.9 percent. Redistributive functions were increased by only 85.1 percent during his administration. See Table 6.3.[24]

Koch attempted to reenter the bond market in the fall of 1980. Felix Rohatyn warned that if New York City attempted to sell its own bonds, it could hurt rather than help the city's fiscal recovery. He said such attempts could jeopardize the credit of the assistance corporation and further delay a full return of the city to public credit markets. Koch held back, but was not deterred for long.

MAYORAL SUCCESS

In June 1980, Mayor Koch succeeded in passing a balanced budget for Fiscal Year 1981. By January 1981, tax revenues were up, the economy was improving, and a surplus of $200 million was expected. In February 1981, Mayor Koch succeeded in getting the city back into the bond market when New York City sold $100 million in short-term notes backed only by anticipated city tax money. In effect, the bond rating agency, Standard & Poor's, gave an investment-grade credit rating to the city's selling $6 billion of general obligation bonds, the first rating since they had suspended the bond rating during the city's 1975 fiscal crisis. This was a year earlier than the city was required to reenter the market. The psychological gains of the note sale were as significant as the fiscal benefits. It marked the first time since December 1974, just before the onset of the city's fiscal crisis, that New York had borrowed money solely on its assurance that it could repay the loan with future tax revenues. "It means," said one banker, "that investors think the city has come far and is in reasonable shape for now. It doesn't necessarily mean they're confident about the city's financial health twenty years from now."[25] In effect, it meant that the city had regained some control over its fiscal policy. The irony in this success is that there were now so many tight state controls through the FCB that getting back in the market may

Table 6.3 Expenditures during the Koch administration, FY1979–FY1990 (in millions)

Categories	FY79	FY82	Annual % Change FY79–82	FY90	Annual % Change FY82–90	Total % Change FY79–90
Total expenditures	$12,892	$15,076	5.6%	$25,932	9.0%	101.1%
Development	190	285	16.8%	584	13.1%	207.9%
Public safety	1,205	1,558	9.8%	3,523	15.8%	192.4%
Human investment	2,477	3,196	9.7%	6,763	14.0%	173.0%
Redistributive	3,945	4,231	2.4%	7,302	9.1%	85.1%
Quality of life	$ 224	$ 343	17.8%	$ 638	10.8%	185.4%

Note: FY78 cannot be used because pensions were included in agency totals for the last time. Expenditures will not total since minor expenditures have been omitted.

Source: NYC Comptroller's reports, FY1979–FY1990.

have been a psychological boost for city officials, but meant little in terms of regaining fiscal control.

In 1982, Mayor Koch again negotiated new labor union contracts, which resulted in 8 percent increases each year for two years. These negotiations occurred during Koch's race for the governorship, which he lost. The FCB at first refused to sign off on Mayor Koch's labor agreement. MAC chairman Felix Rohatyn called the agreement excessive and urged the mayor to reopen negotiations. Mayor Koch sought $600 million in new sales and income taxes to help pay for this increase, bringing immediate resistance from Governor Carey. There was a growing indication that the economy was improving as revenue targets were being met. Mayor Koch submitted a financial contingency plan calling for new layoffs, new taxes, and a cutback in funds for such agencies as the Board of Education and the Health and Hospitals Corporation.

Throughout Mayor Koch's mayoralty, MAC chairman Felix Rohatyn sought to use MAC surplus funds in ways he saw fit, regardless of what city elected officials thought. Tough negotiations among Governor Cuomo, Mayor Koch, and Felix Rohatyn occurred each time there was a surplus. Mayor Koch fought Rohatyn on spending the surplus his way, likening the city to medieval times: "This city is no longer a vassal city. We will not allow an outside committee, whether MAC or anybody else, to decide on an ongoing way what the city will or will not do."[26] The mayor insisted that the MAC surplus consisted of city funds since MAC was financed by city taxes.

The surpluses resulted from refinancing previous MAC bonds with high interest rates to low interest rates and also from interest revenues on reserves that MAC held. In 1984, MAC's first surplus of $1.1 billion was used for a variety of capital projects, including mass transit and school construction. In 1986, in the second surplus, Rohatyn agreed to provide $925 million of MAC surplus to the Metropolitan Transit Authority (MTA) for use in its capital-improvement program. In return, the MTA agreed to freeze fares through 1989, create an oversight committee to monitor its capital spending, hold its wage increases to the rise in the cost of living, and put a labor representative on the MTA board.[27] In 1987, MAC officials offered $600 million to a building program for the city's Board of Education if the board agreed to certain conditions. What is interesting about this is that the mayor had to negotiate with an investment banker, a private person, not an elected official, to spend city revenues. Mayor Koch was not a pushover; he fought for what he thought made sense. But the fact remains that financial interests had succeeded in playing a major role in the city's fiscal policies.

LABOR UNIONS

Union leaders and members were angry and bitter. During the fiscal crisis, wages were frozen. Once the national and city economies improved, the labor unions expected to benefit from the "good times" through salary increases. However, labor unions did not perceive the labor settlements in the Koch administration to be as generous as the financial elites thought they were. During the height of the robust economy of the 1980s, the Citizens Budget Commission demonstrated that union members were no better off than they were during the fiscal crisis if inflation were considered.[28] For example, police officers first grade earned $17,458 in 1977; by 1987, they were earning $32,368, which appears to be a sizeable increase. But, given inflation, it actually was a 0 percent increase.

Of course, the view of contract settlements was one of perspective. The financial elites claimed that the settlements were too rich, given that few productivity improvements were accomplished. Unions saw no financial gain in real terms. The reality was that, over a ten-year period, there was no real financial improvement once inflation was taken into account. Mayor Koch was quite hostile to the unions and the unions reciprocated. Victor Gotbaum was quoted in the press as saying: "Koch is a four-letter word."[29] Mayor Koch used the Citizens Budget Commission to send messages to the unions. In an address before the CBC, the mayor said, to great applause, that 7 percent is out of the question. He said this at a time when 7 percent represented federal guidelines. Victor Gotbaum responded by saying that the mayor projected "amateurish and childish doom and gloom projections."[30]

At the same time, crime soared. Mayor Koch rarely addressed the rising crime rate in the city. Crime rates per 1,000 in population demonstrate that total property crimes peaked at 75.62 in 1988 and that total violent crimes grew steadily from 18.46 in 1984 to 23.00 in 1989, his last year in office.[31] At the same time, Koch let the number of full-time police officers drop to only 25,858 in 1989, the lowest since 1984. The soaring crime rate left New Yorkers fearful. The bond market reflected this. James F. Lynch, a money manager and editor of the Lynch Municipal Bond Advisory in Santa Fe, New Mexico, had been urging investors to sell their New York City bonds since 1987 and warned that a crisis was coming. "The politicians played games when they had all of the money that was generated from the tremendous economic growth in the 1980's," Lynch said. "Everybody was fat, dumb and lazy in giving the store away."[32] Mayor Koch benefited from a booming economy in the 1980s, yet the city suffered an increasing crime rate that Koch did not successfully address. He left that to the next mayor.

CONCLUSION

Mayor Koch's finest achievements came in the first six months of his administration in 1978 when he renegotiated the federal loan guarantees and settled union contracts without disruptions in services. This was a time when the city faced major financial risks on its return to fiscal solvency and Mayor Koch led the way to stability. He was the first mayor after the fiscal crisis who had to deal with the established state institutions put in place during the 1975 fiscal crisis. The FCB, the special deputy comptroller's office, and MAC all put pressure on Mayor Koch to reduce spending. Sometimes they succeeded and sometimes they did not. In his first term, Mayor Koch could not hire the police or sanitation workers that he wanted because FCB objected to an increased city payroll. In his next two terms, the mayor enjoyed surpluses that he spent on municipal labor contracts, much to the chagrin and over the opposition of those financial officials. The financial elites proved most successful in influencing spending policy in times of stress. Although financial structures were put in place to ensure that these state institutions would maintain their influence regardless of who was mayor, what the fiscal environment history reveals is that, in financially flush times, the mayor was able to disregard the protests of financial elites.

In his first term, Mayor Koch succeeded by working closely with financial elites to put the city's house in order. He cooperated by providing tax relief for corporations while shifting the tax burden to individuals. And he improved the fiscal health of the city, at least for his first term. Mayor Koch established an economic development regime and used the state institution of the FCB to legitimize budget reductions and force fiscal discipline on those who sought to spend more for human services.

Mollenkopf charts how Mayor Koch moved from his earlier program of low taxes and improved productivity to his later position as a spender with close ties to real estate developers, who reciprocated with heavy contributions to his campaigns.[33] As demonstrated by Mollenkopf, by the end of his administration, Mayor Koch led a development regime with close ties to real estate interests. Mayor Koch earned his reputation as a spender in his second and third terms of office. As the economy boomed, so did his budget. He no longer pleased the financial elites, particularly with labor contract settlements. The mayor's spending reflected his interests in economic development and improving the quality of life for his constituents. He sought autonomy and fought with officials from the state institutions established to monitor the city's fiscal policies, most notably with the governor's financial expert, Felix Rohatyn.

Mayor Koch shifted his priorities from increased productivity to settlements with the unions that the financial elites opposed. Although he never supported social services and health services for the poor to any great extent, there were increases in these areas in his later fiscal plans. Mayor Koch spent a great deal of time on developing business districts in Manhattan: the Jacob Javits Convention Center, the South Street Seaport, the Columbus Circle Project, and the Times Square Redevelopment Project. The city granted tax abatements worth $650 million over twenty years and allowed office development to exceed prior zoning limits.[34]

In his later two terms, he lost his reputation as a mayor of great competence when several politicians close to him were involved in a major contracting scandal, culminating in a dramatic suicide by Donald Mannes, Queens borough president, who plunged a kitchen knife into his own chest. There was also the general unease in the city as crime rose dramatically during Koch's last term. In the end, as Mollenkopf explains, New Yorkers were just plain tired of Mayor Koch's outspokenness: "Koch encountered minority criticism not just from his bitter enemies among the black political establishment and the white left. The press began questioning him aggressively about the scandals."[35] He sought but did not win the Democratic nomination for a fourth term.

SEVEN

MAYOR DAVID DINKINS AND THE
1989 FISCAL CRISIS (1990–1994)

We've hired 9,000 cops since I've been Mayor, for a net of 5,700, pretty close to 6,000 and more coming. . . . crime is down in the seven major F.B.I. index categories for the first time in 36 years, and for more than two consecutive years.

—Mayor Dinkins, 1993[1]

There was a great deal of racial tension in the mayoral election year of 1989. Racial attacks were common. New Yorkers were shaken in April 19, 1989, when a twenty-nine-year-old female investment banker was raped, beaten, and left to die in Central Park allegedly by a group of black teenagers. Then came Bensonhurst, a largely Italian neighborhood in Brooklyn, where a young African American man, Yusuf Hawkins, was set upon by several white men and then shot. The murder stunned the city. Demonstrators marched through Bensonhurst shouting, "No justice, no peace." On August 30, three weeks before the Democratic primary, Yusuf Hawkins was buried. Twelve days before the primary, demonstrators marched in Brooklyn to the Brooklyn Bridge where police awaited them, and a minor riot ensued. In the midst of this racial turmoil, David Dinkins defeated Mayor Koch in the Democratic primary in September 1989. The voters responded to David Dinkins's calls for racial healing. Dinkins achieved this almost unprecedented level of support (one-third of the white Democratic vote) with white voters. Dinkins's victory speech on primary night reflected New Yorkers hopes and fears: "I'm the guy that brings people together. . . . You voted our hopes and not your fears."[2] Dinkins was referring to the Republican candidate, Rudolph Giuliani, who had won the Republican primary that night. Giuliani said in his victory speech, "Are we going to be a city of crime or a city of law?"[3]

In the general election of November 1989, when Mayor David Dinkins won the mayoralty in a close race against Giuliani, there was much
rejoicing among minorities and liberals who made up Dinkins's constituency.
Wilbur Rich, who closely examined Dinkins's relationship with the press,
commented that "Dinkins had built a reputation as a congenial man and
as a race mediator."[4] In his 1990 inaugural address, Mayor Dinkins said that
his administration would seek social justice and would "speak out against
national policies that offer cold indifference instead of compassion."[5] He was
committed to supporting human services through expansion of government
services, and sought to increase budgets and redistribute resources, even
in the midst of a severe national recession. But Mayor David Dinkins, a
quiet, dignified former Marine, lawyer, and math major in college, had little
experience managing large organizations. He had been a New York State
legislator, the city clerk, and Manhattan borough president. None of these
jobs had prepared him for running the largest city in the nation.

Mayor Dinkins faced fiscal scarcity throughout his mayoralty. Mayor
Abraham Beame, who presided over the city's 1975 fiscal crisis, noted the
difficulties that Mayor Dinkins faced, observing that "no mayor had inherited
a more serious and overwhelming condition in both financial and social problems."[6] He faced it at a time when President Reagan advocated an agenda
of privatization, deregulation, lower taxes, and small government.[7]

EXTERNAL ENVIRONMENT

Much had changed in the city during the Koch administration. The number
of white people in the city had declined dramatically from 51.9 percent of
the population in 1980 to 43.2 percent in 1990.[8] Although New York City
was always an immigrant city, Mayor Dinkins represented an opportunity
to bring a racially diverse population together without the antagonisms that
the Koch administration represented.

Another change was economic. The city was bleeding jobs; this economic collapse has been documented by several researchers.[9] The securities
industry restructured, resulting in fewer available jobs: "NYC securities
employment fell by 26% and the number of commercial banking jobs dropped
by 43% between December 1987 and December 1991."[10] This contraction
accounted for 35 percent of the decline in total real wages paid in the city,
along with a corresponding loss in income taxes to the city.

In the late 1980s, commercial banking institutions began a period of
mergers and consolidations that involved substantial job reductions. Globalization resulted in vast bank mergers with institutions that played on a
world stage. As a result of the mergers, banks laid off thousands of workers. The consolidation of banks also meant that CEOs no longer had the
time nor the clout to play prominent roles in the community.[11] Municipal
securities were not of interest to international bankers. Unlike 1975, when

the banks held a great deal of the city's debt, New York's banks did not buy New York bonds. President Reagan's 1986 tax reform legislation meant that banks did not profit from municipal securities and hence no longer purchased them.[12] For the most part, banks stopped underwriting city debt; they no longer held securities in their portfolios; and mutual funds and individual investors took their place (see the introduction). Traditional bankers, such as Walter Wriston, "were the last at Citicorp that had any interest in New York."[13] Thus, bankers were not as involved in local issues. The exception was Felix Rohatyn, who, although he resigned as chair of MAC in 1993 after eighteen years of service, remained as an advisor to New York's governors and mayors. He was also an important friend to David Dinkins throughout his mayoralty.

When individual investors and mutual funds replaced institutional investors as the largest pool buying municipal bonds, the bond rating agencies assessed the city's finances. During Dinkins's regime, it was the bond rating companies that rose in importance in commenting on the city's finances alongside the FCB and New York State's special deputy comptroller. Comments made by David Rockefeller during the 1975 fiscal crisis were now being articulated by Standard & Poor's. If a credit rating agency reduced its credit rating, the city would pay millions of more dollars in interest on the next bond sale. The credit rating agencies along with state institutions put in place by the state and banking interests took the bankers' place as the watchdogs of fiscal concerns in municipalities.

Although bankers played less of a role, this did not mean that their policies of low taxes, small government, and fiscal restraint were abandoned. Bankers had left in place state institutions created to monitor the city's finances. New York State officials, with the cooperation of the financial elites, had established the New York State's' special deputy comptroller's office and the Financial Control Board that would oversee the city's finances. At the time of the Dinkins administration, two out of the three private members of the FCB were from financial institutions: Heather Ruth, president of the Public Securities Association; Stanley Shuman, executive vice president of Allen & Company, an investment banking concern; and Donald Kummerfeld, president and CEO of the International Federation of the Periodic Press, a trade group. Although it was in sunset mode due to be phased out in Fiscal Year 2008, the FCB continued to review the city's four-year financial plans quarterly and inform the city if its plans were inadequate. The FCB was required to reimpose its rule on the city if it determined the city's financial status had seriously eroded.

INTERGOVERNMENTAL ENVIRONMENT

After the booming 1980s, the October 1987 stock market crash, "Black Monday," signaled the beginning of a national recession. The financial excesses of the 1980s—the junk bond market collapse and the downgrades of commercial banking credit—contributed to the recession. On the intergovernmental level, the lack of growth in state revenue reflected the deteriorating picture of the state's economy. New York State entered a recession. The growth in the state's gross domestic product (GDP) hit an all-time low of 1 percent in 1991 as compared to 9.2 percent in 1988.[14]

New York City's economy suffered; its recession during David Dinkins's mayoralty was severe. In 1992, at the height of the crisis, the city registered an 11 percent unemployment rate, compared to 7.5 percent nationwide.[15] The city's GDP hit a low of –0.2 percent, not seen since the early days of the Koch administration. In the years 1992 to 1993, New York City's number of employed declined by 170,000.[16] The local poverty rate, which had decreased in the 1980s from 25.4 percent in 1982 to 20.8 percent in 1989 along with the unemployment rate, rose again every year during the Dinkins term as the recession deepened.[17]

Revenues increased during the Dinkins administration, but not at the rate of the Koch administration. There were annual tax revenue increases of 5.2 percent, much smaller than those during the Koch administration of 11.4 percent annually. State revenues increased 3.5% annually, a far cry from Mayor Koch's 10.4 percent (see Tables 6.1 and 7.1). This situation was in large part a result of the state's gloomy financial picture. In addition, Allen Proctor, executive director of the Financial Control Board during the Dinkins administration, said that "[Governor] Cuomo always wanted to keep his options open—[he] always distrusted city officials, believed that the city would always want more, no matter what the city got."[18] Although Mayor Dinkins received little financial support from the state, which was going through its own fiscal crisis, the city did see a sizeable increase in its federal revenues—9.4 percent annually over his four-year term. Mayor Dinkins was counting on the 1992 election of President Clinton to provide fiscal relief for the city, and sought even more funding. Unlike President Roosevelt's support for Mayor LaGuardia, Clinton could only offer limited help. Congress defeated President Clinton's proposals before the U.S. Conference of Mayors for a $20 billion stimulus package for urban areas. There were serious limits to federal aid. See Table 7.1.[19]

The external environment had another impact on the city. New York State has numerous laws that affected the city's fiscal policies. One example was the control over negotiating union contracts. Most unions have the right to voluntary arbitration if they cannot agree on a settlement with the city. Arbitration sounds reasonable, but what is not understood is that, since the 1980s, the state legislature removed the explicit requirement that arbitrators consider the city's ability to pay for a settlement.[20] When arbitrators are mediating a settlement between a union and government entity, the arbitrator is not required to consider the cost of the settlement as a factor in the negotiations. Unions benefit from this situation. Consequently, government

Table 7.1 Revenues during the Dinkins administration, FY1990–FY1994 (in millions)

Tax Revenues	FY90	% of Total	FY94	% of Total	% Increase FY90–94	Annual % Increase FY90–94
Total taxes	$15,015	57.9%	$18,115	57.8%	20.6%	5.2%
Federal grants	2,874	11.1%	3,960	12.6%	37.8%	9.4%
State grants	5,172	19.9%	5,903	18.8%	14.1%	3.5%
Unrestricted federal & state	687	2.6%	667	2.1%	-2.9%	-0.7%
Charges & fees	1,077	4.2%	1,277	4.1%	18.5%	4.6%
Other	1,112	4.3%	1,432	4.6%	28.7%	7.2%
Total revenues	$25,937	100.0%	$31,352	100.0%	20.9%	5.2%

Note: Columns will not total due to minor revenues being omitted.
Source: NYC Comptroller's Reports, FY90–FY94.

officials are loathe to turn to arbitration; better to come to agreement in negotiations. In addition, police and fire unions have the right to binding arbitration if the city and these unions reach an impasse. Binding arbitration often favors the unions since, once again, costs are not part of any criteria that an arbitrator uses in negotiations. The state legislature has the right to pass legislation increasing supplements to labor unions' pension funds upon petition by New York City Council.

The Wicks Law is the most famous of New York State's rules that affect the city's fiscal picture. This law requires the city to use multiple contractors for local construction rather than just one. Originally a reform bill, the law has now increased the cost of construction for local governments since it forbids single bid contracting and requires multiple contractors. These types of external financial burdens on New York City can be changed only through the state legislature.

INTERNAL ENVIRONMENT

The First 100 Days

The financial elites' reaction to Mayor Dinkins was at first skeptical. The *Wall Street Journal* set the tone: "It's not Mr. Dinkins' fault that he survived long enough to be in the right place at the right time with the right color—a time of crisis."[21] According to a *New York Times* editorial, "Mr. Dinkins is a product of the regular Democratic organization, a man of modest accomplishment who has fumbled more than once."[22] Few people made open remarks about his race, but the attitude was not far from the surface. His friend, Basil Paterson, explained: "Mr. Dinkins is not only a new mayor; he is also the first black. And black politicians have not been associated with fiscal concerns but with taking care of people."[23] He was under constant attack, sometimes with backhanded compliments. Hy Grossman, the managing director of Standard & Poor's, said about Mayor Dinkins when he was first elected: "So far, Mayor Dinkins's fiscal policy has met the test. He's said that fiscal stability is his Number one priority. He may just be repeating things someone told him to say, but the lesson of the 70's is clear: without financial stability, you can't get anything else done."[24]

Mayor Dinkins established quite early that he would cooperate fully with the financial elites. In his first year, he set up a Council of Economic Advisers, including such leading banking figures as David Rockefeller and Felix Rohatyn, Lewis Rudin, the real-estate developer, and a labor economist, Carol O'Cleireacain.[25] Certainly, the financial elites sought to influence those appointed by Mayor Dinkins. Mayor Dinkins agreed to make Norman Steisel, a former senior vice president at Lazard Freres, his first deputy mayor, and Phillip Michaels, former director of the Emergency Financial Control Board, his budget director.

He also established a business–labor advisory panel on management in his first year. The panel, led by Roger C. Altman and Donald D. Kummerfeld, issued a report that called for managed Medicaid and an early-retirement program for city teachers, both of which would save millions of dollars, and, at the request of the New York City Partnership, merged economic development agencies.

Dinkins asked Nathan Leventhal, president of Lincoln Center and previously a close aide to Mayor Koch, to head his twenty-one-member transition committee to screen appointments to the city's top positions. Although the transition team was ethnically and racially balanced, Mayor Dinkins named other prestigious New Yorkers to the team including Felix Rohatyn, chairman of the Municipal Assistance Corporation, and Peter Goldmark, president of the Rockefeller Foundation, former executive director of the Port Authority of New York and New Jersey, and former state budget director. His appointment of Leventhal was a clear signal to New Yorkers that he intended to include the best and brightest, even those from the Koch administration.

His first executive budget reported his efforts to close "a combined fiscal year 1990 and 1991 gap of some $1.3 billion" only to see the gap grow by another $880 million.[26] Revenues dropped precipitously. Personal income tax in Fiscal Year 1990 grew only 3.8 percent from the year before (Fiscal Year 1989) as compared to growing 17.1 percent from Fiscal Year 1988 to Fiscal Year 1989. Tax revenues on general corporations and financial corporations declined. It was a fiscal nightmare for the new mayor and his staff. The mayor was squeezed by the depressed economy. The impact of this inherited budget meant that Mayor Dinkins had to cut programs immediately, including his anticrime and drug prevention programs. He announced that he would delay the starting date of a police academy class and reduced its size from 1,800 to 750 officers. The financial monitors expressed appreciation. The plan was so well received by the financial community that Felix Rohatyn said, "I can't see that anybody at this stage of the game would have done better than David."[27] Mitchell Moss, director of New York University's Urban Research Center, explained the financial community's reaction: "His performance has been a shock because no one thought he had the reservoir of authority to do the hard things. He came in as Mr. Conciliation, but he's turning out to be much . . . tougher than his persona before the election. He's become a hard-ball mayor on the budget."[28]

The perception was that Mayor Dinkins had appointed a bunch of cronies; however, he did select competent people. His emphasis on harmony in racial relations was reflected in his appointments. He achieved greater diversity than mayors before and after him. He appointed Carol O'Cleireacain, chief economist of the largest municipal workers union, as the city's finance commissioner, along with deputy mayors Bill Lynch, Barbara Fife, and Sally Hernandez-Pinero. He appointed the first Cuban-born hospital chief,

Dr. J. Emilio Carrillo, the first African American commissioner of mental health, Dr. Billy E. Jones, the first Puerto Rican fire commissioner, Carlos M. Rivera, and African American Douglas White as personnel director. An African American, Lee P. Brown, was appointed police commissioner. Mayor Dinkins also appointed more women in higher positions than any mayor before or since. These appointments included Emily Lloyd, the sanitation commissioner; Betsy Gotbaum, the parks commissioner; Catherine M. Abate, the correction commissioner; Barbara Sable, HRA commissioner; and Felice Michetti, commissioner of HPD.

While Mayor Dinkins's fiscal skills were being tested, his reputation as a conciliator was under fire. An alleged racial incident occurred early in his administration. On January 18, 1990, a Haitian woman claimed that a Korean grocer had hit her; African American activists began a boycott of the grocery store and another across from it. In the first hundred days, this incident went unnoticed by the press but it erupted within the first year of the Dinkins administration. The boycott, which continued for a year, was seen by many as an indictment of the Dinkins administration for moving too slowly to resolve racial instances. Within the first hundred days, the mayor was lauded by the financial community, yet in the background lurked the racial tension that proved Dinkins's eventual downfall.

THE REST OF A VOLATILE FIRST YEAR

Mayor Dinkins's first year demonstrated his inexperience in labor contract negotiations, his inability to resolve the deep racial and ethnic divisions in the city, and his failure to control strife within his own staff. He raised taxes, cut the budget, and presented a projected balanced budget. Ronald K. Shelp, president of the New York Partnership and the Chamber of Commerce, said of Mayor Dinkins's first-year budget negotiations: "Business is encouraged that he would bite the bullet on the budget and take a tough stance, even though it may be unpopular."[29] Jeffrey F. Rizzo, Moody's managing director for public finance noted: "The mayor's office has shown a lot of determination and aggressiveness; we are encouraged."[30]

Balancing the budget at one point in time was not enough. As Fiscal Year 1991 began in July 1990, the budget plan deteriorated as revenues declined. Then in October, in the course of a single week, Mayor Dinkins unsettled the financial community. He announced a one-year agreement with the United Federation of Teachers for a 5.5 percent increase in teachers' pay and also announced plans to hire thousands of police officers. Dinkins stayed within a 1.5 percent raise that he had budgeted for union negotiations before going into talks; the remaining 4 percent would be achieved through raising the earnings assumptions for the workers' pension fund investments to 9 percent from the current 8.25 percent. Thus, the city would be required to contribute less money to the pension funds and could then afford the raises. This juggling of accounts did not impress the financial sector.

The UFT settlement was proof of the inexperience of the mayor and his top aides. This inexperience was demonstrated in several ways. First, the Dinkins administration chose to settle with one of the toughest union contracts first—the UFT. The UFT is known for its inflexible negotiating stance. It would have been best to have more experience before tackling the UFT. Second, there were enormous unmet needs for New York City's teachers. The starting salary for new teachers was only $25,000. A real case could be made that the teachers deserved higher salaries, which leads to the third reason. Contracts with many of the city's unions had expired. The other union leaders saw the UFT number—5.5 percent—and said: "That's now our number." If the Dinkins administration had settled with a less powerful union, it probably could have negotiated a smaller price. Fourth, another sign of their inexperience was that the budget director was not present in negotiations. To enter negotiations with the UFT without the city's budget director meant that there was no one to protect the city's fiscal outlook. Fifth, it was only a one-year contract. It was understandable that city officials wanted a short contract because of a gloomy fiscal picture, but the stress and constant battling with unions took its toll on an administration that was heavily supported in the election process by the unions. Lastly, Eric Schmertz, the city's chief negotiator, was not new to negotiating, but was new to representing the city. He was an arbitrator by training and experience and used to making a deal. He had been a member of the city's Board of Collective Bargaining, but Mayor Koch had forced Schmertz out because Koch thought that he favored unions. Schmertz was not used to considering the city's fiscal outlook either.

Certainly, the Dinkins administration was fearful of a teachers' strike at the beginning of the school year, so the team believed it had to tackle the UFT first. In the end, the deal would come back to haunt Mayor Dinkins. He had to renege later and renegotiate the contract to delay payment of part of the raise. The other unions wanted their fair share and negotiations became extremely difficult. The fiscal monitors were up in arms.

Then came even worse news. A few days later, Philip Michaels, the budget director, warned of the possibility of 15,000 layoffs. This split the Dinkins administration. Some staff within the administration were furious that the budget director would announce this without clearing such a pronouncement with the mayor. When newspaper articles quoted unnamed budget officials, such articles added fuel to the fire among the mayor's staff as to who was leaking information to the press. The mixed signals, 5.5 percent increase in the UFT contract, hiring police officers, and laying off city employees, were not welcomed in the state house or in the bond markets: "Worried bondholders quickly dumped large blocks of bonds. Prices fell and

the yields on bonds . . . rose sharply."[31] Standard & Poor's announced that
it was considering lowering the city's credit rating. The private members of
the FCB asked to meet with Mayor Dinkins. News reporters wondered if
Mayor Dinkins had control of his immediate staff, some of whom professed
ignorance about where the 15,000 layoff number came from. The tension
between the budget director, Philip Michaels, and others around the mayor
grew. The outcry was so great that the mayor and the UFT renegotiated
the contract and the UFT agreed to defer part of the salary increases for
four years. The larger fear was being discussed by elected officials and good
government groups—if the teachers get 5.5 percent, then don't all the other
unions get 5.5 percent in a time of deepening fiscal crisis? But Mayor Dinkins
could not take back the number; it was out there. And those mixed signals
of an ample contract settlement while simultaneously calling for layoffs would
come to haunt the Dinkins administration.

To his credit, Mayor Dinkins responded quickly. The FCB asked for
a modified financial plan, and, within a week, Mayor Dinkins presented a
plan that closed a $388 million budget gap through attrition and some ser-
vice cuts. He also called attention to the fact that the 5.5 percent increase
would only cost the city 1.5 percent since the remainder would be taken
from recalibrating the city's pension contribution. The FCB officials were
satisfied as were the credit rating agencies. The New York Times wrote an
editorial stating: "he now offers a prudent and coherent plan for balancing
the budget."[32] The bond market was so nervous that, in December, when
the city was offering a major sale of bonds, Mayor Dinkins announced job
reductions to demonstrate the city's fiscal prudence. He and numerous city
officials met with representatives of bond rating agencies in a successful effort
to convince them that his administration could handle its finances and that
the credit rating should not be lowered. Mayor Dinkins and Comptroller
Elizabeth Holtzman met with Hy Grossman from Standard & Poor's to lobby
to keep the city's credit rating. The Dinkins administration succeeded, kept
its credit rating, and sold $1.3 billion in bonds.

Mayor Dinkins's openness stood him in good stead. When Mayor Dinkins announced his financial plan in January 1991, Allen Proctor, executive
director of the FCB, said that the mayor was "not hiding the deficits, and
financially, he has tried to find enough solutions. We may disagree with his
strategy and the likelihood of it coming to pass, but he's faced up to the
job."[33] Later, Standard & Poor's removed the city from its credit watch and
reaffirmed the city's A– rating: "New York City received a pat on the back
from Standard & Poor's Corp. last week for its handling of its fiscal problems.
But S&P warned that the city still faces major economic problems and that
the bond rating could fall if Mayor Dinkins balances the budget with bond
refinancing and wage deferrals, conserving cash now while costing money
later."[34] Clearly, his creditors were cautiously optimistic.

This attention to financial interests meant Dinkins's supporters were disillusioned. "He seems to want to deal with Wall Street first and the people who brought him into City Hall later," said Mary Brosnahan, executive director for the Coalition for the Homeless. "We've been amazed he's reversed himself so often on our issues."[35] Dennis Rivera, president of one of the largest unions in the city, 1199 SEIU, said: "There is a growing perception among the people in labor that he's paying too much attention to the Wall Street community and the bond raters and not enough to the working people of New York."[36]

This was the hard part for Mayor Dinkins. He struggled to keep his base while dealing with the largest fiscal crisis since 1975. At the end of his first fiscal year, he said, "I'm not saying we ought to be entered into the Fiscal Hall of Fame, but look at what we achieved. Since we did all the things they said we couldn't do, they ought to be saying, 'Wow.' Just maybe, the time will come when people will be a trifle more patient and say, perhaps he does know what the hell he's doing."[37]

In August 1990, Mayor Dinkins was again seen as reacting too slowly when a violent disturbance took place at Rikers Island and 135 people were injured. Over 1,000 correction officers illegally blockaded the island, not allowing any food, medical supplies, or visitors to enter the island for over thirty-six hours. According to many critics, the Dinkins administration did not move quickly enough.[38] Police were not called to remove the demonstrators; the Taylor Law was not invoked to permit fining striking correction officers. Instead, negotiations ensued that finally resulted in corrections officers leaving the bridge after being assured by their labor union leader, Phil Seelig, that "we got just about everything we wanted."[39] The administration did not control correction officers who conducted an illegal blockade.

In September 1990, there was a fatal stabbing of a young white tourist, Brian Watkins, during an attempted robbery by young minority men. This action became national news with countless televised accounts of the stabbing, the family's reaction, the city's high crime rate, and the inability of the city to control crime.

But what Mayor Dinkins did not say at the end of his first fiscal year was that racial strife was increasing and many New Yorkers were uneasy. Mayor Dinkins was not elected because of his fiscal prowess; he was elected because he could bring together the "gorgeous mosaic." In addition to the boycott of the Korean grocery store, the Bensonhurst juries convicted one person but acquitted another. On May 11, 1990, Mayor Dinkins made a televised appeal for racial unity and public order and he was lauded for it. But that was not enough. The boycott of the Korean grocery store continued and the mayor was seen by many as not doing enough to resolve the issue.

Mayor Dinkins also incurred caustic comments from the former mayor, Ed Koch. The irony was that Mayor Koch had allowed the city to accumulate a major deficit and he had contributed to racial strife during his three terms. Ed Koch was a constant critic of Mayor Dinkins's treatment of the Korean grocery boycott. Koch said that the city had not enforced a court order requiring demonstrators to be at least fifty feet from the store. This was not the only time that Mayor Koch criticized the Dinkins administration.

In several ways, Mayor Dinkins did not recover from his first year of intense fiscal and racial confrontations. The media portrayed him as acting too slowly and, even though he was fiscally responsible, it was not enough.

THE WORST FISCAL YEAR, 1991–1992

Mayor Dinkins's plans for his second fiscal year were upset by the financial elites. He faced a budget deficit in his Fiscal Year 1992 projected budget beginning on July 1, 1991. He announced substantial cuts in city services and a plan to use the surplus from MAC bonds to resolve part of the deficit. In Fiscal Year 1991–1992, Mayor Dinkins, in the midst of a depressed economy, faced additional deficits and cut the largest number of employees (7,000 during his term, a 3.0 percent reduction) since the 1975 fiscal crisis.[40] But the credit rating agencies objected. Even though MAC bonds were financed by the city's sales taxes, the agencies saw the plan as simply a scheme for the city to continue to live beyond its means. In May 1991, MAC chairman Felix Rohatyn canceled the plans to refinance MAC bonds, which would produce a one-time cash surplus that could be given to the city, when Standard & Poor's warned that the plan would hurt the city's credit rating. Standard & Poor's was definite—no one-shots to fill budget holes. The mayor had counted on and then had to eliminate plans to use $350 million in MAC bonds as part of his proposed budget. The mayor chose more service cuts rather than see the city's credit rating downgraded.

In the end, the adopted budget for Fiscal Year 1992 was the most difficult since the 1970s, cutting $1.5 billion. Part of the lottery money from the Safe Streets/Safe City Program in the Board of Education's spending plan was used to bridge budget gaps created by the city's falling tax revenues instead of supporting what Dinkins intended: youth programs. When adopting the Fiscal Year 1992 budget, Mayor Dinkins defended raising property taxes to limit the cutting of city services. The choice of the property tax was made for several reasons. First, the city could not raise any taxes except the property tax without permission from the state legislature. Second, the property tax rate was fairly low. Third, any increase was spread over a very large group. "We were going for taxes that had the broadest base and that were deductible," said Carol O'Cleireacain, the city's commissioner of finance.[41] In addition, the top tax rate of the income tax was increased to 4.5 percent and over 6,000 positions were eliminated.

The pressure from financial elites was constant as the recession continued. In November 1991, Mayor Dinkins submitted a five-year financial plan to the Financial Control Board in which he announced a $1.2 billion deficit for the following year's projected budget. He also proposed using $1 billion in MAC funds to avoid more property tax increases. Since the financial elites did not wish to see borrowing taking the place of tax revenues, the FCB and MAC officials rejected Dinkins's plan. An example of sheer power by financial elites was the reaction of the mayor's office after sharp criticism by Felix Rohatyn, who, in November 1991, objected to Mayor Dinkins's financial plan. Two days later, Dinkins's financial staff met in Rohatyn's office to redraft the plan to Rohatyn's satisfaction.[42] One labor union official described it in this cynical way: "The non-government government has decided that the four-year plan that the government government gave did not meet the non-government government's needs."[43] The nongovernment government referred to is the credit rating agencies and MAC and FCB officials.

There is no mistaking the dominant role of the financial elites during this fiscal crisis. Expanding on its earlier complaints, the FCB issued in December 1991 a sharply critical report on Mayor Dinkins's long-term plan to balance the city's books, saying the administration's predictions about future tax revenues, debt, and demands on welfare and the schools were unrealistic. The city budget director, Philip Michael, insisted that the city's economic assumptions were sound. But he said the administration would take many of the board's criticisms to heart while revising the plan. The report had special significance because the state's Municipal Assistance Corporation, led by Felix Rohatyn, said: "it will not provide $1 billion in crucial aid unless the Dinkins administration can satisfy the board that it has a feasible plan to permanently shrink the government."[44] This was the common theme from oversight agencies—shrink government, cut spending.

In August 1991, only eight months after Mayor Dinkins was sworn in, there was another horrifying racial incident that involved the death of a seven-year-old Guyanese boy and the resulting Crown Heights riot and death of an Australian rabbinical student, Yankel Rosenbaum. The African American rioting in Crown Heights against Jews lasted for three days. The Jewish community blamed Mayor Dinkins for not controlling the rioting sooner. This incident still resonates today, and was another racial conflict that Mayor Dinkins could not live down.[45]

1992–1993

In its first two years, the Dinkins administration was criticized for acting slowly in the face of the coming crisis, even granting municipal employees a 5.5 percent wage increase at the same time it was discussing layoffs. The recession was relentless and efforts to balance the budget were continuous. Then, at the end of Fiscal Year 1992, tax revenues rose and the city announced a $566 million budget surplus.[46] But that surplus was quickly absorbed in new municipal labor contracts.

With this surplus came praise. Allen Proctor, executive director of the New York State Financial Control Board, a fiscal oversight panel, said that the city managed to take control of its daily problems. It was like night and day. For example, Mr. Proctor said the Dinkins administration trimmed $2 billion from its budget the previous year and instituted tight controls on all its agencies. "I am astonished at the surplus and the general fiscal stability," said Howard Sitzer, director of municipal bond research with Greenwich Partners Inc., who added that he did not expect the stability to continue without a major turnaround in the local economy.[47] Also in 1992, the city froze corporate taxes and at the same time announced that Morgan Stanley would remain in the city with approximately $39.6 million in incentives over ten years. "The company generated over $2 billion in economic activity within the city every year and was expected to pay $911 million in direct taxes over the decade."[48]

Mayor Dinkins had a terrific start at the beginning of the new fiscal year, Fiscal Year 1993. The New York Times reported:

Imagine a mayor who trims $2 billion from New York City's vast bureaucracy in a single year, cobbles together a $500 million surplus despite a recession, moves aggressively against possible police corruption, stands up to the city's labor unions and demonstrates toughness and guile in outwitting state legislators. David N. Dinkins? Precisely.[49]

The major credit agency that rated New York City's bonds, Standard and Poor's, had consistently threatened to reduce the city's credit rating of A– if the mayor raised taxes or borrowed money to close gaps in his operating budgets. In May 1992, when Mayor Dinkins released his Fiscal Year 1993 executive budget, which announced cutbacks in government positions, Standard and Poor's applauded him: "This . . . is the third in a series of improving financial plans since November 1991 to address the substantial budget gaps facing New York City over the next several years."[50]

It was in this fiscal year that Mayor Dinkins reached an agreement with the largest municipal union, DC 37, for modest increases of 8.25 percent over three years. Allen Proctor, head of the FCB, said that the city could not afford the contract and would have to examine spending cuts. Raymond D. Horton, the president of the Citizens Budget Commission, was, as usual, critical, pointing out that there were no productivity gains to offset the raises. But there was not the outcry that accompanied previous settlements. That outcry came a few months later.

MAYOR DINKINS'S LAST BUDGET, FISCAL YEAR 1993–1994

This was the fourth year of a major recession. In the spring of 1993, the year he would run for reelection, the mayor proposed a Fiscal Year 1994 budget projecting an optimistic future and assuming $115 million in new taxes that needed to be passed by the state legislature. However, the projected budget was in deep trouble. The economy remained mired in recession; tax revenues continued to be sluggish. He faced a gap of over $500 million in his proposed budget and neither Governor Cuomo nor President Clinton was supportive of more aid. Then the three private members of the FCB, Heather L. Ruth, Robert R. Kiley, and Stanley S. Shuman, issued a public statement condemning the mayor's proposed budget, stating that Mayor Dinkins had failed to shrink the size of the city government to fit its revenues and had saddled the city with a permanent deficit.[51] Robert R. Kiley, president of Fischbach Corporation and former MTA chairman, said that the Dinkins administration had never closed the permanent deficit as they stretched further and further to fill larger and larger gaps.[52] Heather L. Ruth, president of the Public Securities Association, said that the FCB's private members saw a growing sense of urgency about the deteriorating budget crisis that the city clearly did not share.[53] Such public statements by the private members of the FCB could not have come at a worse time. It was election year and Mayor Dinkins's opponents used these statements as they sought to convince voters that the Dinkins team was incapable of resolving the city's financial issues. The Dinkins team believed that such a statement on the part of the private members of the FCB was political. Certainly no such outcry ever followed Mayor Koch during his twelve years, eight years of which saw the city's budget and payroll soar.

The mayor and his aides pointed out that, over the course of the Dinkins administration, the payroll had been slashed from 252,584 in Fiscal Year 1990 to 246,783 in Fiscal Year 1994 after years of growth under Mayor Koch.[54] The administration had cut 15 to 20 percent of the agencies' budgets except for police and education. It had frozen property and corporate taxes while shrinking the size of government, even though the state had not delivered promised reforms such as taking over Medicaid costs.

A few weeks later, Standard & Poor's was not as laudatory as in previous statements. They were withholding judgment on the Fiscal Year 1994 $31.2 billion budget, with the ominous comment that "there were some disturbing elements" in it.[55] Moody's Investor Services complained that "the new level of spending, given the current size of the budget gaps, is not affordable on an ongoing basis . . . some of the one-time savings and revenue items in the budget were not likely to be there next year to support the higher level of city spending."[56]

These comments from the FCB and credit rating agencies registered clearly with Mayor Dinkins. A few weeks later, the mayor announced that he planned to trim his Fiscal Year 1994 budget by $400 million and proceeded with spending cuts that would narrow the estimated budget gap for Fiscal Year 1995. Mayor Dinkins trimmed his budget during an election year, an unheard-of action for most mayors. In addition, Mayor Dinkins and a team of OMB and comptroller staff met at Standard & Poor's offices for hours to convince the staff of the credit rating agency not to lower the city's rating. Dinkins's strategy worked with the credit rating agencies; that same day Standard and Poor's reaffirmed its rating.[57] Mayor Dinkins was so successful with the credit rating agencies that he obtained letters of credit from banks in order to offer long-term variable-rate bonds with maturities from twenty to thirty years. "Three of those banks, the Industrial Bank of Japan, Sumitomo Bank and Sanwa Bank, are Japanese and were wooed by the city when both Mayor David N. Dinkins and City Comptroller Elizabeth Holtzman visited Tokyo earlier this year."[58]

Mayor Dinkins's settlement with the United Federation of Teachers in 1993 after a bitter nineteen-month negotiation led to an outcry from the financial elites that not enough was done to force productivity savings from the unions. In response, Mayor Dinkins announced the formation of a productivity panel led by three experienced fiscal experts—former congressman and House of Representative's budget committee chairman, Bill Gray; former state budget chief, Dall Forsythe; and former city budget director, Don Kummerfeld. Their charge was to come up with $2 billion in productivity savings by December 1. The tension eased at the annual August meeting of the FCB when all of the FCB members, including the three private members, issued a public report praising Mayor Dinkins for responding so positively to their criticisms and promising such bold action.

RELATIONSHIPS WITH FINANCIAL ELITES

In addition to credit rating agencies that assessed the city's finances, the New York City Partnership, formed in the aftermath of the 1975 fiscal crisis by David Rockefeller and other key financial leaders, sought to pressure the mayor to adopt conservative fiscal policies. They were successful. In 1991, the New York City Partnership called for consolidation of all economic development agencies. Mayor Dinkins complied. By next summer, the six economic development agencies would be consolidated into two agencies, the Department of Business Services and the New York City Development Corporation with an efficiency savings. The New York City Partnership also called for the development of managed Medicaid within the public hospitals. Much later, managed Medicaid became a reality when the Health and Hospitals Corporation (HHC) created its own HMO in early 2000. Enormous pressure on Mayor Dinkins to freeze the property tax came from the New York City Partnership and the Chamber of Commerce. In 1992, the Partnership called for the freezing of the property tax. They succeeded in 1993.

The Citizens Budget Commission (CBC) continued their criticism of the city's mayors, complaining that the workforce was too large and not as productive as it could be. The CBC advocated no salary increases without productivity improvements when the Dinkins administration negotiated contracts with the municipal unions. Report after report called for employing a smaller and more productive workforce; reducing subsidies such as rent control for those who are not poor; cutting the number and size of the municipal hospital system, and making the tax system more effective and efficient.

Mayor Dinkins was proactive in trying to win over investors. He played an active role in reassuring the bond market. In his first year, he and City Comptroller Elizabeth Holtzman met at least three times with officials from each rating agency. Deputy Mayor Sally Hernandez-Pinero said officials from both rating agencies were given helicopter tours of development sites and an intensive round of briefings. Although nationwide bonds offered by localities were yielding 6 percent to 7 percent interest, the city's underwriters had to offer more than 8 percent to attract investors.[59] The city had to prove that it could maintain a balanced budget.

On another front, Mayor Dinkins courted investment firms throughout his mayoralty. He succeeded in keeping the Morgan Stanley Group, one of the nation's largest investment firms, from leaving the city by offering a package of tax credits. He also offered tax incentives and energy savings to Prudential Securities. When four of the five commodities exchanges sought to move to Jersey City, the mayor and his team again came to agreement with the help of tax incentives.

TAXES

Since the mayor could not wrest enough financial support from the federal or state governments, he turned to taxes. He could not count on sales, mortgage, or transfer taxes. With the economy collapsing, these taxes decreased. So he turned to property taxes which had increased almost 19 percent in current dollars during his tenure.

There are four classes of property tax in the city: the first class is one- to three-family homes; the second class is apartment houses (cooperatives, condominiums, rentals); the third class is utility companies; and the fourth class is commercial property other than utilities. There was a history in the city of property taxes for homes being kept quite low while cooperatives and other apartment buildings paid higher taxes. The disparity in tax burdens was quite large. A study by Dean Michael Mead of the Citizens Budget Commission demonstrated that small residential properties were only assessed at 9 percent of their market value while large apartment houses were assessed at 45 percent.[60] Regardless of the disparities, homeowners in the outer boroughs—Queens, Brooklyn, the Bronx, and Staten Island—were furious at the tax increases. These are the same homeowners who voted for Mayor Dinkins's opponent.

In four years, Mayor Dinkins raised taxes three times. In his first budget (Fiscal Year 1991), Mayor Dinkins proposed and got a property tax increase on one- to three-family homes from a tax rate of 9.452 percent to 9.840%

and a reduction for class two properties from 9.229 percent to 9.154 percent. Class four, utilities property, jumped from 12.903 percent to 15.079 percent and similarly class four, utilities commercial, increased from 9.539 percent to 9.924 percent.[61] He also raised the mortgage recording tax from 0.625 percent to 1.0 percent for small residential mortgages and greater amounts for larger residential and commercial mortgages. The second tax increase was in the Fiscal Year 1992 budget in which the personal income tax's top rate was increased from 3.91 percent to 4.5 percent as well as another property tax rate increase across all four classes. He paid for a major program, the Safe Streets/Safe City Program, "through a property-tax increase, a personal income tax surcharge, and a new $2 scratch-off lottery game for New York City to pay for the hiring of 3,500 new police officers."[62] The increase in taxes on three separate occasions may have been financially sound, but was remembered when Mayor Dinkins sought reelection. Even with those tax rate increases, the national recession meant that the tax revenues increased slowly during the Dinkins years. Tax revenues increased by 5.2 percent a year as compared to Mayor Koch's 11.4 percent a year shown in Table 6.2. The prime indicator of a booming real estate market, the mortgage recording tax, dropped precipitously (−3.4 percent annually) during the Dinkins years, a far cry from the growth during the Koch administration of 45.1 percent a year. See Table 7.2.[63]

In response to pressure from the financial and business community, Mayor Dinkins agreed to freeze the corporate tax rate in 1992 and the property tax rate in 1993. His State of the City in January 1993, his final year as mayor, demonstrated his collaboration with the business community as he called for relieving small businesses of the "single most onerous tax" in the city, the commercial rent tax. Ronald K. Shelp, president and CEO of the New York City Partnership, was quite pleased, however, by the mayor's terminology: "We've been using the phrase for years that this is the most onerous tax in New York and it's nice to hear him say it," Shelp said.[64] Mayor Dinkins, during very difficult economic times, responded to business calls to deal with rising tax rates.

CITY COUNCIL

In 1989, the Supreme Court ruled that the Board of Estimate was unconstitutional because it did not constitute one person, one vote. The city needed to change its governance structure.[65] After much deliberation, ballot proposals eliminating the legislative capacity of the borough presidents and upgrading the city council powers were put before the voters. The 1989 Charter Revisions expanded the city council from thirty-five to fifty-one members, eliminated council members at large, and expanded its powers. For the first time, the city council had control over land use and became the only body passing the mayor's budget. The speaker, Peter Vallone, sought

Table 7.2 Tax revenues during the Dinkins administration, FY1990–FY1994 (in millions)

Tax Revenues	FY1990	% of Total	FY1994	% of Total	% Change	Annual % Change FY90–94
Property tax	$ 6,542.6	43.6%	$ 7,773.3	42.9%	18.8%	4.7%
Personal income	2,537.6	16.9%	3,555.6	19.6%	40.1%	10.0%
General sales	2,431.2	16.2%	2,503.7	13.8%	3.0%	0.7%
General corporation	1,122.9	7.5%	1,386.3	7.7%	23.5%	5.9%
Financial corporation	195.7	1.3%	683.2	3.8%	249.1%	62.3%
Unincorporated business income	356.5	2.4%	407.6	2.3%	14.3%	3.6%
Mortgage recording	154.4	1.0%	133.7	0.7%	-13.4%	-3.4%
Commercial rent	684.7	4.6%	703.5	3.9%	2.7%	0.7%
Conveyance of real property	215.3	1.4%	154.0	0.9%	-28.5%	-7.1%
Other taxes	773.9	5.2%	813.6	4.5%	5.1%	1.3%
Total taxes	$15,014.8	100.0%	$18,114.5	100.0%	20.6%	5.2%

Source: Independent Budget Office of New York City, "Revenues since 1980."

to increase the council's prestige to a coequal branch of government with the mayor by aggressively questioning the mayor's proposed budgets. The city council, led by Speaker Vallone, sometimes fought the mayor's budget cuts and tax increases, but there was little room to maneuver.[66] Dinkins's Safe Streets/Safe City Program (adding thousands of police officers to the payroll) was a compromise with Speaker Vallone since the city's political leaders had to be in agreement in order to approach the state legislature. After much negotiation, Mayor Dinkins and Speaker Vallone combined forces to persuade the state legislature to increase taxes earmarked for more police positions in the city.[67] The Safe Streets/Safe City Program involved more than hiring police officers. Mayor Dinkins called his program "cops and kids" because he included funds for an expansion of youth programs. The most popular kids program, the Beacon program, remains his legacy today as thousands of kids attend afternoon and evening recreation and educational programs in schools throughout the city.

MAYORAL SPENDING GOALS

In the midst of the fiscal crisis, Mayor Dinkins during his four-year term sought to reallocate funding to the poor; he was a redistributive mayor. In his first executive budget, Dinkins wrote: "Some say quality of life is best defined by spotless parks and sparkling roadways. But for me it is best exemplified by a happy, healthy baby or by a teenager with a diploma in hand and a sparkle in the eye."[68] He did exactly what he said he would do as a mayoral candidate, even in the midst of a major recession. He increased redistributive expenditures—an annual increase of 7.9 percent. But, due to the recession, Dinkins cut into the affordable housing program.[69]

Even in the midst of a major downturn in the economy, Mayor Dinkins sought to invest in human services, demonstrating a commitment to education and libraries. Youth programs, libraries, community colleges, and education all had increases in expenditures during Dinkins's reign. He succeeded in shifting resources to redistributive services from 28.2 percent of the budget in Fiscal Year 1990 to 30.6 percent in Fiscal Year 1994. He invested less in the area of development. City planning, finance, transportation, and buildings departments all had only small increases. In public safety, Mayor Dinkins began the Safe Streets/Safe City Program and increased the number of police on the street, but the proportional amount of expenditures for public safety declined. In 1989, before Dinkins became mayor, there were 25,858 police officers; in 1993, his last year as mayor, there were 29,327 for an increase of 3,469, a growth of 13 percent. There was a small increase in expenditures for public safety (police, fire, and judiciary). Debt service declined as the city refinanced its debt to take advantage of lower interest rates. The annual percentage increase in expenditures was up 5.2 percent while Mayor Koch's annual percentage increase was 9 percent. See Table 7.3.[70]

Table 7.3 Expenditures during the Dinkins administration, FY1990–FY1994 (in millions)

Categories	FY90	% of Total	FY94	% of Total	% Change FY90–94	Annual % Change FY90–94
Total expenditures	$25,932.0	100.0%	$31,348.0	100.0%	20.9%	5.2%
Development	584.4	2.3%	607.0	1.9%	3.9%	1.0%
Public safety	3,522.9	13.6%	3,846.1	12.3%	9.2%	2.3%
Human investment	6,762.9	26.1%	8,078.1	25.8%	19.4%	4.9%
Redistributive	7,302.0	28.2%	9,596.7	30.6%	31.4%	7.9%
Quality of life	638.4	2.5%	730.7	2.3%	14.5%	3.6%

Note: Columns will not total since minor expenditures have been omitted.
Source: NYC Comptroller's Reports FY90–FY94.

ECONOMIC DEVELOPMENT

Unlike his successors, Mayor Dinkins participated in few subsidy programs for corporations. Eight companies received $364.1 million in subsidies from the city and state during the Dinkins administration—far less than under Mayor Giuliani ($2,198.5 billion) or Mayor Bloomberg ($332.9 by 2005).[71] An example of the types of subsidies given to corporations is the deal between the city, the state, and Prudential Securities in December 1992. The city agreed to a sales tax exemption of $29.5 million, property and commercial rent tax breaks of $24.1 million, a mortgage recording fee waiver of $4.2 million, and an energy benefits package of $48.4 million. The state also gave Prudential Securities a $16.7 million package of sales tax breaks and mortgage reduction fees for a total subsidy of $122.9 million. Mayor Dinkins supported economic development projects such as the Times Square Renovation, but he did not give tax breaks to corporations as easily as those who followed him.

CONCLUSION

In times of recession, "the nongovernment government" topped "government government" every time. But as soon as the recession receded, nongovernment government said that the mayor performed quite well fiscally. Part of this scenario was a repeat of the 1975 fiscal crisis when Mayor Beame could not do anything right.

Even though financial elites praised Mayor Dinkins at the end of four hard years, the base of Mayor Dinkins's support was not pleased. To his constituents, Mayor Dinkins represented a redistributive regime that emphasized human investment policy. But he could not satisfy his constituency and the financial community at the same time. The external constraints were too great; thus, Mayor Dinkins could not sustain his emphasis on redistribution. The Independent Budget Office stated that Mayor Dinkins faced budget gaps that were "on the same order of magnitude as those faced during the fiscal crisis."[72] The state was in fiscal crisis and could not financially support the city to the extent the mayor expected. On the federal level, President Clinton never delivered on his promises to help the cities.

In addition, the city remained in racial turmoil throughout Mayor Dinkins's term in office. The Korean grocery store boycott in Brooklyn and the racial rioting in Crown Heights greatly weakened the mayor. The unsophisticated way his administration handled those two incidents defined his mayoralty.

Mayor Dinkins began with a solid relationship with Governor Cuomo whom he had supported in the gubernatorial primary in 1982 when Cuomo won against Koch. The governor and his son, Andrew, helped Dinkins during his election bid for mayor. But the recession was hurting the state and the governor had his own fiscal problems. When the governor heard about the teachers' 5.5 percent settlement in 1990, Governor Cuomo publicly said that the city's finances were in disarray, much to Mayor Dinkins's dismay. In the spring, the two sparred over labor negotiations. In June 1993, when the mayor was up for reelection, Governor Cuomo, who faced his own budget deficit, was seen as orchestrating members of the FCB to complain about the mayor's budget. Governor Cuomo had also agreed to let Staten Island, a Republican stronghold of New York City, have a nonbinding referendum on the issue of its secession from the city. Many African Americans condemned the governor's action because it meant that voter turnout on Staten Island would be quite high. And Staten Island voters had never voted for the mayor. The finishing blow to the mayor by the governor occurred shortly before the 1993 elections, when Governor Cuomo released a state report criticizing the city administration for the handling of the Crown Heights affair of two years before.[73] The governor put the racial disturbance back into the public eye during Dinkins's reelection campaign. Clearly, Mayor Dinkins could not turn to Albany for support. In effect, the inability to keep racial peace, a platform on which he was elected, haunted Mayor Dinkins throughout his term.

Over time, Mayor Dinkins won over some financial leaders with his comprehensive and thoughtful approach to fiscal policy. "It's sort of ironic that David Dinkins, considering his platform and commitment to so many things, is becoming most of all an expert on austerity," observed Ronald Shelp.[74] Shelp and Preston Robert Tisch, chair of the New York City Partnership, worked closely with the mayor, advising him to travel to Europe and Asia on trade trips and also to create a new position in March 1992, deputy mayor for finance and economic development, a first in New York City history. Felix Rohatyn remained his friend and supporter. Yet *Crain's New York Business*, a trade magazine for businesspeople in the city, conducted a fax poll in July before the election in which business leaders rated his performance as poor. "It reflects the problem that none of the city's attempts to balance the budget that year addressed the underlying problems," Allen Proctor of the New York State Financial Control Board said in a recent interview.[75] The mayor had taken aggressive actions two years before, cutting thousands of city jobs, Proctor said, but Crown Heights was such a distraction that he did little during the present fiscal year to trim further. In Proctor's view, the city had never fundamentally rethought the role of local government or the range of services that it delivered to New Yorkers, since the city had never said that some service would end. Hence, the financial elites, along with the state, controlled the environment in which Mayor Dinkins sought to achieve his goals.

In the race for his second term, the distinction between Mayor David Dinkins and his challenger once again, Rudolph Giuliani, was clear. Mayor Dinkins said, "We don't need a mean mayor. We need someone who understands that you have to reach out to people. We don't need to build jails, we need to build jobs."[76] On November 3, 1993, Rudolph Giuliani defeated David Dinkins in a very close race, winning by 97,156 votes out of 1.8 million votes cast. Dinkins could not overcome his prevailing image as "one of a nice man out of his depth."[77] By a narrow margin, New York City residents voted to enter the third American Revolution.

EIGHT

MAYOR RUDY GIULIANI'S FIRST TERM

AND THE ONGOING FISCAL CRISIS

(1994–2002)

Freedom is about authority. Freedom is about the willingness of every single human being to cede to lawful authority a great deal of discretion about what you do and how you do it.

—Mayor Giuliani[1]

Rudolph Giuliani had lost a very close race to David Dinkins in 1989 after which he spent the next four years studying the city and talking to numerous New Yorkers. Running again in 1993 on a law and order campaign theme, he narrowly defeated Dinkins. Giuliani was a Republican candidate assembling disgruntled Democrats, Republicans, and Liberal Party members to support him. In effect, the election of Giuliani was a backlash by many citizens in the outer boroughs who no longer felt that New York City represented them. The city had changed. Its population had shifted from majority white at the time of the city's fiscal crisis to only one-third white at the time of Giuliani's election. The whites who remained lived in the outer boroughs of Queens and Staten Island and voted for someone whom they thought would represent their concerns.

    Mayor Giuliani gained a reputation as authoritarian, aggressive, and combative. He challenged all who disagreed with him. The speaker of the city council, Peter Vallone, said: "The problem with the mayor has always been that he has the right goal, but he has a sledgehammer approach to get there."[2] A typical incident was when Mayor Giuliani ignored the independent panel to review judicial candidates created by former Mayor Koch and instead appointed his own judges with caustic comments about the former mayor. One *New York Times* editorial said: "It was one of Mr. Koch's great achievements, and Mayor Giuliani's refusal to acknowledge that during this spitting match is a stark example of his worst failure as a leader—the compulsion to demonize everyone who disagrees with him."[3] Mayor Giuliani sought to control the press through intimidation. Another *New York Times* editorial stated that "the challenge for reporters and editors is to respond professionally to the administration's unprofessional behavior."[4] Within a year, Giuliani had forced the resignation of the school chancellor, argued publicly with the governor, was sued by the city council, and terminated the city contract for the Legal Aid Society that represented indigent criminal clients. All these actions reinforced his reputation as a tough guy.

His caustic manner alienated him from many voters, particularly African Americans and Hispanics. The U.S. attorney general found the New York Police Department under the Giuliani administration to have engaged in "racial profiling," unjustifiably stopping and frisking citizens of color. According to the 2000 annual report of the Civilian Complaint Review Board, cops were more likely to use physical force or pull a gun on blacks during stop-and-frisks than on whites. Police allegedly used force to detain 45 percent of the blacks who complained during stops, the report said, compared to 25 percent of whites.[5] When blacks asked for meetings to discuss police harassment, the mayor refused to meet with them. "Moderate black leaders, like State Comptroller H. Carl McCall, say they had only one or two meetings with Giuliani during his eight years in office, and those were only 'for show' after the Amadou Diallo police shooting in 1999 in which an unarmed Haitian was killed, with no follow-up. McCall told me that Giuliani ignored his requests for a meeting for five years. Queens Congressman Gregory Meeks says he didn't have a single meeting or even phone conversation with Giuliani in eight years."[6] The black community remained estranged throughout the mayor's two terms. In a Quinnipiac poll taken August 2, 2000, toward the end of his mayoralty, 63 percent of blacks disapproved of the way Mayor Giuliani handled his job as compared to only 30 percent of whites.[7]

His aggressiveness carried over into his fiscal policy as well. Rudolph Giuliani called for a new vision for government: operating more efficiently, shedding government functions to the private sector, and improving public safety. "It is the responsibility of the City administration to provide the climate that will make it possible for the private sector to earn profits and provide jobs."[8] He was the city's first mayor to totally embrace the fiscal conservatism of his day in which the state and civil society are restructured in a Darwinian market economy calling for privatization of government services, reduction in the safety net, and creation of a favorable climate for business. Reducing taxes was the stimulus needed for private sector growth. This was the city that Mayor Giuliani wished to make and he often succeeded.

EXTERNAL ENVIRONMENT

Mayor Giuliani faced the same weak economy and a $2.3 billion deficit as the previous mayor, and, for the first two years, had similar problems balancing his budget while maintaining positive relationships with voters and the financial elites. And those problems existed while he dealt with a deficit that was not as deep as what was outlined in chapter seven, given what Mayor Dinkins had faced when he was elected. The state's gross domestic product began recovering in 1996 and achieved 6 percent growth.[9] This was far from the all time low of 1.0 percent growth that Mayor Dinkins faced.

After the first two years, as the economy improved, the number of people employed in New York City from 1994 to 1998 increased from 2,973,000 to 3,284,000.[10] Mayor Giuliani took full credit for the improving economy. In a speech before the Real Estate Board of New York in June 1995, he stated: "I believe that we lost it [loss in private sector jobs] because of the policies the city has selected, put into effect, and enforced. That's what drove businesses out of here."[11] Yet the city does not exist in a vacuum. From an economic perspective, the start of the 1990s and the end of the 1990s were opposites in the nation. "In April 1990 . . . the nation teetered on the verge of an economic recession. Within one year, the unemployment rate rose to seven percent, and the economy shed 1.3 million jobs. But between 1992 and 2000, the U.S. GDP grew at a blistering 4.3 percent annual pace. By the time of Census 2000, the unemployment rate was 3.9 percent, the lowest in a generation."[12] Mayor Giuliani was the beneficiary of a booming national economy.

INTERGOVERNMENTAL ENVIRONMENT

Unlike Mayor Dinkins, Mayor Giuliani benefited from increases in both federal and state dollars. Federal dollars increased by almost 6.7 percent yearly and state dollars by 4.5 percent. President Clinton came to the mayor's aid in 1998 when he offered a $120 million Justice Department grant to pay for 1,600 new police officers in the city (see Table 8.1).[13]

Governor Pataki facilitated the state role of increasing city spending by signing expensive pension packages passed by the state legislature into law, but paid for by the city. The governor and state legislature agreed in 1996 to allow pension funds to set their own budgets and pay administrative expenses from their contributions and investments. The city was then required to reimburse the funds for those costs. Mayor Giuliani was furious with the state legislature when, despite his heated objections, the legislature "overrode the governor's veto of a bill giving a state agency [Public Employment Relations Board PERB] jurisdiction over contract disputes involving city police officers and firefighters."[14] In 1999, after a successful reelection campaign, Governor Pataki, who had had support from the correction officers

Table 8.1 Revenues during the Giuliani administration, FY1994–FY2002 (in millions)

Revenues	FY1994	% of Total	FY2002	% of Total	% Change FY94–02	Annual % Change FY94–02
Total taxes	$18,114.0	57.8%	$21,696.2	53.1%	19.8%	2.5%
Federal grants	3,959.6	12.6%	6,096.7	14.9%	54.0%	6.7%
State grants	5,902.9	18.8%	8,030.5	19.7%	36.0%	4.5%
Unrestricted federal & state	666.9	2.1%	518.8	1.3%	-0.2%	0.0%
Charges & fees	1,277.0	4.1%	1,458.0	3.6%	14.2%	1.8%
Other	1,432.0	4.6%	3,065.0	7.5%	114.1%	14.3%
Total revenues	$31,352.4	100.0%	$40,865.3	100.0%	30.3%	3.8%

Note: Columns will not total since minor revenues have been omitted.

Source: NYC Comptroller's Reports, FY94–FY02.

union, agreed to sign a bill that provided annual bonuses to retired correction officers like those retired police and firefighters receive. Mayor Giuliani opposed the signing. In 2000, Governor Pataki agreed to cost-of-living adjustments to city pensions and to relieve city workers from contributing 3 percent of their salary to their pensions after ten years on the job. City officials feared that these pension enhancements, particularly the cost-of-living adjustments, would cost as much as $1 billion in 2001. Under pressure from the mayor and city council, state legislative leaders agreed to phase in the pension enhancements over five years. It would not be until 2005, after Mayor Giuliani left office, that the annual cost of pension enhancements would reach over half a billion dollars.

INTERNAL ENVIRONMENT

Mayor Giuliani appointed well-qualified people, many of whom he knew. Deputy Mayor Peter J. Powers, a CPA and lawyer from Gibney, Anthony & Flaherty, was his lifelong friend and first deputy to the mayor. The deputy mayor for finance and economic development, John Dyson, had been chairman of the New York State Power Authority and of the Urban Development Corporation and was previously commissioner of commerce for Governor Carey and owner of the Millbrook Winery. One of the budget directors was Joe Lhota, previously director of public finance at First Boston. Randy Mastro, deputy mayor for operations, had been a lawyer in the firm, Gibson, Dunn & Crutcher, and had worked with the mayor when he was U.S. district attorney. One key person in his first few years, Abraham Lackman, an experienced financial expert from Albany named as the first budget director, was unknown to the mayor. There was one prominent black man—Rudy Washington, who became deputy mayor for community development and business services after Dyson stepped down. The mayor also hired two prominent Hispanics—Ninfa Segarra, deputy mayor for education and human services, and Herman Badillo, mayor's special counsel on education policy.

REVENUES

The mayor set a revenue pattern in his first three years—projecting more revenue than was realized to get his budget adopted. When these projected revenues did not materialize, continued deficits resulted throughout the year. On July 1, 1994, the mayor had a $31.6 billion budget. Midway through the year in November, he had a $1 billion deficit that he announced he would eliminate by cutting services. The city council members were furious when he proceeded to cut much of the $75 million in programs that the council had restored to the mayor's budget during budget negotiations in June. The speaker had used this $75 million to assemble votes to pass the budget; the mayor then sought to eliminate those funds.

But the revenues continued to deteriorate. It was clear that his adopted budget had been inadequate. There are two explanations for this. One is that the Giuliani team deliberately overestimated revenues in their proposed budget in order to demonstrate a balanced budget so that the FCB would approve their financial plan. The other is that no one in the Giuliani team expected the revenues to deteriorate further than they already had. It is understandable that the deterioration was unexpected. As Abe Lackman reported in his first year as budget director in 1994, "It (revenues) was worse than we thought. Then it continued to be worse than we thought."[15] As well prepared as Mayor Giuliani was to be mayor of the New York City, nothing could prepare him for the falling revenues.

As with most city budgets, the mayor had to sell his financial plan. Mayor Giuliani sought to sell his plan to businesses, the Partnership, and other corporate forums, starting on the day of its release. His team was aggressive and on message—we are cutting taxes and we need your help. To that end, businesses were enthusiastic. The development community was also upbeat over taxpayer-friendly proposals, and builders were jumping on the bandwagon. "When was the last time a big-city mayor said he wanted to cut taxes? It's like man bites dog," noted Samuel J. LeFrak, who developed Newport Center. "If it serves as a wake-up call to the banks to start lending again, it's enough to get me to start building again."[16] Although Mayor Giuliani's combative stance wore on people, his attempts to cut taxes were always welcomed in the business community.

Mayor Giuliani's tax cuts were substantial and controversial. The IBO reported that Mayor Giuliani's tax cuts cost the city $2.3 billion by the time he left office in Fiscal Year 2002.[17] This is almost the same amount that Mayor Giuliani was in deficit in the latter part of his term before 9/11. These tax cuts became problematic when the city's economy took a nosedive during 2000, as well as after the terrorists attacks of 9/11 in 2001 when once again the city faced large deficits. But Mayor Giuliani justified his tax cuts as necessary to encourage business. At the same time, the mayor experienced a growing economy so that even though he cut taxes, tax revenue grew.

The increased revenues came from a revived national economy. Although property tax rates did not increase, property tax revenues did. Sales tax collections were up 4.8 percent a year. The real estate market took off and mortgage and transfer tax collections rose. Personal income tax collections increased dramatically, by $1 billion. Mayor Giuliani provided tax relief to the cooperatives and condominiums in the city that cost the city $439.3 million, $424 million from the commercial rent tax, $823 million in the elimination of the 12.5 percent personal income tax surcharge, as well as others. Although Mayor Giuliani was cutting tax rates, because of the improvement in the economy his total tax revenues still increased by 2.5 percent a year for almost a 20 percent increase over eight years (see Table 8.2).[18]

Table 8.2 Tax revenues during the Giuliani administration, FY1994–FY2002 (in millions)

Revenues	FY1994	% of Total	FY2002	% of Total	% Change FY94–02	Annual % Change FY94–02
Property	$ 7,773.3	42.9%	$ 8,760.9	40.4%	12.7%	1.6%
Sales & use	2,855.0	15.8%	3,957.4	18.2%	38.6%	4.8%
Mortgage recording	133.7	0.7%	476.9	2.2%	256.7%	32.1%
Personal income	3,555.6	19.6%	4,555.1	21.0%	28.1%	3.5%
Corporate & utility	2,724.9	15.0%	3,192.1	14.7%	17.1%	2.1%
Unincorporated business income	407.6	2.3%	829.1	3.8%	103.4%	12.9%
Other taxes	1,148.7	6.3%	1,181.9	5.4%	2.9%	0.4%
Conveyance of real property	154.0	0.9%	518.7	2.4%	236.8%	29.6%
Total taxes	$18,114.0	100.0%	$21,696.2	100.0%	19.8%	2.5%

Source: Independent Budget Office, "Trends in Revenues since 1980."

RELATIONSHIPS WITH FINANCIAL ELITES

In many ways, Mayor Giuliani hit the ground running. He had been studying New York City for four years, and knew a great deal about the city and its fiscal problems. As soon as Mayor Giuliani took office, in January 1994, he set up an Agency Advisory Group Program in cooperation with the New York City Partnership to assist commissioners in improving the performance of six major agencies: Office of Management and Budget, Department of Housing Preservation and Development, Department of General Services, Department of Transportation, Department of Business Services, and the Police Department. The emphasis was on performance and managed competition. The mayor and his staff took the program seriously and recruited people from well-known firms: Lehman Brothers, Rockefeller Group, and Deloitte & Touche. Not only did some of the advisory groups create excellent recommendations but the mayor was the recipient of goodwill from many business leaders. Although there was no evaluation of how well these recommendations worked over time or were even implemented, there is no question that the private sector was pleased at being asked to participate in the program.

Mayor Giuliani's initiatives included regulatory reform. There were three task forces in the areas of inspection consolidation, one-stop licensing and adjudication, and regulatory changes. Peter Powers, Giuliani's closest friend and first deputy mayor, oversaw the implementation. Powers adopted five key initiatives in the restaurant industry that had complained that extensive requirements were excessively burdensome. He wrote extensive requests to commissioners with whom he had met to follow up on meetings and insist on progress reports. It was clear that these types of management issues were of the highest priority. The archives of the Giuliani administration in the Municipal Library demonstrated the administration's keen interest in regulatory reform that spilled over into privatization efforts.

The mayor's immediate fiscal strategies were to slash the budget, cut taxes, and divest the city of city assets. These actions, at first, pleased the financial sector. When Mayor Giuliani outlined his first financial plan on February 2, 1994, he advocated reducing the payroll and cutting taxes. "Allen J. Proctor, the executive director of the Financial Control Board, the state agency that oversees the city's fiscal management, called it bold and courageous. Richard P. Larkin of Standard and Poor's Corporation, a bond rating agency, described it as a good start that needed the test of time."[19]

However, in Mayor Giuliani's first proposed budget (Fiscal Year 1995) in the spring of 1994, the state's Financial Control Board warned that city hiring had increased in the past few months when it should be shrinking, thus compounding the difficulty of cutting back, and that overtime had gotten out of control. The revenue pattern of projecting more revenue than realized was frowned on by the credit rating agencies and the agencies

balked. "My initial reaction to this kind of scheme is still decidedly negative," Larkin said. "I'm getting concerned that every time something major
is suggested for city government restructuring, it always involves someone
else's money or borrowing."[20]

The Citizens Budget Commission was quite firm that the mayor's first
budget was overly optimistic. In October, responding to his midyear cuts, the
CBC stated: "The plan does not go far enough in dealing with the City's
fiscal problems; more than $400 million in risk remains, and $519 million
or nearly half of the gap-closing plan is comprised of one-shot actions; and
the plan fails to take full advantage of opportunities to gain savings through
productivity improvements that protect citizens from service reductions."[21]
In effect, Mayor Giuliani had trouble implementing his ideal of smaller
government during a recession.

But the credit agencies turned more positive again. When Mayor
Giuliani announced increased cuts in late 1994, they responded positively.
The bond raters on Wall Street praised the plan as a prudent step toward
restoring stability in the city's finances. "It's a good plan," said Richard P.
Larkin, managing director of Standard & Poor's. "After looking at at least
five years of budgets with varying degrees of gimmickry and one-shots, this
plan addresses the problem head-on."[22]

In January 1995, Mayor Giuliani fielded the idea of refinancing debt to
get through the year. The credit rating agencies were not pleased. Richard
P. Larkin said of a refinancing: "Most people know what we think of this
kind of gimmick. It is certainly not a positive development for the city, and
it would cause us concern."[23]

The credit agencies reversed their appraisal a year later because another
deficit was looming. In July 1995, Standards & Poor's reduced the city's A
rating by one level, to BBB+. This was the first Standard & Poor's downgrade
of New York's long-term debt since the 1975 fiscal crisis. "Of thirty major
cities, only Philadelphia, Detroit and Washington are considered a worse
credit risk."[24] Standard & Poor's cited "sluggish local economy and fiscal
gimmickry" that prevented the mayor from resolving the city's continued
structural deficit. However, Fitch, another credit rating agency, did not lower
its rating, citing Giuliani's deep spending cuts as being responsive to the
recession. Giuliani used Fitch's rating to complain that Standard & Poor's
downgrade was "political," in that Standard & Poor's should have lowered
its rating in 1993 when Dinkins faced similar issues. This produced a letter
to the New York Times editor from Mayor Dinkins explaining the great care
that his administration had taken with the credit rating agencies, and adding
that the Giuliani administration had fallen short.[25] Mayor Dinkins wrote that
Giuliani was unable to address the concerns of Standard & Poor's.

Mayor Giuliani's second-year budget of $31.1 billion had deep cuts
and debt refinancing. The Citizens Budget Commission complained that
the deal relied on too many rosy assumptions and fiscal gimmicks, such as

delaying hiring 1,700 police until the last second of the year, to avoid even more painful budget choices. "This really doesn't get the city any closer to permanent structural budget balance," said Raymond D. Horton, the commission's president.[26] The city comptroller, Alan Hevesi, and the state comptroller, Carl McCall, both agreed; they also worried about fiscal gimmicks. The credit rating agencies were not pleased. Announcing his second financial plan for Fiscal Year 1996 in January 1995, Giuliani noted that his second budget faced a shortfall of $2.7 billion. He was caught, like other mayors before him, in a stagnant economy with decreasing revenues, yet with some costs continuing to rise, such as pensions, Medicaid, and debt service. This second year continued with a terrible economy and constant budget cuts. And those budget cuts affected Mayor Giuliani's poll ratings; his disapproval rating went from 27 percent to 40 percent. In January 1996, with his financial plan for Fiscal Year 1997, Giuliani announced more cutting of both taxes and human services. Standard & Poor's criticized his plans. Richard P. Larkin said the mayor would eventually have to reconsider his ambitious tax-cutting plans. Larkin added that Giuliani's reliance on one-shot financing and risky revenues confirmed Standard & Poor's decision to lower the city's bond rating the summer before. Larkin drew attention to Giuliani's reliance on $244 million in airport lease payments that the Port Authority had refused to pay and $150 million in still-unapproved state and federal aid.[27] The creditors were unhappy.

At the same time, the city's comptroller was critical of the mayor. Comptroller Alan Hevesi rejected the mayor's proposed municipal bond refinancing. The mayor sought a half-billion dollar refinancing, giving the cash-strapped city $157 million up front, but costing taxpayers $50 million in higher interest costs for seven years, starting in 2002. Standard & Poor's sided with the comptroller. Larkin noted, "The longer the city has to use these refundings to balance its budget, the farther away are the city's chances of getting its rating back."[28]

The end of Fiscal Year 1996 (June 1996) was a disappointment for Giuliani, who was accused, once again, of advocating one-shot revenues to solve the current deficit by refinancing the city's debt. There were two kinds of one-shot savings. Mayor Giuliani was criticized for using funds from asset sales for the operating budget. These were called one-shots because they were not recurring revenues. In addition, there were one-shot savings through refinancing. Richard P. Larkin noted that the refinancing seemed to be intended to give a current cash infusion by putting off payment of principal. That, he said, provided one-shot savings without addressing rising costs in next year's budget. Larkin said his agency lowered the city's rating—BBB+ from A- —because of these kinds of budgetary ploys; "I guess the best way to put it is the city is living down to our expectations."[29] The Fiscal Year 1996 city budget relied on $1.4 billion in nonrecurring revenues to remain in balance. "McCall's report showed that only one other budget in the last decade contained more one-shots. That was the 1994–95 spending plan, when Giuliani and the city council included more than $2 billion in one-time revenues."[30]

In his proposed Fiscal Year 1997 budget, the mayor drew back from reducing taxes. Instead, he maintained the temporary income tax surcharge of 12.5 percent, which generated about $400 million in annual revenue. The budget was agreed to by the city council, but it was not well received by the credit rating agencies. Richard P. Larkin called the mayor's willingness to use one-shot solutions and other manipulations "business as usual." He said Mr. Giuliani, like other mayors, turned to them "because the alternatives—raising taxes or making dramatic cuts in services—were politically unpalatable. As long as the city relies on temporary relief, he said, it would continue to have lasting problems. He called on the city to decide what services it should no longer provide. Until that happens, he said, it will always be a chronic budget problem."[31]

As his first term drew to a close, Wall Street revenues picked up. The finance commissioner reported in November 1996 that revenues were up by $142 million. "The bulk of the surplus is related to the strong performance of Wall Street firms, which has bolstered city business income tax collections. The impact of the strong market also carried over into personal income tax collections, which are up nine percent compared to year-to-date collections for the comparable period in Fiscal Year 1996."[32] Revenues poured into the city, just in time for the 1997 elections. The mayor estimated over an $800 million surplus. The actual "surplus roll" was over $1 billion.[33]

Both the state comptroller's office and the CBC criticized the Giuliani administration for refinancing so much of its debt in order to seek lower interest payments, claiming that this refinancing "added costs to future years' budgets by pushing out maturities and capitalizing interest payments. Our analysis shows that these refundings added on average some $200 million per year to debt service costs over the FY 1996-through-FY 2007 period."[34]

In effect, Mayor Giuliani, regardless of his rhetoric, was incapable of balancing the budget without using one-shots, just as the mayors who came before him had, and this led him into constant conflict with financial elites. It was on his watch that Standard & Poor's lowered the city's credit rating which it had avoided doing since 1975. After the first two years as the economy improved, the credit rating agencies were less critical.

PRIVATIZATION AND MERGERS

Mayor Giuliani sought to privatize some city services. He met several times with gurus of privatization: E. S. Savas, professor at Baruch College School of Public Affairs known as the father of privatization and author of numerous books on privatization; Steve Goldsmith, former mayor of Indianapolis and an advocate of privatization; David Osborne, author with Ted Gaebler of *Reinventing Government*; and Mayor Edward Rendell of Philadelphia who dramatically cut government costs. Within a year, the city had contracts with private contractors to pave streets and maintain several city parks. He sold off the city's AM and FM radio stations as well as WNYC-TV, the city's public television station. He sold the United Nations Plaza Hotel, and unloaded the city's stock of "In-Rem" housing (housing that was taken over for nonpayment of taxes) to the private sector. These were small items. When he sought to sell more costly institutions, such as the city's water system and three public hospitals, he failed, stopped by the courts, the city council, the comptroller, and outraged city residents. The New York State Appeals Court stopped the mayor from privatizing Coney Island Hospital. The court said that the mayor had overstepped his statutory authority by trying to lease the hospital to a private, for-profit company without the approval of the state legislature and city council.[35] Mayor Giuliani's relentless criticism of the Health and Hospital Corporation (HHC), which operated the city's public hospitals, crippled HHC's ability to sell additional bonds. Moody's and Standard & Poor's bond rating agencies downgraded HHC's bonds to a step above junk bonds, citing cuts in Medicaid and the mayor's plan to privatize three hospitals.

The mayor's harsh cuts to the city's welfare population became part of his privatization efforts.[36] During his tenure, the welfare population was reduced from 1,141,000 in Fiscal Year 1994 to 516,000 in Fiscal Year 2001, a 54.8 percent decline.[37] The 1986 federal reform of welfare gave states a great deal of latitude in redesigning welfare programs. New York State allowed localities the ability to design their own programs. Mayor Giuliani awarded large contracts to private companies to train and place welfare recipients in jobs. He brought in Jason Turner, an architect of "Wisconsin Works" welfare program in Wisconsin. Maximus, a contractor in Milwaukee, Wisconsin, won $104 million in New York City contracts to run job training and employment programs in the welfare-to-work program. Its contract was rejected by the city's comptroller, Alan Hevesi, for reasons of corruption. After a bitter court battle between the mayor and the city comptroller, the mayor won and Maximus received its contract. The court ruled that, under the 1989 Charter Revisions, the mayor had complete control of the procurement process.

The most difficult part of the mayor's welfare reduction plans was his insistence that as many people on welfare work as possible. One of the most disturbingly punitive actions by New York City officials was the imposition of a requirement that all nineteen-year-old students had to report to Work Experience Programs (WEP) rather than attend high school. This action was taken by the Giuliani administration in defiance of a state education law that provided secondary education to all interested up to the age of twenty-one. This illegal act also was prevented only by court action.[38]

Throughout the country, the dropout rates in four-year colleges by women on welfare ranged from 29 percent to 82 percent.[39] At the City

University of New York, 28,000 welfare recipients were in college in Fiscal Year 1996, and only 7,000 welfare recipients were at CUNY in Fiscal Year 2000, a 75 percent loss.[40] At the University of Wisconsin at Madison, the school lost 60 percent of its students who were on welfare.[41] The loss of educational opportunity to these students was enormous.

Research demonstrates that welfare recipients benefit significantly from higher education. In 1990, a New York City study found that of 158 former welfare recipients who were college graduates, 83 percent were working and 87 percent were off welfare.[42] The study was replicated in Illinois, Tennessee, Pennsylvania, Washington, and Wyoming with similar results. A 1990 Ford Foundation study showed that welfare recipients who completed a two- or four-year degree earned significantly more than other former welfare recipients. Another study of 253 welfare recipients who graduated from college in 1995 and 1996 found that, seventeen months after graduation, 88 percent of these students were off welfare, and their median wage was $11 an hour. The most worrisome aspect of these welfare reductions was that only one study, an inadequate one of less than 125 people, was conducted in New York City to discover what happened to the hundreds of thousands of people, most of them women and children, who were cut from the welfare rolls.

In addition to privatization attempts, the mayor sought to merge city agencies to make them cheaper and more efficient. He succeeded in the police department, merging the Housing Authority Police Department (2,700) and the Transit Authority Police Department (4,600) into the city's police force. This was the mayor's most successful administrative merger. Since police officers held administrative jobs, and those positions were eliminated in the merger, it was thought to have put an extra eight hundred officers on the streets.

Although some of these privatization efforts saved dollars, the emphasis was as much on competition as it was on saving money. E. S. Savas documented the mayor's privatization efforts in his book, *Privatization in the City: Successes, Failures and Lessons*.

LABOR UNIONS

At first, Mayor Giuliani demonstrated toughness with labor unions. The first labor contract up for negotiations in 1994 was with the school custodians and it was negotiated by the Board of Education. Mayor Giuliani refused to approve it. Chancellor Raymond Cortines had no choice but to return to the bargaining table and attempt to gain further concessions. This time Labor Commissioner Randy Levine was in charge and the mayor got concessions. For the first time, custodians were placed under the control of the principals, future salary increases were tied to productivity, and privatization efforts were permitted. The mayor's team negotiated their first contract with sanitation workers in September 1994 in which the city gained productivity improvements; the city was able to extend routes on which workers collect garbage in exchange for a contract. Facing layoffs, the sanitation union believed it had no choice; it wanted to avoid massive layoffs.

Mayor Giuliani used the fiscal picture in a clever way to intimidate labor unions. Allen Proctor, executive director of the FCB, described it this way: "In our initial meetings with the Mayor (1994), we told him that property taxes would hit a squeeze in 1997 and 1998—FCB told him—you need to know the wall you are going to hit so you can make changes now. But Giuliani wanted to hit the wall in 1997. He wanted to cry poverty in 1997 to break the unions."[43] And he did.

Mayor Giuliani faced deficits; he wanted to cut the payroll. The Giuliani administration approached the unions and said that, instead of layoffs, the administration would like to create voluntary severance plans similar to cutback patterns that had been utilized in the private sector: the Severance Reduction Incentive Program. Severance plans were more palatable than layoffs to the unions; they were less disruptive. Fearing layoffs, the municipal unions accepted two voluntary severance plans that reduced the city's payroll and gave the mayor authority to transfer employees between agencies to compensate for problems that arose when too many people from one agency applied for a severance package.

Coming closer to reelection, Mayor Giuliani was less insistent on productivity improvements. Instead, he signed five-year labor contracts with few productivity increases and a no-layoff clause. In November 1995, first the United Federation of Teachers (UFT) and then a coalition of seventeen unions representing more than sixty locals negotiated five-year contracts guaranteeing no layoffs for three years, and no raises for the first two years. In return, Mayor Giuliani did not emphasize productivity, even though he had been stressing productivity improvements for two years. The Giuliani administration's agreement that teachers need no longer monitor hallways and the cafeteria meant that the city had to spend over $100 million to hire DC 37 educational aides to take the teachers' places. In terms of security, it was problematic to have teachers disappear from the school during class changes and lunch. The 13 percent wage increase came with a promise of no layoffs and no need to pay for increased wages with productivity increases. The UFT membership voted the contract down when the mayor announced major raises for himself and his commissioners, but, by spring 1996, all was agreed to and the contract was passed. In return, Queens Assemblyman Brian McLaughlin, president of the New York City Central Labor Council (CLC), the umbrella organization of city AFL-CIO affiliates, announced that the CLC was joining just about every other major union leader in supporting Giuliani for his reelection bid.

But Eugene Keilin, president of the business-funded Citizens Budget Commission, criticized Giuliani and city labor negotiator Randy Levine, saying that what they call productivity gains is "embarrassing" and that his labor strategy has failed:

With most major collective bargaining agreements coming up for renewal within the next eighteen months, there is an urgent need to define and dramatize the case for efficiency. The goal should be a workforce with more pay, more skills and more productivity. Recent growth in the number and cost of municipal workers reinforces the need to increase productivity. After a 13,731 decline in headcount between fiscal years 1993 and 1996, your plan will increase employment by 9,836 between fiscal years 1996 and 2000. In addition, real personal services spending is growing and will be at its highest level in decades.[44]

By Giuliani's second term, financial interests were calling attention to the absence of productivity improvements to gain savings. The Citizens Budget Commission reported: "the new financial plan represents a retreat from earlier city promises to reinvent government. As local economic fortunes have improved, the city has abandoned its attempts to lower costs and reduce the size of its work force."[45] Mayor Giuliani was no longer holding firm on labor contracts.

MANAGING DEBT

Mayor Giuliani hid the amount of debt to which he was committed. The Transitional Finance Authority was created in 1997 explicitly to avoid the city's debt limit. The state, at the request of the city, created the Transitional Finance Authority (TFA) as a tool to fund part of the city's capital program. The city anticipated that it would reach the limit on the amount of borrowing state law allowed by Fiscal Year 1998. As explained earlier, the state sets a general obligation debt limit for the city that is equal to 10 percent of the average full value of taxable real property over five years. The TFA had the authority to issue up to $7.5 billion in revenue bonds backed by the city's personal income tax; the TFA was also outside the state's constitutional limit. In his Fiscal Year 1999 executive budget, the mayor hid the TFA debt. As Raymond D. Horton, president of CBC, indicated: "The executive budget does not show debt service obligations of the TFA as part of regular City expenses and eliminates the portion of the personal income tax revenues devoted to this purpose as regular tax revenue. . . . The executive budget in effect hides from citizens debt service expenses that grow from $17 million in fiscal year 1998 to $560 million in Fiscal Year 2002."[46] This surge in TFA debt, which resulted in an increased debt service payment each year in the city's operating budget, was seen as justified by the credit rating agencies because of the severe underfunding of the city's capital needs during the 1975 fiscal crisis.

Another mechanism established outside of the state's required debt limit was the creation of the Tobacco Settlement Asset Securitization Corporation (TSASC) in 1999. The city used its share of the settlement (a national lawsuit against tobacco companies) to support revenue bonds for its capital budget.

CITY COUNCIL

Mayor Giuliani did not share the making of fiscal policy easily. The mayor's relationship with the city council quickly deteriorated in his first year. As speaker, Peter Vallone continued his efforts to work closely with whoever occupied the mayoralty. When the midyear budget crisis occurred and the mayor announced budget cuts without consulting the city council in October, the council was so angry that it passed its own version of $1.1 billion in cuts over Mayor Giuliani's version. The irony is that they disagreed on less than $100 million. The battle became an institutional one, with the city council stating that it had the right to designate spending of new monies. The city council sued; the first time a city council had sued the mayor since the council's inception in 1938. The State Supreme Court threw out the case and the mayor and city council compromised and settled.

The deterioration in the Giuliani/Vallone relationship reached its height in 1998 when Vallone ran for governor and did not support Mayor Giuliani's dream of bringing the Yankees to the West Side of Manhattan. Mayor Giuliani refused to spend funds appropriated by the city council; again, the council went to court. But the real issue was the city council's lack of support for the West Side stadium. Giuliani was relentless and the city council refused to give in. The conflict did not end until after the fall elections when Speaker Vallone, losing the gubernatorial race, returned to the council, and a settlement was reached between the mayor and Vallone. Speaker Vallone concluded that the mayor "had a tendency to bear a grudge . . . it may have had something to do with his background as a prosecutor."[47] Whatever the origins, Vallone believed that Giuliani's "mean streak" was quite well developed.

MAYORAL SPENDING GOALS

First Term

Mayor Giuliani stated in his first financial plan: "New York City government is too large; it has grown beyond our ability to afford it." Abe Lackman, the first budget director, explained, "New York City has enormous need; at some point we have to recognize that we cannot spend beyond our means. It doesn't mean that we don't care."[48] When Mayor Giuliani got elected, his first financial plan, released on February 3, 1994, represented his campaign pledges: deep cuts in government spending except for police and fire, privatization including street resurfacing and water pollution control plants, and reductions on commercial rent tax, hotel tax, and unincorporated business tax, agency consolidations, and a phased-in lowered sales taxes for retail clothing under $100. His plan was generally well received by the credit agencies and financial monitors, but met with disdain by union leaders. However, his protection of police and fire agencies from budget cuts was too much for the Citizens Budget Commission. Raymond D. Horton, its president, pointed out that cuts should come from reform in police and fire operations; very little of local government would be left if these two agencies were exempted. Eugene Keilin, chair of MAC, discussed Giuliani's unwillingness to examine police and fire department budgets; Keilin wanted no sanctuaries and no exemptions. But Mayor Giuliani refused to even consider bringing efficiencies to the police and fire department that would result in budget cuts. He embraced CompStat, a police intelligence computer system, introduced by Police Commission William J. Bratton.

Throughout his mayoralty, Mayor Giuliani's budget cuts in welfare drew wide criticism and editorials condemning his actions: "A policy of requiring recipients to work, if need be at community service at minimum wages, could be a sensible way to help put dysfunctional adults back on their feet. But to threaten to cut off people who, through no fault of their own, cannot find work demeans New York's proud history of helping the destitute."[49] He slashed any type of redistributive function, which resulted in an annual percentage change of −1.6 percent. In the first three years of his tenure, 1994–1996, the Health and Hospitals Corporation (HHC), which served mostly low-income residents, lost over 20 percent of its staff and its subsidy from City Hall went from $235 million in Fiscal Year 1995 to $48 million in Fiscal Year 1997. Public safety, however, received large increases each year, a 7.1 percent annual percentage increase.[50] Giuliani paid little attention to economic development agencies and slashed those budgets more than −3.7 percent in annual percentage change. Debt service took an increasingly large share of expenditures, with an average yearly change of 12.5 percent. The annual percentage increase in total expenditures for his first term was quite small—only 2.9 percent. See Table 8.3.[51]

Even in the midst of the fiscal crisis, Mayor Giuliani proposed tax cuts, albeit small, for the first year, 1990–1991, at $35 million and $250 million for the second year, 1991–1992.

Slashing the city budget meant cutting the education budget. In his first financial plan, he called for a reduction of 2,500 employees at the central Board of Education whom he labeled "useless bureaucrats." When Chancellor Ramon Cortines refused, Giuliani asked for his resignation. The New York Times chastised the mayor for "bullying" the chancellor, and Governor Cuomo negotiated a cease-fire, but, within a year, Ramon Cortines was gone (September 1995). And it is here that another pattern became clear—Mayor Giuliani's propensity to insist on his way even if it meant that he would end up in court.[52] He ordered the mayor's office of management and budget (OMB) to freeze educational spending in supplies,

Table 8.3 Expenditures during Giuliani's first term, FY1994–1998 (in millions)

Categories	FY1994	% of Total	FY1998	% of Total	% Change FY94–98	Annual % Change FY94–98
Total expenditures	$31,348.0	100.0%	$34,923.0	100.0%	11.4%	2.9%
Development	607.0	1.9%	517.3	1.5%	-14.8%	-3.7%
Public safety	3,846.1	12.3%	4,945.6	14.2%	28.6%	7.1%
Human investment	8,078.1	25.8%	9,369.3	26.8%	16.0%	4.0%
Redistributive	9,596.7	30.6%	8,981.0	25.7%	-6.4%	-1.6%

Note: Expenditures will not total since minor expenditures have been omitted.
Source: NYC's Comptroller's Reports, FY94–FY98.

travel, and consultants. This exceeded his authority; he had no right to do this. The Board of Education was a semiautonomous organization led by a chancellor and board. Even *Crain's New York Business* expressed concern about his overreaching.[53]

Mayor Giuliani's popularity suffered as the service cuts were implemented. In April 1995, the poll from the Marist College Institute for Public Opinion indicated that 44 percent of registered voters approved of the job the mayor was doing, which was down from 51 percent in a December Marist College poll.[54] By the end of his second year, December 1995, Mayor Giuliani's poll numbers were the lowest ever—35 percent approval rating, a decrease of sixteen points in one year, according to a Marist College poll that also showed a deep divide among the races. Fifty-four percent of whites interviewed approved of Giuliani's job performance, compared to only 12 percent of blacks and 8 percent of Latinos.[55]

Throughout his first term, the mayor relied on one-shots to balance the budget. Such maneuvers meant that the financial situation would be problematic in future years. But Mayor Giuliani's response was to question the political motivations of the monitors, including the State Financial Control Board, the state and city comptrollers, and Wall Street bond-rating firms. Martin Arrick, a director at Standard & Poor's, said, "We see continued chronic budget stress."[56] Standard & Poor's lowered the city's rating last year to BBB+ because of its financial troubles.

Second Term

The economy improved and Mayor Giuliani increased his spending accordingly. He experienced major "surplus rolls" in five of his eight years in office: 1997—$1.4 billion; 1998—$2.1 billion; 1999—$2.1 billion; 2000—$3.1 billion; and 2001—$2.7 billion.[57] Mayor Giuliani used these "surplus rolls" to repay expenditures in the next year. His spending grew dramatically: average yearly increases in expenditures were 4.3 percent in current dollars, more than a two-thirds increase from his first term. His investments in public safety and education resulted in almost 8 percent annual increases. His support of economic development was demonstrated by an annual increase of almost 10 percent. Redistributive categories increased as well, by 4.3 percent annually. Debt service decreased as the mayor sought to refinance debt at a lower interest rate. Pension contributions were kept low as the mayor cut these contributions during the stock market increases; Mayor Bloomberg would be forced to deal with this issue when the city had to once again begin to contribute to the pension funds. Part of Giuliani's neglect of growing expenditures was a result of term limits that passed as a referendum in 1993, limiting elected city officials to two terms. One real consequence of this law was that elected officials did not need to worry about the future. The mayor would move on.

In his second term, Mayor Giuliani continued to advocate tax cuts and privatization of government services in the face of an improved economy. But a policy of tax cuts without corresponding expenditure reductions created budget deficits in the outlying years. Mayor Giuliani's four-year financial plans constantly showed budget deficits in the second through fourth years (outlying), and financial monitors raised serious objections. Mayor Giuliani solved his outlying deficits by rolling over his surpluses into the next year to pay debt service costs—a strategy that angered fiscal monitors. The CBC wrote to the mayor: "Using the fiscal year 1998 surplus to pay fiscal year 1999 debt service is fiscally imprudent. Nonrecurring resources should be used to improve the long-run financial condition of the city—not to support recurring operating expenditures. For instance, the surplus could be used to pay off outstanding debt, invest in infrastructure on a pay-as-you-go basis, or fund one-time operating expenses that yield benefits in the future."[58]

Mayor Giuliani increased his spending in his second term, averaging an increase in expenditures of 4.3 percent annually. Public safety continued to benefit from his attention as did education. The economic development sector received a large proportion of resources—spending increased 9.5 percent. See Table 8.4.[59]

Mayor Giuliani's second term was marred with personal problems that undermined his reputation and again led to low poll numbers. Voters became quite skeptical about Giuliani's misuse of authority. Floyd Abrams in his book, *Speaking Freely*, noted that "over thirty-five separate successful lawsuits were brought against the city under Giuliani's stewardship arising out of his insistence on doing the one thing that the First Amendment most clearly forbids: using the power of government to restrict or punish speech critical of government itself."[60] The excesses of the New York City police force documented in life and death situations with young black men further eroded support for the mayor. Many New Yorkers were shaken over the torture of Abner Louima (1997) in a Brooklyn police station, the forty-one shots fired by police in the death of Amadou Diallo (1999), and the police shooting of Patrick Dorismond (2000), son of a prominent Haitian immigrant family. For each of these tragedies, thousands of people protested the police excesses in the streets. The lawyer representing the family of Abner Louima put it in perspective, "There was skepticism during the Giuliani years and fear of the police. And there was a concern that the polarization was coming from City Hall."[61]

ECONOMIC DEVELOPMENT COSTS

Mayor Giuliani participated in an enormous number of development projects in which his administration provided large tax breaks and subsidies to major corporations. The corporations read like a who's who of corporate America such as the *New York Times*, NASDAQ/Amex, Arthur Andersen, StarMedia,

Table 8.4 Expenditures during Giuliani's second term, FY1998–FY2002 (in millions)

Categories	FY1998	% of Total	FY2002	% of Total	Annual % Change FY98–02	Annual % Change FY94–02
Total expenditures	$34,923.0	100.0%	$40,860.0	100.0%	4.3%	3.8%
Development	517.3	1.5%	713.0	1.7%	9.5%	2.2%
Public safety	4,945.6	14.2%	6,462.4	15.8%	7.7%	8.5%
Human investment	9,369.3	26.8%	12,238.9	30.0%	7.7%	6.4%
Redistributive	8,981.0	25.7%	10,510.5	25.7%	4.3%	1.2%
Quality of life	820.3	2.3%	921.6	2.3%	3.1%	3.3%

Note: Expenditures will not total since minor expenditures have been omitted.
Source: NYC's Comptroller's Reports, FY1998–FY2002.

Bloomberg, Scient Corporation, Met Life, Ernst & Young, New York Board of Trade, Time Warner, Reuters, PaineWebber, and Bear Stearns. Job First quoted these subsidies as totaling $2,198.5 billion for eighty-four separate packages for corporations between the city and the state.[62] A typical small subsidy would be the $5.8 million in sales tax benefits to ING Barings and $1.6 million in energy benefits. Along with the city's subsidy, the state granted $1.6 million of sales tax exemptions.[63] One of the largest deals was the package of incentives for the New York Mercantile Exchange on state-owned land in Battery Park City ($183.9 million in subsidies between the city and state). After Mayor Giuliani left office, his firm benefited from city subsidies through ZEA credits (Zone Equivalent Area) of $1,500 to $3,000 for each employee. Recipients who benefited from these ZEA credits in Times Square included

> Ernst & Young, Morgan Stanley, Lehman Brothers, White & Case, Giuliani Partners, Giuliani Group, Giuliani-Kerik [which was re-named Giuliani Security and Safety, following the recent departure of former Police Commissioner Bernard Kerik from the firm], and Giuliani-Van Essen. The Giuliani firms are registered to receive benefits at 5 Times Square, a building, which pays no property tax as part of the 42nd Street Redevelopment Project and which is also home to ZEA beneficiary Ernst & Young, which collaborated closely with the former mayor to launch Giuliani Partners in 2002.[64]

9/11

But 9/11 made Mayor Giuliani a national hero. He was seen as the man in charge during a terrorist attack, keeping the city's citizens calm and working together. Much has since been written that disputes Mayor Giuliani's cool-ness under fire.[65] It was his poor choice of placing the Office of Emergency Management (OEM) at Seven World Trade Center that was destroyed in the attack in part because of thousands of tons of fuel oil kept by OEM in its offices. He never resolved the issue of phone communications between the firefighters and police officers and the dead zones of phone communications and defective radios that could very well have cost some of their lives.[66] One of the most offensive shortcomings was the Giuliani administration's laxity over fire codes for the World Trade Center. After the 1993 bombing, the Dinkins administration signed a memo of understanding with the Port Authority that the Port Authority would adhere to city code and expeditiously resolve any disagreements. But in 1995, during the Giuliani administration, the city's building commissioner, Joel Miele, eliminated the requirement that the Port Authority review and examine all plans to determine whether ten-ant improvements conformed to code; instead, the tenant's architect could certify compliance. But worse still was the fact that Mayor Giuliani's fire commissioner, Howard Safir, signed a similar 1995 amendment to the fire department agreement with Port Authority. He eliminated any requirement that the drawings and specifications of any fire safety system changes be submitted to the Bureau of Fire Prevention.[67] Again architects could simply certify compliance. Fire codes hold standards for fireproofing, stairwells, and access to the roof—all of which proved inferior on 9/11.

It has become clear that the city did not enforce health and safety standards at the World Trade Center site after 9/11. In federal court, Judge Alvin K. Hellerstein rejected the city's motion to dismiss lawsuits brought against it because of the deteriorating health of thousands of Ground Zero workers after 9/11.[68] Years later, the World Trade Center Worker and Volunteer Medical Screening Program funded by the National Institute of Occupational Safety and Health studied the health of nearly 10,000 rescue and recovery workers at Ground Zero on or after 9/11 between 2002 and 2004.[69] The results were that 69 percent of the 9,442 subjects reported new or worsened respiratory symptoms. The *Daily News* issued a special report describing the deteriorating health of firefighters: "In the Fire Department, more than 600 firefighters—soon to be 700—have been forced into retirement because they were deemed permanently disabled. Most suffer from asthma that disqualifies them from battling blazes. And fully 25% of the FDNY's active fire and EMS forces have lung-related conditions—more than 3,400 people in all."[70] Mayor Giuliani was one of those government officials who stood by and watched thousands of workers toil at Ground Zero without adequate equipment. After the *Daily News* published reports that toxic chemicals and metals were above accepted safety levels, Mayor Giuliani said, "the problems this created are not dramatic, are not health-threatening."[71]

The International Association of Fire Fighters criticized Mayor Giuliani's handling of 9/11 and attacked his positions when he ran for president of the United States. The association focused on several issues, including the inadequate radio system emergency workers used on 9/11 and the placement of the city's emergency command center in the trade center.[72] Hearings about 9/11 were held in May 2004 in which former Mayor Giuliani testified. In the midst of this testimony, "a firestorm of protest was ignited by victims' families and their advocates who believed that he and his administration had been grossly negligent before and on September 11, 2001."[73] But none of these shortcomings appeared to matter. What mattered to the nation was that the mayor went on television and said that we were going to pull together and get through this. He gave people hope and ended up a hero.

CONCLUSION

Mayor Giuliani's fiscal rhetoric does not match his fiscal results. Although he never admitted it, Mayor Giuliani did not control the size of government. His cutbacks resulted in a reduction in government payroll for a few years.

In Fiscal Year 1994, there were 246,783 employees; by Fiscal Year 1996, there were 235,069, a reduction of almost 5 percent of the workforce. However, this reduction quickly disappeared. From Fiscal Year 1994, Mayor Giuliani added over 4,000 people to the payroll (1.63 percent) at the height of the payroll (250,856) in Fiscal Year 2000.[74] In Fiscal Year 2000, this was the second highest payroll since Fiscal Year 1980, and remained so until Mayor Bloomberg surpassed it in Fiscal Year 2004. Mayor Giuliani insisted that he had reduced the number of government employees.[75] And for a few short years, he did. But the economy improved and, with that improvement, Mayor Giuliani spent money hiring more teachers and police in particular.

In addition to declaring victory about reducing the payroll, Mayor Giuliani had trouble with his budgets during hard times. He managed to hold any increases in expenditures in Fiscal Year 1995 to a bare minimum so that the increase in expenditures from his first to second year was less than 1 percent. And this was quite an achievement in fiscal controls. But the constant overestimating of revenues and then having to modify the budget during the first two years took its toll in credibility with financial interests. The mayor's attempt to hide the increased debt amounts was also a mistake. And his inability to obtain sizeable productivity improvements from the unions was something he never acknowledged. However, he did advance his privatization goals, even in the face of fiscal retrenchment. The issues around 9/11 will not disappear. What was most notable about Giuliani was the presentation, not the reality. Mayor Giuliani talked the talk of cutting government and increasing productivity but reality need not interfere.

Yet, in the midst of his early unpopularity, he received accolades for the reduction in crime. "New York is leading all major cities in drops in murder, burglary and motor vehicle theft. Ranked by the Justice Department as the 88th most crime-ridden city out of 183 with populations of 100,000 or more in 1993, New York dropped to 101 in 1994, and to 136 in the first half of this year measured on a per capita basis."[76] At no time did Mayor Giuliani acknowledge former Mayor Dinkins's role and that of former police commissioners, Lee Brown and Ray Kelly, for adopting the strategy of community policing that resulted in the first reduction of crime in a decade.

His challenge to the big-city liberalism of Republican mayors before him—LaGuardia and Lindsay—struck a cord in many people. Yet he was not successful in reducing government. Privatizing government functions during his first term was confined to smaller agencies; he failed to privatize larger institutions, such as the public hospitals and the city's water system.

His success in getting five-year union contracts, although a combative process, was useful to him since he could run for reelection and not be negotiating contracts in the same year. On the one hand, he and his staff demonstrated a great deal of sophistication in dealing with the unions. He wanted to create a situation in which there were no surpluses at the time of union negotiations. But, by the end of his first term, there was no focus on productivity improvements and some contracts lost ground. His contract with the custodians, although lauded at the time, was disappointing; years later the custodians were still entrenched. Diana Fortuna, the president of the Citizens Budget Commission, said: "Rudy Giuliani's rhetoric was a lot tougher than his results. He signed some pretty generous contracts."[77] Mayor Giuliani talked tough, but the results did not necessarily match the toughness.

His strident tone was deliberate. Why not show people his kinder, gentler side? "I don't know that I have a choice," he said. "The only way I could be less combative would be if I would compromise more. If I compromised more, I would achieve less."[78] But it wasn't simply his combativeness—his aggressiveness and his vindictiveness frightened people. Ruth Messinger, who ran against Giuliani for his second term, described finding a job after she had lost the election: "I was intent on finding a not-for-profit organization that I could direct . . . I had meetings with the boards of a couple of good organizations and then was the runner-up. And in one of these I was really surprised that they didn't choose me. I actually called a couple of people and said, 'What's the matter?' And those people said to me, 'You must be out of your mind; no one who runs a not-for-profit in the city is going to hire you because they think the mayor will punish them!' "[79] This fear was prominent among many people who had interactions with city services. And it affected his popularity. At the end of 1995, Mayor Giuliani's popularity was lower than Mayor Dinkins's had been. What worked for Mayor Giuliani was the improvement of the city's economy. Tax revenue increased and the mayor no longer needed to constantly cut the budget. He ended his mayoralty with a surplus for five of his eight years in office.

As the economy grew, voters forgot about his first three years in office when he used fiscal gimmicks and one-shot revenues to balance the budget. He cut revenues in good times and used any surpluses to prepay next year's expenses instead of paying down the massive capital debt. His major reductions in taxes came in his second term, when surpluses reigned. If Mayor Giuliani had demonstrated prudence during his second term when he ran surpluses, he could have created long-term savings that would have meant a much smaller deficit facing the city after 9/11. Good times were back and the electorate gave him credit for it. However, he lost credibility with many voters when his personal life became public gossip.

Mayor Giuliani clearly ignored the law when it suited him. In his reknowned struggle with the city council in 1998, he simply ignored the budget that the city council passed over his veto. Ester Fuchs, a highly respected political scientist, put it succinctly: "He is very good at ignoring the law when it suits his political purposes. It is amazing to any of us who read the City Charter that the Mayor would actually say that he does not have to follow the budget passed by the City Council."[80]

When Bloomberg took over the reins, the city projected a $5 billion budget gap, which was in sharp contrast to the healthy budget surpluses experienced by his predecessor, Rudolph Giuliani, for the five years prior. The tragic events of 9/11 and a recession certainly explained part of the looming deficit, but not all of it. The other part of the answer lay in Mayor Giuliani's embrace of tax cuts and his lack of control over expenditures. In a booming economy, Giuliani advocated deep reductions in taxes and, along with state officials, achieved those reductions to the tune of $3 billion a year in loss revenue. But the issue surrounding such tax cuts is that the city has flourished for many years with the highest taxes in the nation. The problem is not taxes; the problem is that recessions force the city into deficits that must be eliminated through service cuts. At the same time, he was a public order mayor, most concerned with reducing crime.

Clearly, the city's economy was already in trouble before the 9/11 attack, with four out of five economic indicators deteriorating. In the third quarter of 2001, the comptroller's office reported that the economy was slumping. Commercial vacancy rates rose quickly, private-sector jobs fell, with the securities industry leading the way, and unemployment rose sharply. The 9/11 destruction of the World Trade Center provided an opportunity for Mayor Giuliani to rescue his reputation. He received high accolades from federal and state officials and voters for managing those difficult days following the attacks. Jim Pasco, executive director of the National Fraternal Order of Police, said: "Everybody likes a Churchillian kind of leader who jumps up when the ashes are still falling and takes over. But two or three good days don't expunge an eight-year record."[81] He left office a hero on the world stage and bequeathed his fiscal troubles to the next mayor. Mayor Giuliani knew before September 11 that his fiscal year 2002 budget was in trouble, but his term was up and his deficit fell to the next mayor.

NINE

MAYOR MICHAEL BLOOMBERG AFTER 9/11

(2002–PRESENT)

> During the fiscal crisis of the 1970s, services were cut so much that crime gripped whole neighborhoods, fires gutted whole blocks and garbage littered the streets. We haven't permitted and I won't permit that history to repeat itself.
>
> —Mayor Bloomberg, 2003[1]

After 9/11, the city once again faced a fiscal crisis and the financial interests were calling for cutbacks and increased federal aid. Steve Rattner, formerly of Lazard, worried over the city's debt and its annual payments.[2] A *New York Times* editorial stated that closing the budget gap would be almost impossible without a great deal of sacrifice. Felix Rohaytn called for massive state and federal aid: "The city is in greater economic jeopardy today than it was in the fiscal crisis of 1975. . . . We were able to deal with the last fiscal crisis mostly with our own resources. . . . This is no longer possible . . . we cannot do this alone."[3]

The mayoral race was divided between a Republican (Michael Bloomberg), albeit not as conservative as Mayor Giuliani, and a Democrat (Mark Green) who openly advocated a progressive voice in the city's safety net. Mayor Bloomberg, a bond trader and entrepreneur, who began his own company, Bloomberg L.P., had been incredibly successful in revolutionizing information systems for Wall Street brokerage firms. Owning the leading financial news and data company in the world, he became a multibillionaire. Certainly, Mayor Bloomberg was the most experienced business manager to ever run for mayor. In November 2001, Bloomberg, wealthy, liberal Republican, won a very close race against Green, a liberal Democrat, in an overwhelmingly Democratic city. City residents were reeling from the terrorists' attack and voted for a person whom they thought could manage this difficult time. They wanted someone who was not seen as a politician.

Mayor Bloomberg had to struggle with the devastating shock of 9/11 and the collapsing economy. His term began just four months after 9/11. When Bloomberg first took office—in January 2002—many New Yorkers were pleasantly surprised. His inaugural ceremony was modest and low-key, and, with his predecessor sitting in the front row, he emphasized that he disavowed divisiveness as a tactic when dealing with the public. Unlike Giuliani, he reached out to the African American community; he reintroduced the Committee on the Judiciary to independently assess judicial candidates, which Giuliani had ended; and he traveled extensively to Washington and Albany to create close ties with state and federal officials. He reopened City Hall to the public, and, unlike Giuliani, permitted his commissioners to speak during mayoral press conferences and to hold their own press conferences. Within five months, Mayor Bloomberg reversed several of Giuliani's fiscal decisions: he stopped the plan to privatize city-owned buildings used by the United Nations, and he ended city support of Lincoln Center's renovation.

His appointments were filled with experienced managers and few politicians, many of whom he did not know. He relied on the same person whom Mayor Dinkins had relied on to head his transition committee—Nat Leventhal, who had been deputy mayor of operations for Mayor Koch and president of Lincoln Center. His budget director was Mark Page, long-time OMB staff person, and the deputy was Alan Anders, a senior investment banker at JP Morgan. He appointed Michael Cardozo, former president of the city's bar association as his corporation counsel, and Daniel Doctoroff, president of NYC 2012 (the Olympic Bid Committee) and former CEO, to become deputy mayor in charge of economic development. He appointed insiders from the agencies as agency commissioners in the Departments of Parks and Homeless Services. And he brought over a few people—Deputy Mayor Patricia Harris, special advisor Kevin Sheekey, and Communications Chief Bill Cunningham—who had worked in his media information company and mayoral campaign. In addition, he hired Katherine Oliver who was charged with turning around the city's Office of Film, Theatre, and Broadcasting. Since he was not elected by the political parties, he owed them nothing.

EXTERNAL ENVIRONMENT

Much had stayed the same since the structural changes in the 1975 fiscal crisis. Financial monitors were ever present (the FCB and special deputy controller were still in place), and financial information systems and required financial planning, implemented as a result of the 1975 fiscal crisis, resulted in far greater understanding of the city's financial problems. This understanding meant that mayors could take immediate steps to meet a crisis, and that monitors would have the information to understand both the issues and the strategies adopted to deal with those issues.

Mayor Bloomberg faced a severe fiscal environment. The terrorists' attacks resulted in an economic downturn not just in the city but also in the state. The growth in the state's gross domestic product declined sharply after 9/11, slowing to 1.6 percent in 2002 from a 4.0 percent change the year before.[4]

This downturn dramatically affected the city. Tax revenues took a beating after 9/11. Sales taxes decreased by –8.3 percent in one year. Personal income taxes plummeted, down –20.9. Corporate taxes decreased –18.0 percent in one year.[5] 9/11 was an economic disaster for the city. See Table 9.1.

Mayor Bloomberg had his work cut out for him. After two years, the economy improved and the city benefited. His increase in the property taxes brought in over $1 billion. Taxes increased significantly in Mayor Bloomberg's first term, 14.4 percent annually; the bellwether indicator of the real estate market, the mortgage recording tax, increased by 45.9 percent. Federal grants declined when comparing Fiscal Year 2002 to Fiscal Year 2006, but increased if the amount is compared to Fiscal Year 2001 before 9/11. State aid increased 4.8 percent a year. See Table 9.2.

The State and Labor Unions

When Governor Pataki sought reelection in 2002, he courted the support of the hospital workers union, Local 1199. He ensured that union's backing when he passed the $3 billion Health Care Reform Act of 2002, which increased Medicaid reimbursement rates. The governor had an agreement to pass the Medicaid increases onto raises for the workers. Needless to say, Governor Pataki got Local 1199's endorsement. New York City had to bear part of the costs since the city paid 16 percent of the Medicaid costs.[8]

Governor Pataki also sweetened city pensions. City labor unions must negotiate their contracts with the city, but labor unions can go to the state legislature to win measures that add to their pensions. In August 2006, Governor Pataki signed a law that would pay more generous death benefits to relatives of city workers who took part in the rescue and cleanup efforts at the World Trade Center site and later died from certain cancers or respiratory illnesses. Mayor Bloomberg, who had no objections to the concept of the bill, asked the state to pay for the costs. The state refused. In September 2006, Governor Pataki signed into law a pension law that permitted police and firefighters to claim a disability if they had a stroke. A disability allows a worker three-quarters of his or her pension. There were other pension bills signed that day as well. First there was a bill to allow city carpenters who had been laid off in the 1990s and then rehired to get credit toward their pensions for the time that they were out. Another pension bill refunded

Table 9.1 Tax revenues during 9/11 and Bloomberg's first term, FY2002–2006 (in millions)

Tax Revenues	FY2001	FY2002	% Change FY01–02	FY2006	% Change FY02–06	Annual % Change FY02–06
Property tax	$ 8,245.6	$ 8,760.9	6.2%	$12,636.4	44.2%	11.1%
Personal income	5,757.1	4,555.1	-20.9%	7,675.8	68.5%	17.1%
Sales	3,678.7	3,373.4	-8.3%	4,439.4	31.6%	7.9%
General corporation	1,977.7	1,621.4	-18.0%	2,738.5	68.9%	17.2%
Financial corporation	469.1	366.9	-21.8%	925.0	152.1%	38.0%
Unincorporated business income	859.8	829.1	-3.6%	1,366.4	64.8%	16.2%
Mortgage recording	406.7	476.9	17.3%	1,352.6	183.6%	45.9%
Commercial rent	399.6	403.1	0.9%	499.4	23.9%	6.0%
Conveyance of real property	479.7	429.0	-10.6%	1,305.5	204.3%	51.1%
Other taxes	903.1	880.4	-2.5%	1,272.4	44.5%	11.1%
Total taxes	$23,177.1	$21,696.1	-6.4%	$34,211.2	57.7%	14.4%

Source: Independent Budget Office, "Trends in Revenues since 1980."

Table 9.2 Revenues during Bloomberg's first term, FY2002–2006 (in millions)

Revenues	FY2002	% of Total	FY2006	% of Total	% Change FY02–06	Annual % Change FY02–06
Total taxes	$ 21,696.2	53.1%	$ 34,211.2	63.3%	57.7%	14.4%
Federal grants	6,096.7	14.9%	5,243.4	9.7%	–14.0%	–3.5%
State grants	8,031.0	19.7%	9,586.0	17.7%	19.4%	4.8%
Unrestricted federal & state	665.8	1.3%	494.2	0.9%	–25.8%	–6.4%
Charges & fees	1,458.0	3.6%	1,837.0	3.4%	26.0%	6.5%
Other	3,065.0	7.5%	2,632.0	4.9%	–14.1%	–3.5%
Total revenues	$ 40,865.3	100.0%	$ 54,003.7	100.0%	32.2%	8.0%

Note: Columns will not total since minor revenues have been omitted.

Source: NYC's Comptroller's Reports, FY2002–FY2006.

contributions that TA bus drivers had made into a pension plan. Governor Pataki also signed a law that included emergency medical technicians and paramedics in the "heart bill" along with police officers and firefighters. Any heart ailment makes these workers eligible for a tax-free (city and state), lifetime pension at 75 percent of their salary.

All of these bills were costly and almost all were opposed by Mayor Bloomberg. In his 2007 State of the City speech, Mayor Bloomberg said, "It's time for Albany to stop playing Santa Claus with the city's money!"[9] While Mayor Bloomberg complained, he was not telling the full story. The impact on the city was less than it appeared. The pressure on the city concerning pensions began in the 1980s when a strong stock market resulted in pension funds being so well endowed that the city did not contribute to the funds. The change in the city's cost was dramatic. In Fiscal Year 1981, 15.3 percent of the city budget went to pay for pensions. By Fiscal Year 2000, that figure had dropped to 2.3 percent.[10] In 2004, the governor and legislature passed a law requiring a minimum pension payment of 4.5 percent of the city payroll. The downward spiral of the stock market hit pension funds and the city was once again required to pay into the funds. Pension costs in Fiscal Year 2006 amount to only 7.2 percent ($3.9 billion) of the total budget—much less than the early 1980s but more than in 2000.

The bulk of city pension costs come from only a small portion of the city's workforce—police and firefighters—and these are the pensions that politicians, particularly those in Albany, refuse to control. In Fiscal Year 2005, the city paid almost as much to fund the pensions of 46,000 cops and firefighters ($1.5 billion) as it did to fund those of 235,000 other city workers, including teachers ($1.6 billion).[11] Since fire, sanitation, and police workers work only twenty years before being eligible to collect a pension and often collect three-quarters of their salary through disability, these workers constitute a disproportionately large share of the pension costs. Mayor Bloomberg cannot cut current pensions; that is prohibited by the state constitution. But he can reduce pensions of new hires by asking the state legislature to create a Tier Five of the four-tier pension system with lower pension rates.

INTERNAL ENVIRONMENT

After 9/11, poverty remained high, as did unemployment. From 2001 through 2003, the city's number of employed was reduced from 3,454,000 to 3,413,000.[12] The poverty rate stood at 20.2 percent when Mayor Bloomberg took office, up slightly from 19.8 percent from 2000.[13] This rate is similar to other times of fiscal scarcity. New York City's economy was reeling, and the national economy was also problematic: "Wages for New York City residents declined by nearly 2%, and the annual unemployment rate reached an anxiety-producing 7.9%. The effects of the struggling economy were evident in the 5.4% decline in the gross city product and the 24.6% plunge in personal income tax collections."[14]

Also, the city was far more heavily dependent on Wall Street than before the 1975 fiscal crisis. "In 1970, [Wall Street] accounted for just 2% of all New York City jobs and 4% of New Yorkers' wages. At the end of the most recent bull market, Wall Street's share of New York workers had more than doubled to 5%, while its share of total wages paid in the city had soared to 22%."[15] Basically, one in nine jobs in the city was on Wall Street and two additional jobs in retail and professional services were dependent on Wall Street. As the stock market continued its slump, the city lost millions of dollars in corporate and personal income tax revenues. The jobs were leaving Wall Street.

However, after Fiscal Year 2002, the Wall Street employment growth bounced back. As of August 2004, New York City securities industry employment totaled 161,900, up from a ten-year low of 157,500 in April but below the peak of 200,300 in December 2000. In 2006, it was almost 180,000. Wall Street rebounded and with it came tax revenue for the city and state. Collections in Fiscal Year 2007 were 45.8 percent, which accounted for 9 percent of the city's tax revenues and more than the $2.3 billion collected in Fiscal Year 2001.

How long Wall Street will continue to add strength to the city's employment numbers is questionable. Certainly, the largest New York-based Wall Street firms are investing in overseas markets—in Fiscal Year 2006, the seven largest firms received 43 percent of their revenues from non-U.S. sources, an increase of 5 percent from Fiscal Year 2004. The seven largest New York-based Wall Street firms are Goldman Sachs, Morgan Stanley, Merrill Lynch, Citigroup, Lehman, JP Morgan, and Bear Stearns. The largest increases in non-U.S. sources were Citigroup (63 percent), JP Morgan (50 percent), and Lehman (53 percent). Such increases bode poorly for future employment figures in the city.

> New York City has held up well as a world financial market: The share of global capital that flows through New York is steady, even rising. But because of the increased automation of the industry, this does not portend continued high levels of employment and office-space consumption by the city's financial-services sector. The days when financial services acted as a well-paid affirmative action program for presentable, moderately literate Ivy League graduates are ending—as, sadly, are the days when the stock market provided ready employment for legions of semiskilled clerks and runners.[16]

In addition, the demographics had changed. In 2000, the city had almost 670,000 more residents than in the 1990 census, an increase of 9.4 percent. The composition of the population had also changed. The proportion of the white population declined from 43 percent of the total to 35 percent. The proportion of the Latino population grew from 24 percent to 27 percent while the proportion of the African American population remained about the same, from 25 percent to 24 percent. Asians grew proportionately from 7 percent to 10 percent of the population.

HIS FIRST YEAR

In his inaugural address in January 2002, Mayor Bloomberg said, "We cannot make the mistakes of the past. We cannot drive people and business out of New York. We cannot raise taxes."[17] Mayor Bloomberg declared two priorities: rebuilding Lower Manhattan and improving education. But first he had to resolve the deficit. In his first day of office, he sent a letter to all agencies asking for plans to slash their budgets 5 percent to 20 percent. In his first executive budget (Fiscal Year 2003), Mayor Bloomberg did exactly what two previous mayors had done. He filled the budget with one-shot revenues, such as refinancing the debt and selling a water tunnel to private interests. Using one-shot solutions did not bring the condemnation of the credit agencies, as previous mayors experienced because New York City had a very good reason for part of the deficit—the terrorist attacks. Also, Wall Street respected Bloomberg's expertise in finance and he benefited from his willingness to brief Wall Street analysts early and often. According to Robert Kutter, a senior vice president at Moody's Investors Service, "Of course, [one-shots are] a concern from a credit perspective but this appears to be a necessary action that the city must take to get the budget balanced."[18] Standard & Poor's said the "city has demonstrated an ability to manage the budgetary pressure associated with economic cycles," though it warned of "some risks" in Mayor Bloomberg's preliminary spending plan.[19]

Bloomberg went to great lengths to develop close alliances with business leaders. He worked closely with the Partnership for New York City, which represented a network of business leaders who sought to enhance the city's economy. With the Partnership, Mayor Bloomberg created NYC Counts, which tracked each congressperson's vote to ensure that elected officials were supporting the city financially. NYC Counts informed New York's vast number of large political contributors of the position of these elected officials, and, in this way, also informed potential contributors about elected officials' financial support or nonsupport of the city.

TAXES

Mayor Bloomberg did not experience the luxury of revenue increases as Mayor Giuliani had. The city lost almost 21 percent in incomes taxes immediately after 9/11 and 18.0 percent in corporate and utility taxes, with an overall loss of 6.4 percent. At first, he adamantly refused to raise taxes: "I would not consider tax increases. . . . It is exactly the wrong time to even contemplate raising taxes I think, considering it does a disservice to New York City."[20] He instituted cuts, including position reductions through attrition at the police department, which had been a sacred cow for the previous mayor, and borrowed money, almost $1.5 billion. One difference between his budget and Giuliani's was that, unlike Giuliani, Mayor Bloomberg provided a more realistic picture of the revenue side and did not underestimate how much revenue could be expected.

In the fall of 2002, looking at the next year's budget projected deficit, and demonstrating flexibility, he rethought his position on new taxes and sought a major increase in the property tax. He reversed himself, clearly, irrevocably, and openly—"Like all parents, I love my children dearly. I want to leave them: hope and opportunity, not our problems. We will not borrow our way out this time. I was elected to stand up and face the music now—and rest assured—I'll do exactly that. Last month, we took the difficult but necessary step of raising the property tax rate."[21] He placed higher taxes on the table by proposing a 25 percent increase in the only tax the city controlled, the property tax. After extensive negotiations, the city council agreed to an increase of 18.5 percent.

Other taxes were in the mix. He went to the state legislature with proposed tax increases—a cigarette tax increase of $1.50 a pack, higher water fees, and the use of parking meters on Sundays. In his deal with the state legislature, the combined state and local sales tax went to 8.625 percent and an income-tax surcharge was applied on taxable incomes of more than $100,000.[22] He sought the renewal of the commuter tax, which had been rescinded by the state legislature in 1999 during the Giuliani administration. The attempts to bring back the commuter tax led to open disagreement among financial interests. The Partnership for New York City supported the mayor's tax increases, which outraged conservatives. "Is it a business advocacy group, or is it a social-welfare group?" one Giuliani deputy mayor was quoted as saying about the Partnership.[23] The Manhattan Institute, a conservative think tank, criticized Mayor Bloomberg for raising property taxes and attempting to renew the commuter tax. Crain's New York Business, one of the voices of the financial elites, was apoplectic, predicting thousands of businesses adversely affected: "The tax hike's impact will be the same as in 1991. No one will announce that they are laying off people or leaving the city because of the Bloomberg tax increase. But such decisions will be made, and they will cost the city thousands of jobs."[24]

Most New Yorkers did not approve of instituting increased taxes or greater cutbacks. The mayor's poll numbers plummeted; New Yorkers did not like increases in the property tax and he faced the same outcry that Mayor Dinkins experienced when he raised the tax. In a New York Times poll in June 2003, Mayor Bloomberg had the lowest approval rating of any mayor—24 percent—since the *Times* began the poll in 1978.[25] Only 20 percent approved of his increasing the property tax.

Mayor Bloomberg's choice to increase the property tax was based partly on the fact that it was the only tax that the city controlled without needing permission from the state legislature. There was another reason. Property taxes on single-family homes were extraordinarily low in the city.

The effective tax rate for Class 4 commercial properties used to be more than three times higher than Class 1 houses. Now they are almost eight times higher. The rate for the commercial properties is 3.56. The rate for the houses is .46. Co-ops used to be lower than houses. Now they are 1.5 times higher. Elevator apartment buildings (Class 2) used to be almost three times houses (Class 1). Now they are more than eight times. The elevator apartments buildings have a rate of 3.72. The rate for houses, again, is .46.[26]

Mayor Bloomberg was the first mayor on record to seek such a hefty increase in property taxes.

Mayor Bloomberg was quite strategic in his dealings with the bond rating companies and the fiscal monitors. In July 2002, just sixteen days into his first full fiscal year of 2003, he called for more than $1 billion in savings from city agencies, saying that revenues were not meeting targets. Such a move preempted the monitors from anticipating their worries over falling revenues. By November 2002, as the budget struggle with Albany took place, Standard & Poor's did lower the city's financial outlook to negative from stable, while keeping the city's A general obligation rating. "The outlook is basically a tool to signal there are certain trends emerging that could lead to a lower rating," said credit analyst Robin Prunty. "She called the mayor's plan 'reasonable,' and she praised the city council for quickly approving this week a combination of tax increases and spending cuts."[27] By May 2003, Standard & Poor's had returned the financial outlook to stable, based on the mayor's Fiscal Year 2004 projected budget and his actions to lay off 3,400 city workers as part of a gap-closing measure. Bloomberg won the game with the credit agencies.

Fortunately for the city and for Mayor Bloomberg, tax revenues began to increase in the latter part of Fiscal Year 2004. In his first term, property tax revenues rose by 11.1 percent annually and personal income taxes increased by 17.1 percent. Within three years, the pattern in revenues was clear—the real estate market was back. Although small in absolute dollars, mortgage taxes and the transfer of property increased dramatically—183.6 percent and 204.3 percent, respectively (see Table 9.1). According to the city comptroller, the economy in the city grew 2.9 percent at the end of 2003, which was the highest growth rate since 2000. The Independent Budget

Office projected an increase of 13.2 percent in tax revenues as compared to Fiscal Year 2003.[28] The mayor was placed in the awkward position of having greater revenue only two years after raising property taxes. He offered a $400 tax rebate to property owners when he projected ending the year in a $1.9 billion surplus this fiscal year. By 2006, the mayor received the highest-ever credit rating from Standard & Poor's, which raised the city's rating on its general obligation debt to AA– from A+.

However, the looming problem was that part of the revenue increase relied on Wall Street. The increases in personal income and corporate taxes in Bloomberg's first term represented the large profits and high incomes of Wall Street. Mayor Bloomberg said: "We have a tax structure in this city that's more dependent than ever on high-income businesses and individuals."[29] New York City always has had a high tax burden, but the revenue growth makes the city quite dependent on the health of the financial services sector.

ECONOMIC DEVELOPMENT COSTS

Mayor Bloomberg seemed more than willing to spend city dollars on the economic development front. And it is in this arena that many question his choices. Bloomberg's support of building a stadium in Manhattan's West Side caused widespread opposition. His design was a complex one—extending a subway line, enlarging the Jacob Javits Center, and constructing a platform over the Hudson rail yards to support the stadium. The entire project was described as the center of New York City's Olympic bid. Such a proposal was extremely expensive; the Independent Budget Office estimated that the cost to the city would be $3 billion.[30] Bloomberg proposed creating a separate corporation with bonding authority, the Hudson Yards Infrastructure Corporation (HYIC), which would rely on short-term borrowing to pay interest since the project would not have had the revenues necessary to cover repayment of the debt. The Transitional Finance Authority would be the backup to pay a "significant portion of the debt service on the bonds issued by HYIC if revenues from the project do not materialize."[31] In addition, attempting to finance the project through a separate corporation, and not through the city's capital budget, meant that city oversight would not exist. With a separate corporation, the project need not go through the city's land-use approval process (ULURP) and thus Bloomberg would not require city council approval. In the end, capital projects of authorities had to be approved by the New York State Public Authorities Board on which sat the governor, Assembly and Senate leaders; the latter two did not support the project, and Bloomberg's dreams of a stadium on the West Side died.

This was not the only stadium Mayor Bloomberg was involved with; he supported rebuilding the Mets' Stadium in Queens on city-owned land with tax breaks to the Mets worth $276 million and a cost to the city of $155 million in forgone revenue and a cost to the state of $89 million.[32] George Sweeting, deputy director of the Independent Budget Office, examined the costs in a letter to the city council: "because a large share of sports business income flows to a relatively small number of owners and players—few of whom reside in the city—much of these earnings will be spent elsewhere with only a small effect on the local economy."[33] Even though he was roundly criticized for support of private ventures with public taxpayers' monies, the mayor also gave tax breaks to the Yankees for the renovation of their new stadium. In the same memorandum, George Sweeting updated an earlier memo he had written about the subsidies involved with Yankee Stadium. The Yankees saved $361 million in the property tax and sales tax exemption. The new stadium will cost the city $154.9 million, mostly in the replacement of parkland that is being used for the Mets. In addition, the state and the Metropolitan Transportation Authority will lose about $92.8 million, only because the state is losing access to the revenue generated by the Yankees' parking garages. Much of the literature regarding public financing of stadiums has demonstrated that the costs to the cities outweigh the benefits.[34]

In December 2005, the mayor announced the largest proposed economic development project in Brooklyn: the Atlantic Yards, a twenty-one-acre development for an arena for the Nets basketball team, office buildings, and housing in cooperation with one of the city's most experienced developers, Forest City Ratner. The disruption to the neighborhoods of Prospect Heights, Fort Greene, and Park Slope would be major. At first, many people and organizations supported the project because the mayor announced a strong affordable housing component. However, by 2008, Ron Shiffman, a recognized authority in the city's urban planning, announced his withdrawal of support for the project, stating: "The density proposed by Forest City Ratner far exceed the carrying capacity of the area's physical, social, cultural, and educational infrastructure. The Atlantic Yards density is extreme and the heights of the proposed buildings totally unacceptable."[35]

The IBO once again provided cost estimates. The city would make a slight profit on the venture of $28.5 million.[36] The controversy continued to rage as Mayor Bloomberg signed a Memorandum of Understanding with Forest City Ratner Companies, Empire State Development Corporation, and the New York City Economic Development Corporation in February 2005.

Although Mayor Bloomberg raised property taxes significantly, he also focused on tax breaks to keep corporations in the city and subsidize further development. In addition to these economic development projects, the mayor awarded more than $900 million in tax breaks and other subsidies for commercial projects in his first five years in office, including those for Bank of America, Pfizer, Hearst Corporation, and Bank of New York.[37] The $1.5 billion tax break awarded to Goldman Sachs is the best example of this aid.

REBUILDING LOWER MANHATTAN

Unlike previous mayors, Mayor Bloomberg had the unenviable job of rebuilding Lower Manhattan after the devastating 9/11 terrorist attack. City officials did not control this project. The governor and private sector had a great deal of power through financing incentives using federal dollars and the State Lower Manhattan Development Corporation (LMDC). Congress passed the Job Creation and Worker Assistance Act of 2002, and through that act arranged financing to rebuild using Liberty Bonds and Community Development Block Grants (CDBG). These federal resources, which could have been used to finance the building of low- and middle-class housing, were instead used for financing luxury housing and providing tax breaks to large corporations to attract them to Lower Manhattan.

Congress waived the two most obvious requirements of CDBG funds—the majority of funds must benefit low- and middle-income communities and public hearings must be held prior to the allocation of the funds. The LMDC was free to administer these funds without public input. The LMDC was created by the state "to implement the programs and allocate the cash grants after the attacks and therefore should have been respectful of inclusiveness and transparency. Instead, state officials took full advantage of the federal waivers by implementing restricted public comment opportunities and allocating a disproportionate amount of funds to prominent firms."[38] The mayor appointed half of the board and the governor the other half.

The $8 billion in Liberty Bonds were tax-exempt private activity bonds created by the federal government for nonresidential property and some residential property ($1.6 billion) in rebuilding Lower Manhattan. Any federal requirements that a certain percentage was to be used only for low-income housing were lifted. The bonds could be used to finance activity in other parts of Manhattan and regulations also required a large minimum size to build so that small businesses found it difficult to qualify for Liberty Bonds. The results were that Lower Manhattan boomed in luxury housing and the rebuilding of large commercial space. However, small businesses were constantly complaining that they got little help in rebuilding in their previous space in Lower Manhattan.[39] After many complaints, the governor and mayor agreed that the remainder of the LMDC funds (about $1 billion) would be distributed through a variety of city and state agencies.

It was unclear how much power Mayor Bloomberg would have had to influence Congress in the details behind the federal financing structure. The mayor certainly had been an advocate for low- and middle-income housing. He created a five-year housing initiative in 2003 that called for building and preserving 65,000 units, but how successful he will be is unclear. At the same time, he advocated the tax giveaway programs for large corporations that were focused overwhelmingly in Manhattan.

LABOR UNIONS

Mayor Bloomberg was successful in demanding productivity increases in return for higher wages. The Citizens Budget Commission (CBC) applauded his efforts. In 2002, within a few months of becoming mayor, Mayor Bloomberg announced a settlement with the UFT. In exchange for hefty pay increases of 16 percent to 22 percent over two and a half years, the union had agreed to extend the school day by twenty minutes. He was less successful with the police union. It demanded state arbitration (which under state law is compulsory if one of the parties demands it) and got agreements from the state arbitrators for an 11.5 percent raise over two years without the ten additional work days the mayor wished to add to the work schedule. Again, the state intervened and the city paid.

A year later, the mayor played hardball. He faced another deficit and sought $600 million in concessions from the unions. The labor unions disagreed; 2,000 city workers were laid off. The labor union officials were shocked that the mayor's negotiators would walk away from negotiations. James Hanley (the administration's top negotiator) said after leaving the bargaining session: "They asked us to stop the clock on layoffs, and we said we weren't going to do it. We said there was nothing further to talk about."[40] This was a serious split between the unions and Bloomberg, who wanted the unions to play a major role in helping the city close its $3.8 billion budget gap through productivity improvements.

The struggle continued until December when the unions agreed to $100 million in health care savings through out-of-pocket health outlays. In January 2004, when the budget forecast was positive, the mayor agreed to property tax rebates and, playing hardball, added that labor unions were not to benefit from the positive budget forecast. "The taxpayers . . . stepped up to the plate and bailed the city out of the fiscal crisis," Ed Skyler, his press secretary, said. "The unions still haven't made any sacrifices."[41]

Finally, in June 2004, DC 37, the largest municipal union with 121,000 workers, settled. They "overwhelmingly ratified a contract that provided for a one-time $1,000 payment, a 3% raise in the second year, a 2% raise in the third year, and the potential for an additional 1% pay hike based on productivity. It also reduced the salaries of new workers by 15%."[42] Mayor Bloomberg wanted other city unions to follow this same settlement. However, teachers, police, and firefighters sought higher raises because of their special skills. There were three-day strikes by daycare workers and home health aides as well as a protest by the uniform unions and teachers objecting to this settlement. This protest was not minor. On June 8, 2004, there were 60,000 workers massing at City Hall condemning what union members considered a paltry settlement. The mayor's demands for more productivity from labor unions did not hurt him in the polls. The settlement came in the same week that his approval rating rose above 50 percent.

The struggle over productivity with labor unions continued. In October 2005, the UFT again settled, with the city agreeing to pay raises of 14.25 percent over fifty-two months and also requiring teachers to work an additional fifty minutes a week and two additional days. And it eliminated some seniority rights in staffing decisions and established a new master teacher position with higher pay. A few days later, the sanitation union settled for using one sanitation worker instead of two on some additional trucks and increasing tonnage collection per shift. In addition, trucks would go to dump sites as part of their regular route. The salary increases were for 17.1 percent over four years. A few days later, the firefighters settled for 17 percent over four years and made many concessions, including a cut in wages for new hires, a reduction in vacation time, and the withdrawal of several grievances.[43] The concessions followed a pattern that had characterized the city's negotiations with other municipal unions over the previous few months. The mayor won his point—no increases without productivity improvements.

SPENDING

In Fiscal Years 2005 and 2006, greater tax revenues and an improved economy meant that the budgets of over $50 billion could demonstrate growth. Mayor Bloomberg's priorities differed from Mayor Giuliani's. He de-emphasized public safety, demonstrating only a small growth in expenditures. The mayor's commitment to public health was substantial and is reflected in his quality-of-life programs. He added $200 million to help HHC's deficit and also "increased the corporation's capital budget by roughly $700 million since he came into office at a time when he has scaled back projects on other agencies. Among his plans are a major modernization of Harlem Hospital Center, budgeted at $225 million, a new outpatient center at Jacobi Medical Center, and new clinics at Queens Hospital Center."[44]

His commitment to human investment was clear: 6.8 percent annual increases in his first term.[45] He gave the largest increases to the community colleges since the 1975 fiscal crisis and also provided increases to libraries. His commitment to education was unlike any other mayor's. Mayor Bloomberg was convinced that K–12 education could be substantially improved. In his time in office, in exchange for productivity improvements, he increased average teacher salaries by 40 percent. Although some disagreed with the implementation of his educational plans, few disagreed with his goal of public school students being successful academically. Unlike Giuliani, Mayor Bloomberg invested in the community boards and the Business Improvement Districts. What he did not invest in with additional resources was public safety, which hardly grew—0.9 percent. This was not to say that the mayor did not focus on reducing crime, but his emphasis was on obtaining efficiencies of resources rather than adding more resources. He established

Operation Impact, deploying up to 1,000 new and veteran officers to targeted high-crime zones with great success.

His hard-to-control expenditures were indeed hard to control. Debt service increased as did pensions and benefits. His trips to Albany to stop the governor and legislature from increasing police and firefighter pensions were to no avail. Mayor Bloomberg spent a total of 8 percent annually in his first term emphasizing elementary and secondary education as well as quality-of-life agencies such as parks, public health, and environmental concerns. See Table 9.3.[46]

His second term differed from his first—it began in a time of surplus. In Fiscal Year 2006, Mayor Bloomberg demonstrated a thoughtful budget when he set aside a surplus of $2.5 billion to fully fund the city's retirees' health fund. This act was, in budget terms, the right strategy, but not one often seen by the previous mayor who had used surpluses to pay off next year's expenditures. It was also a time to commit to dealing with poverty in the city. His innovations included an affordable housing plan. His ten-year housing plan, the largest municipal affordable plan in the nation, was quite comprehensive, including tax-incentive programs for the private sector. Over a ten-year period, Mayor Bloomberg planned to provide enough homes for half a million New Yorkers.

However, as the surpluses continued to flow ($4.7 billion in Fiscal Year 2008 alone), Mayor Bloomberg took a page from previous mayors, and, instead of using them to pay down the city's debt or to invest in pay-as-you-go capital projects, Mayor Bloomberg prepaid future expenses (debt service).[47] Even more worrisome was that Mayor Bloomberg provided large tax cuts in Fiscal Year 2008—the average property tax cut was 7 percent, and cost the city $1 billion. Yet, the tax cuts remained conditional in good times. If the surpluses ended, presumably so would the tax cuts. Since large tax cuts are easy to make in times of surplus but are usually regretted when the economy declines and tax revenues are drastically reduced, Mayor Bloomberg demonstrated his fiscal responsibility theme when making the tax cuts conditional. The city council sought to create a rainy day fund, but the mayor was not interested since the legislation would give the council a role to play in how surplus funds were spent.

Then in Fiscal Year 2008, the mayor acknowledged the downturn in the national economy. He proposed a $58.5 billion budget for Fiscal Year 2009 that contained spending cuts over eighteen months and the use of surplus funds from Fiscal Year 2007.[48] The mayor's four-year plan projected deficits of $5.6 billion in Fiscal Year 2011 and $5.3 billion in Fiscal Year 2012. However, the mayor's financial plan extended the big property tax cuts through all four years. This would cost the city over $1.3 billion in lost revenue.[49] The 2009 budget finally adopted by the city council in June 2008 cut human services, particularly the Department of Aging and the Department of Youth and Community Development. In addition, major

Table 9.3 Expenditures during Bloomberg's first term, FY2002–2006 (in millions)

Categories	FY2002	% of Total	FY2006	% of Total	% Change FY02–06	Annual % Change FY02–06
Total expenditures	$40,860.0	100.0%	$53,999.1	100.0%	32.2%	8.0%
Development	713.0	1.7%	811.6	1.5%	13.8%	3.5%
Public safety	6,462.3	15.8%	6,693.9	12.4%	3.6%	0.9%
Human investment	12,256.6	30.0%	15,605.8	28.9%	27.3%	6.8%
Redistributive	10,510.5	25.7%	12,144.9	22.5%	17.0%	3.9%
Quality of life	921.6	2.3%	1,131.6	2.1%	22.8%	5.7%

Note: Expenditures will not total since minor expenditures have been omitted.
Source: NYC's Comptroller's Reports, FY2002–FY2006.

spending reductions were made in Child Health Clinics and the Infant Mortality Initiative. Mayor Bloomberg advocated for these cuts while cutting property taxes.

In his second term, he also announced a program using private money to provide conditional cash transfers to create financial incentives for poor people. "In the private sector, financial incentives encourage actions that are good for the company: working harder, hitting sales targets or landing more clients. In the public sector, we believe that financial incentives will encourage actions that are good for the city and its families: higher attendance in schools, more parental involvement in education, and better career skills."[50] The Bloomberg administration created the program as a pilot funded by foundations and designed by MDRC, one of the top evaluation firms in the country. Mayor Bloomberg was determined to make his second term a broad attack on poverty.

However, Mayor Bloomberg faced a growing homeless problem. There are now more homeless in the city than in the last twenty years. In its eighth annual report, the Coalition for the Homeless said: "[We found] that in the past year the number of homeless New Yorkers in shelters increased by 11.1% (to 35,113), the number of homeless families in New York City shelters increased by 17.6% (to 9,190) and the number of homeless children increased by 18.1% (14,219). Most striking, the report found that the average number of families in shelters hit an all-time record high—with the Department of Homeless Services reporting a monthly average of 9,287 families in the city's shelters in February. These numbers come less than a month after the Mayor's management report documented a 24% increase in the number of new families entering the shelter system."[51] Clearly, the high cost of housing had had a devastating impact on poor New Yorkers. Mayor Bloomberg came under increasing attack for his inability to house the poor, even in the midst of his ten-year housing plan. He received low grades on a report card from housing groups, and was severely criticized when his administration introduced a new program, "Work Advantage," that required homeless families to save $107 a month and contribute $50 toward their rent without regard to the employment status of the worker.[52] Clearly, Bloomberg's affordable housing plans were not sufficient. The latest research report from CSS detailed the ongoing loss of federally subsidized affordable housing units in New York City. It found that, since 1990, the city has lost 27 percent of its subsidized housing stock, with more than 4,000 units lost in 2006 alone.[53] But Mayor Bloomberg was interested in tax cuts, not more investment in affordable housing.

In April 2007, Mayor Bloomberg presented *PlanNYC: A Greener, Greater New York*, which contained 127 separate initiatives emphasizing sustainability goals. These goals included "increasing access to parks, playgrounds and open spaces; reclaiming brownfields; developing critical backup systems for our aging water network to ensure reliability; providing additional reliable power sources and upgrading our existing power plants; reducing water pollution so we can open our waterways for recreation; and reducing our greenhouse gas emissions by 30%."[54] The initial emphasis focused on environmental issues, and not affordable housing about which community advocates remain skeptical.[55]

Another area of concern in Bloomberg's public policies involves his actions regarding civil liberties. The New York Police Department (NYPD) spied on lawful political activity during the policing of the 2004 Republican National Convention. Because of the discovery process in lawsuits surrounding the NYPD's actions, it became clear that the NYPD had "amassed information on plans for peaceful protest and created political dossiers on innocent individuals."[56] The NYPD's actions were not the first issue concerning civil liberties during the Bloomberg administration. In 2003, the NYPD forbade an antiwar rally to march; rather, the protestors were required to remain stationary. And in one of the most shocking decrees, Mayor Bloomberg forbade war protestors from using Central Park, a long-standing demonstration site. One of the more recent transgressions in 2007 was Bloomberg's press office taking away the press credentials from Rafael Martinez Alequin, a reporter from a long-time blog. And Mayor Bloomberg's plans to install thousands of cameras on street corners stirred a tide of discord among New Yorkers. The tension around Bloomberg's public policies on civil liberties was questioned even by the mainstream press in a series of articles in the New York Times.

CITY COUNCIL

Mayor Bloomberg's ability to work with others was demonstrated in his relationship with the city council. Unlike Giuliani, Mayor Bloomberg worked closely with the new city council speaker, Christine C. Quinn, and New Yorkers benefited. Mayor Bloomberg in Fiscal Year 2006 appointed a citywide task force of developers, bankers, and affordable housing advocates to study the tax breaks available to developers for building affordable housing alongside luxury housing and make recommendations about how to improve the law. The mayor sought to bring disparate groups together and urged them to forge a compromise. That compromise was eventually worked out with the city council and a new law was proposed that needed state legislative approval. Most were satisfied with the process. And the mayor demonstrated that he understood how to move his agenda among very powerful real estate economic interests.

In another situation, the mayor and city council announced a budget plan in Fiscal Year 2007 that would stabilize funding for the arts, park maintenance, libraries, summer jobs, and family childcare programs. In the past, these functions had been part of a budget dance every year as to whether or not the mayor would include them in his proposed budget. They would no longer be part of the annual budget chop. These functions would now be base lined and part of any future proposed budget by the mayor. The mayor and speaker also agreed to reform the capital budget process and give the city council more information from OMB.

It was difficult to examine the capital budget. Commitments were not the same as appropriations and appropriations were not the same as what was actually spent. If expenditures were examined, it was clear that the mayor had shifted spending in capital items from public safety to environmental protection and public health. Public safety had a far smaller share of the capital expenditures while environmental protection had a 10 percent increase in its share. Education remained about the same, a 1.1 percent increase, while the health area vastly increased its share of capital expenditures (142.5 percent increase), indicating the mayor's interest in this area.[57]

THE CITY AND THE CHARTER

In Mayor Bloomberg's first term, he sought to address fiscal policy that would be adrift once the FCB expired in 2008. He did this through a Charter Revision Commission that drafted a ballot proposal addressing concerns over fiscal policy that would be eliminated when the FCB expired. The law supporting the FCB, the NYS Financial Emergency Act (FEA), required the city to plan and maintain a balanced budget and to incur a deficit of no more than $100 million at year-end. The ballot proposal would require the city to balance its budget each year. In addition, the FEA required the mayor to create a four-year financial plan and include a balanced budget, maintain a reserve of at least $100 million each year, pay down any deficit accrued from the previous year, and not issue debt inconsistent with the financial plan. The ballot proposal included all these points. The FEA limited the amount of short-term debt that the city issued; it had high standards for the annual audit and these high standards were included in the proposal. The ballot proposal passed and became law. The city's residents registered a resounding vote that the city keep its fiscal house in order.

In 2008, the state legislature fully funded the Financial Control Board and the Office of the Special Deputy Comptroller. The Financial Board will no longer have the power to declare a control period. It has become only a monitoring body, not an oversight body.

CONCLUSION

Mayor Bloomberg breezed through reelection. His popularity matched the upgrade in bond ratings given by the major credit rating agencies. Standard & Poor's general obligation credit rating of A+A– was highly praised. The words used to describe him were intelligent, expert, and determined.

Divisiveness was not part of his vocabulary. His popularity at the time of his reelection was based on a confidence that citizens had in him to manage the city. He succeeded through his expertise with good management and sober reflection to win voters to him, even though he had little in the way of charisma. His willingness to meet everyone, including angry African American leaders over the ill-advised police shooting of an African American, was highly respected by city citizens, and very different from his predecessor. His reaching out to the many different ethnic and racial groups in the city through attending church services was a welcome relief after the harshness of the former mayor.

Although more congenial with the city's labor unions, the mayor was far tougher than Giuliani. Diana Fortuna, president of the Citizens Budget Commission, said, "Bloomberg started off much more smoothly with the unions, but now he's showing he's prepared to stand up to them and take a lot of heat from them."[58]

If the economy had not picked up, it is very doubtful that he would have won reelection. Raising property taxes by almost 20 percent in his first year in office was courageous—it was not something politicians usually did. But he did it and it paid off. The mayor was not faced with huge budget deficits that required an enormous number of layoffs. His deficits were manageable because he raised the property tax. And the financial elites were divided over the tax increase, which also was to his advantage.

Mayor Bloomberg invested in education as he said he would. He sought to invest in luxury economic development schemes of which several are on track. The economic development ventures demonstrated Mayor Bloomberg's determination to support very high-end real estate ventures regardless of the cost to the city's neighborhoods. He continued the development schemes of his predecessors and initiated others.

If the mayor had an Achilles' heel, it was that he was perceived as being unable to focus on poor and working-class issues, particularly housing; rather, he invested his time and resources into upper-class development projects that were quite controversial. His tax cuts were worrisome, and his stance on civil liberties continued to be contentious. His budget cuts in Fiscal Year 2009 were directed at human services agencies. He chose property tax increases over human services.

By nature an optimist, Mayor Bloomberg portrayed a spirit of civic pride and know-how even though he lacked traditional political savvy. Because he belonged to the financial elite, his fiscal actions were not as highly scrutinized as those of the previous mayors, much to his and the city's benefit. And, within a few years, the economy was booming so that his first term when he struggled with incredibly low polls was forgotten. In addition, he demonstrated a shrewd understanding of the city's financial condition. He and Senator Charles Schumer commissioned an in-depth report on the financial services industry, *Sustaining New York's and U.S.' Global Financial Services Leadership*, with major recommendations on improvement for the industry.[59] This type of leadership can prove crucial to the city's future.

The financial services crisis of 2008 resulted in five of the 12 largest arrangers of municipal bond sales having being taken over or having left the business during 2008: two top underwriters, JP Morgan and Bear Stearns, combined their businesses when JP Morgan bailed out. Bear Stearns and Lehman Brothers went bankrupt, and top ranking Swiss firm, UBS, bowed out of the municipal bond market. Merrill agreed to be bought by Bank of America Corporation. This upheaval in the municipal bond market will result in higher priced bonds as liquidity dries up and the market remains uncertain. The result will be enormous tax revenue losses for New York City, New York State, Connecticut and New Jersey, which are all dependent upon the fiscal health of the financial services sector. Mayor Bloomberg's term of office is ending as the city faces an enormous crisis—9 percent of the city's tax revenues and 20 percent of the state's tax revenues are dependent upon Wall Street.

In his second term, Mayor Bloomberg left the Republican Party. This was widely interpreted as the beginning of his testing the water for a race to the presidency. The mayor was independently wealthy and could afford to throw his name in the ring. The mayor pointed out that, although he is Jewish, divorced, supports antigun legislation, and is pro-gay and pro-abortion, voters could respond to his successful record as a business-minded executive: "Any successful elected executive knows that real results are more important than partisan battles and that good ideas should take precedence over rigid adherence to any particular political ideology."[60] Although his record of fiscal responsibility and solid management style could have been very appealing to voters in both major parties at a time when political party leaders lack credibility with many voters, the dream was not to be. No mayor of New York City has gone on to the presidency; Mayor Bloomberg is no exception. His future lies in state or political office, federal service, or the world of philanthropy. His legacy to the city is mixed. New Yorkers are proud of their well-run city under Mayor Bloomberg, but his large-scale development projects in his second term, along with his inability to solve the affordable housing problem, left some New Yorkers skeptical. Mayor Bloomberg helped to secure the city as a global entity, but the price was awfully high.

As this book goes to press, Mayor Bloomberg announced his intention of running for a third term as mayor. This requires the city council to extend term limits from two to three four-year terms, a legislative act in which they would be happy to participate. If Mayor Bloomberg succeeds in extending term limits, many New Yorkers will welcome the mayor to a third term because of his acknowledged financial acumen.

TEN

CONCLUSION

The realignment wrought by Franklin Roosevelt dominated American politics for years after he was out of the White House. . . . it dominated American politics until the election of Ronald Reagan. And the realignment wrought by Ronald Reagan dominates us still today.

—Mayor Rudolph Giuliani, 1999[1]

My position has not always been understood in the Republican Party. But let me tell you. I want to preserve this country. Who's got more to preserve?

—Governor Nelson Rockefeller[2]

The second American Revolution grew out of the collapse of capitalism. President Roosevelt changed the role of government to remake a primitive capitalism into a more collaborative capitalism in which labor unions benefited. When this era ended, due to the intense competition among nations in the 1960s and 1970s and the changing technologies, so too did the collaborative capitalism. We turned to the third American Revolution, a primitive capitalism with global overlays in which multinational corporations became dominant. New York City's fiscal crisis took place in the midst of this turmoil.

Along with this turmoil, cities had little power to take financial steps to end deficits without appealing to their state legislature. New York State was no different. Mayor Lindsay looked to New York State's constitutional convention to gain power over revenue issues. But the convention refused to add to New York cities' home rule. Governor Rockefeller was not about to give power to the cities as opposed to the state legislature, which he dominated. In the popular literature of urban fiscal crises, little attention is paid to the legal structures within which cities make fiscal policy. Few authors, other than Gerald Frug and Lawrence Tribe, have fully discussed state limitations on cities while a wealth of researchers have limited their discussion on fiscal crises of cities to largely internal reasons such as the inadequacy of mayoral leadership or the power of municipal unions.[3]

In a time of increased globalization, the financial elites in New York City in close cooperation with individual states were quite effective in imposing their will on local decision-making, particularly when municipal finances were dire. Business interests did dominate because of the intense competition that elected officials face when dealing with scarce resources. As credit rating agencies grew in their comprehensive, in-depth assessments of municipal stability, these agencies also grew in power. "By regulating the connection that municipalities have with the wider bond market, rating agencies affect more than just the immediate ability to access credit. They influence local autonomy by controlling the interaction that cities have with markets."[4] Indeed, beginning with the 1975 fiscal crisis, the financial elites had sufficient controls over the city governmental process that mayors were quite constrained during tough fiscal times.

In several ways, the third American Revolution is recognized as having failed. On the national level, we have more inequality in income and poverty has grown. On the international level, we have growing inequality and deepening poverty in the developing world. But one of the most disturbing parts is that, on the local level, we are so accepting of subordinating our needs to the demands of the financial elite. The most striking observation about several of these fiscal crises is that, in a republic, elected officials had so little control. During fiscal crises, an equal partnership between elected officials and financial elites did not develop. Elected officials had far less power for spending decisions. The financial elites often dominated the city's major policy decisions concerning budgets. Throughout the city's fiscal crisis of 1975, citizens lost their representative democracy. Bankers ran the city:

> When Ellmore Patterson (CEO of JP Morgan) went golfing, he would see a golf cart speeding toward him and know it carried a message from the mayor. "He kept calling me and he'd say, 'What's going on?' " Patterson recalled. As Beame lost more control, we gradually had to tell him what he could and couldn't do.[5]

Less than two decades later, Mayor Dinkins's staff members sat in Felix Rohaytn's office and renegotiated the budget. No one elected Felix Rohaytn; no one elected the Financial Control Board. When the credit agencies threatened to lower the city's credit rating, the Dinkins administration downsized his proposed budget. The power of the financial elites overwhelmed the mayoralty.

No one presented other choices; the money providers dominated. The other power arena, the labor unions, which were service demanders, remained silent. Challenging the banks rather than acceding to their demands for cutbacks was problematic. The lack of challenge arose because of New York City's isolation. This is what Savitch and Kantor pointed out—intergovernmental factors are important. Unlike in LaGuardia's time, when every city was in fiscal distress and LaGuardia found support from the president, there was no support in the nation's capital for the city's fiscal issues in 1975 and after, thus New York City officials had little choice. Unions were boxed in. If unions did not cooperate, the city could enter bankruptcy proceedings, which meant that union contracts would be null and void, thus negating years of advances in working conditions for city employees.

Another striking observation is the degree of Mayor LaGuardia's fight with financial elites. The actions of other mayors were in stark contrast to LaGuardia, who fought furiously for his budget, but, unlike modern mayors, he was well positioned because of powerful allies—the president and his aides. In the midst of the nation's greatest Depression, Mayor LaGuardia identified the needs of the city's citizens and fought to create a city that met those needs. In later fiscal crises, city officials were unable to protect these successes.

In many ways, LaGuardia was the great communicator. He traveled frequently to Washington and Albany, and constantly wrote and called officials in the two capitals. He would not take no for an answer. LaGuardia understood that too much debt meant that the city could not control its destiny but that bankers would. It is easy to see that the personality of an individual mayor made a difference. But would LaGuardia have been successful without FDR? Of course not. Millions of federal dollars poured into the city during Roosevelt's tenure. LaGuardia's leadership did not matter as much as the partnership. At the same time, it was LaGuardia's leadership that led to FDR's committing millions to the city. It was LaGuardia's leadership that led to the passage of the Economy Act, giving future mayors more control over local government. Of course, leadership mattered. But LaGuardia had FDR in his pocket; without FDR, LaGuardia would not have succeeded.

Governor Rockefeller left the state in a mess. The state might have avoided its steep economic decline if the governor had not built a mountain of debt for his construction projects. Certainly, New York City would not have gone down the road of financing expenditures through debt without the help of both the governor and the state legislature. Mayor Lindsay counted on the Constitutional Convention to enlarge home rule so that he could pass the tax packages he required. But he lost that battle.

We can see how critical revenues are to the mayors when we compare tax revenues growth across mayors. Mayor Dinkins had sustained retrenchment throughout his term. In Table 10.1, we note the lack of revenue growth that Dinkins experienced, particularly in the real estate market.[6] The mortgage tax and the real property tax indicate the strength of the real estate market.

Table 10.1 Annual percentage change in tax revenues among post-1975 fiscal crisis mayors, FY1980–FY2006

Tax Revenues	Koch FY1980–1990	Dinkins FY1990–1994	Giuliani FY1994–2002	Bloomberg FY2002–2006
Property tax	10.5%	4.7%	1.6%	11.1%
Personal income	18.9%	10.0%	3.5%	17.1%
Sales	11.3%	0.7%	4.3%	7.9%
General corporation	11.1%	5.9%	2.1%	17.2%
Financial corporation	0.3%	62.3%	-5.8%	38.0%
Unincorporated business income	26.5%	3.6%	12.9%	16.2%
Mortgage recording	36.4%	-3.4%	32.1%	45.9%
Commercial rent	21.3%	0.7%	-5.3%	6.0%
Conveyance of real property	49.1%	-7.1%	22.3%	51.1%
Other taxes	2.2%	1.3%	1.0%	11.1%
Total taxes	11.6%	5.2%	2.5%	14.4%

Source: Independent Budget Office, "Trends of Revenues since FY1980."

Mayor Beame is a much more difficult case study. Could he have formed an alliance with the labor unions? Mayor Beame, completely isolated from his natural allies, the unions, lost complete control to the financial elites. Could Beame if he had been in the same leadership mode as LaGuardia taken on the bankers? What if he had threatened to close the schools, hospitals, parks, and libraries? We will never know, but it is doubtful. The bankers held all the cards. They forced city and state officials to adopt stringent fiscal policy—severe cutbacks or no access to the financial markets. It is hard to imagine that any mayor could have successfully fought the financial interests. It is easier to construct a scenario in which a mayor, like Koch, endorsed fiscal responsibility and worked with financial interests. That did not happen with Mayor Beame; he was quite clear that the financial interests were blackmailing the city and the unions had caved. There are no heroes in the 1975 fiscal crisis. It is fashionable in books about this crisis to praise Governor Carey, Felix Rohatyn, and Victor Gotbaum, the leaders who put together the deal, the deal that saved the city. The city wasn't saved. It was a disaster from which it is still recovering.

Mayor Koch certainly helped the city when it gained four more years of federal loan guarantees. But the city was a mess in the 1980s under Koch's watch, a fact seldom acknowledged. The crime rate soared; the number of police fell dramatically. The middle class fled the city while he was mayor. Corruption among political officials ran rampant. Since Mayor Koch is an entertaining fellow and has had years after office to create a record, he appears to have weathered any criticism of his time in office. Later historians may not be so kind.

Dinkins was not Beame. He was not isolated. Mayor Dinkins was far more competent in fiscal matters than the press portrayed. But he and his team did suffer from a lack of expertise in managing interest groups and communicating their message. Mayors Giuliani and Bloomberg hit the ground running in terms of dealing with labor contracts. Mayor Dinkins had a painful first year until he had gathered the necessary experience. Felix Rohaytn endorsed him for reelection as did Governor Cuomo. Mayor Dinkins lost the election due to racial issues, not fiscal ones. He was elected at a time when citizens were fearful of the growing racial unrest, and Mayor Dinkins, originally voted in on a platform of bringing everyone together, did not succeed in controlling that unrest.

Mayor Dinkins stands in sharp contrast to Mayor Giuliani who controlled the image he wished to convey to the press. Mayor Giuliani was not successful in the eyes of voters or the financial elites during the recession of the first three years; he emerged triumphant only when the recession ended. Giuliani was a great communicator only after the recession. His need for control and his disdain for those who disagreed with him worked only during the good times. His last five years were quite different from his first three. When faced with a miserable economy, Giuliani's popularity declined rapidly; it was only as the economy picked up that Giuliani's popularity improved. This difference was due to more than personality; it was also due to the economic and social environment in which mayors found themselves, isolated from federal help and losing control to the financial elites during fiscal scarcity.

Another factor is the extent to which bankers were accepted in later crises as part of the solution, which was vastly different from what had occurred during the 1929 depression. The Great Depression was so vast and so deep that bankers lost their credibility; they had no credit in Albany and Washington, where congressional hearings were being held to castigate bank officials. President Roosevelt in his inauguration address pledged to "drive the money changers from the temple." This was not so in 1975 or 1990. Bernard Baruch said: "The stereotype of bankers as conservative, careful, prudent individuals was shattered in 1929."[7] In later fiscal crisis, the financial elites were instrumental in creating solutions—undemocratic solutions, but solutions nevertheless, ones that were devastating to city services.

Then along came Mayor Bloomberg, the ultimate successful business executive. To deal with his inherited deficit, he borrowed and he extended debt. None of these strategies would have been acceptable in the eyes of the financial elites during the Dinkins era. During the 1975 fiscal crisis, borrowing was only agreed to when the city gave up its budgetary and expenditure powers to the Emergency Financial Control Board. What Bloomberg achieved, facing the greatest fiscal crisis since 1975, was no loss in mayoral power, very little disruption in city services, and credibility with the financial elites, Albany, and Washington. How did he do it? A large part of Bloomberg's success with the city's finances was because he came from Wall Street. His hardware and software were in every Wall Street office. His clients were the financial elites; he had built a highly successful company that served them. New York City, the financial capital of the world, had one of their own in power.

But there is another answer. Mayor Bloomberg believed that his non-political approach to city issues made a difference: "It's an administrative job. I never ran anything this size—nobody's going to run anything this size—but I have a lot of administrative experience. I would argue those who work their way up the legislative branch of government have absolutely no skills to do the job."[8]

Financial elites, however, do not elect mayors; voters have a choice once every four years. Mayor Bloomberg extended his support from the conservative base of Mayors Koch and Giuliani to the rainbow base of Mayor Dinkins. His attention to the ethnicity of New Yorkers has paid off. Unlike Mayor Giuliani, Mayor Bloomberg is welcomed in African American churches and Hispanic ones. Immigrants have flooded the city in the 1990s; only 35 percent of the population is white. It is now a nonwhite city. Although Bloomberg alienated his conservative base—small property owners in the outer boroughs—by raising the property tax, he regained them over his first four years through solid management and property tax rebates.

Certainly, his strategies at first alienated him from the Democrats. In an attempt to closely align himself with his Republican colleagues, he alienated the rank and file of the political world by seeking to replace the closed primary system with an open one. He invited the Republican president to his home for a $15,000-a-head fund-raiser for Republican Governor George Pataki within his first month in office.[9] His relationships with unions became strained when he insisted on productivity improvements in return for wage increases. And he got far more than previous mayors. Certainly, he won reelection easily. He left the Republican Party; he no longer needed it. He was term limited and briefly thought about running for the presidency. He abandoned his wish to run for the presidency once Barack Obama became popular.

Over time, the resolutions of the budget issues during these fiscal crises resulted in the financial elites gaining incredible long-lasting control over the ways the city used its resources. There is no doubt that creditors controlled the mayors' ranges of options and reduced city services in times of recession. Mayor LaGuardia created and was the best protector of these services. But after the 1975 fiscal crisis with the state Financial Control Board in place, the financial elites kept future mayors on a short lease during recessions. Giuliani was lucky. Although financial elites and voters were alienated during his first three years, the economy improved, and so did his ratings until his last year in office when his personal problems overtook him. Bloomberg differed from these previous mayors—he was a businessman, not a politician—and he won over the electorate; his handling of the financial elites was certainly masterful. Mayor Bloomberg asked the state legislature to continue the Financial Control Board, which was due to expire in 2008. He succeeded. Already, city residents have voted in financial controls that make it more difficult for mayors to practice deficit spending.

What does this say about regime theory that claims that political considerations are not necessarily subservient to economics? Yes, each mayor had the option to approach fiscal problems with his own policy goals and leadership style. These mayors may have been successful on occasion in the allocation of resources in ways intended by the mayor even in the harshest of times. This is witnessed by the actions of Mayor Dinkins as he succeeded in shifting resources to social services and Mayor Bloomberg when he raised the rate of property taxes. As can be seen in Table 10.2, when we compare the expenditure growth for each of the post-1975 fiscal crisis mayors, we see the stark contrast among them.[10] Koch had his commitment to economic development; Dinkins, in a time of enormous retrenchment, had his commitment to redistributive services; Giuliani had his commitment to public order; Bloomberg had his commitment to education and economic development.

But, by and large, the financial elites won on most occasions whenever times were hard. Regime theory ignores the sheer power of financial elites to dictate the parameters within which mayors function. There is the complexity

Table 10.2 Percentage comparison of mayoral expenditures, FY1979–FY2006 (in millions)

Expenditures	Koch			Dinkins		Giuliani		Bloomberg	
	FY79	FY90	Annual % Change FY79–90	FY94	Annual % Change FY90–94	FY02	Annual % Change FY94–02	FY06	Annual % Change FY02–06
Total expenditures	$12,892	$25,932	9.2%	$31,348	5.2%	$40,860	3.8%	$53,999	8.0%
Development	189.8	584.4	18.9%	607.0	1.0%	713.0	2.2%	811.6	3.5%
Public order	1,205.0	3,522.9	17.5%	3,846.1	2.3%	6,462.4	8.5%	6,693.9	0.9%
Human investment	2,477.0	6,762.9	15.7%	8,078.1	4.9%	12,256.7	6.4%	15,605.8	6.8%
Redistributive	3,945.2	7,302.0	7.7%	9,596.7	7.9%	10,510.5	1.2%	12,144.9	3.9%
Quality of life	$223.7	$638.4	16.9%	$730.7	3.6%	$921.6	3.3%	$1,131.6	5.7%

Source: NYC Comptroller's Reports, FY1979–FY2006.

that financial elites are not homogeneous and often disagree about resource allocation at the local level. And of course, in the United States, each state provides sizeable resources to its cities, and state officials have their own relationships with financial elites. Thus, individual states can have enormous influence on financial decision-making at the local level. Savitch and Kantor give center stage to intergovernmental support. But, in the end, on most occasions, financial elites have won and continue to do so.

The creditors from banks and credit rating agencies reflected time and again the accuracy of Sinclair's thesis that private power can dominate public policy. First bankers then, later, credit rating agencies had considerable influence over the public policy choices that mayors made. Did this amount to diminished public government? New York City was pressured to eliminate its free university, to cut services deeply in order to satisfy financial interests, and to reduce taxes as a symbol of shaping up. This was required from the city, not just in 1975, but continually up to the present time whenever revenues lagged. Although mayors sometimes outmaneuvered these financial forces, they remained limited in their responses in times of retrenchment.

Yet even in fiscally hard times, mayors clearly had some discretion and achieved some of their goals—whether it was Koch demanding and finally winning the right to control the MAC surpluses, or Dinkins who insisted on money for "cops and kids" not just "cops," or Giuliani who was determined to spend dollars on public safety and education, or Bloomberg who claimed that an increase in property taxes was the only sound choice. And certainly, in good times, mayors were in charge within the regulatory framework established during the 1975 fiscal crisis.

And it is a framework that New York City residents agree with, as demonstrated by their vote to place more fiscal regulation in their own charter. It is certainly the case that private power won out over public policy on numerous occasions during and after the 1975 fiscal crisis. We lost the free university system; we endured years of cutbacks in city services. But it is almost thirty-five years since 1975. Savitch and Kantor remind us that our local political culture is also important, not just our economic circumstances. Indeed, the city's liberal tradition has been severely limited in the last thirty-five years. As this city takes its place as a global city, its very culture has shifted from a liberal tradition to a far more conservative one that calls for balanced budgets and less public spending.

Whoever becomes mayor in 2009, the mayor will face an uncertain financial future as tax revenues decline and the city's major industry, financial services, suffers an uncertain future. In 2008, the municipal bond market was in confusion; cities were finding it difficult to attract the capital they needed; their bond offerings went unanswered. New York City will have to pay high interest rates in order to attract investors. Once again, it will be a very difficult time financially. And once again, the mayor may have few choices.

EXPENDITURE CATEGORIES

DEVELOPMENT

City Planning
Business
Finance Department
Transportation
Buildings Department

PUBLIC SAFETY

Police
Fire
Other includes district attorneys, CCRB, PAS, Corrections, Board of Corrections, Juvenile Justice, Probation, Special Prosecutor, and Emergency Departments

HUMAN INVESTMENT

Colleges
Education Department
Libraries

REDISTRIBUTIVE

Hospitals
Housing
Human Rights
Legal Aid
Social Services includes Department of the Aging, HRA, Homelessness, Social Services, Administration of Children's Services, and Department of Employment

QUALITY OF LIFE

Cultural Affairs
Environmental Protection Agency
Parks
Public Health includes Health and Mental Retardation
Sanitation and Trade Waste Commission

APPENDIX B

CONSTANT DOLLARS

These tables have been created for readers who are interested in revenue data translated into constant dollars. Patterns in constant dollars are similar to those found in current dollars.

Table B.1 Comparing revenues among post-1975 fiscal crisis mayors in constant dollars (in millions)

Revenues	Year		% Change	Annual % Change
Koch	FY78	FY90		
Total taxes	$20,691	$23,926	15.6%	1.3%
Federal grants	8,097	4,579	–43.5%	–3.6%
State grants	7,498	8,242	9.9%	0.8%
Unrestricted fed & st	3,234	1,094	–66.2%	–5.5%
Charges & fees	2,213	1,716	–22.4%	–1.9%
Other	127	1,772	1299.4%	108.3%
Total revenues	41,859	41,330	–1.3%	–0.1%
Dinkins	FY90	FY94		
Total taxes	23,926	25,271	5.6%	1.4%
Federal grants	4,579	5,524	20.6%	5.2%
State grants	8,242	8,235	–0.1%	0.0%
Unrestricted fed & st	1,094	930	–15.0%	–3.7%
Charges & fees	1,717	1,781	3.8%	0.9%
Other	1,772	1,997	12.7%	3.2%
Total revenues	41,330	43,739	5.8%	1.5%

continued on next page

Revenues		Year	% Change	Annual % Change
Giuliani	FY94	FY02		
Total taxes	25,271	24,952	–1.3%	–0.2%
Federal grants	5,524	7,012	26.9%	3.4%
State grants	8,235	9,236	12.2%	1.5%
Unrestricted fed & st	930	596	–36.0%	–4.5%
Charges & fees	1,781	1,677	–5.9%	–0.7%
Other	1,997	3,525	76.5%	9.6%
Total revenues	43,739	46,998	7.5%	0.9%
Bloomberg	FY02	FY06		
Total taxes	24,952	34,211	37.1%	9.3%
Federal grants	7,012	5,243	–25.2%	–6.3%
State grants	9,236	9,586	3.8%	0.9%
Unrestricted fed & st	596	494	–17.0%	–4.3%
Charges & fees	1,677	1,837	9.6%	2.4%
Other	3,525	2,632	–25.3%	–6.3%
Total revenues	$46,998	$54,004	14.9%	3.7%

Note: CPI: Metropolitan New York. All items; Series Id: CUURA101SAO,
CUUSA101SAO, Based Period: 1982–84 = 100. Not seasonally adjusted.
Source: New York City Comptroller's Reports, FY1979–FY2006.

Table B.2 Comparing expenditures among post-1975 fiscal crisis mayors in constant dollars (in millions)

Koch	FY79	FY82	FY90	Annual % Change FY79–82	Annual % Change FY82–90	Annual % Change FY79–FY82
Total Expenditures	$38,606	$34,914	$41,323	-3.2%	2.3%	0.6%
Development	568	660	931	5.4%	5.1%	5.8%
Public safety	3,608	3,609	5,614	0.0%	6.9%	5.1%
Human investment	7,418	7,401	10,777	-0.1%	5.7%	4.1%
Redistributive	11,814	9,798	11,636	-5.7%	2.3%	-0.1%
Quality of life	$ 670	$ 795	$ 1,017	6.2%	3.5%	4.7%

Dinkins	FY90	FY94	Annual % Change FY90–94
Total Expenditures	$41,322.7	$43,732.6	1.5%
Development	931.2	846.8	-2.3%
Public safety	5,613.7	5,365.6	-1.1%
Human investment	10,776.7	11,269.5	1.1%
Redistributive	11,635.8	13,388.1	3.8%
Quality of life	$1,017.3	$1,019.4	0.1%

continued on next page

Table B.2 (Continued)

Giuliani	FY94	FY98	Annual % Change FY94–98	FY98	FY2002	Annual % Change FY98–02	Annual % Change FY94–02
Total expenditures	$43,733	$44,398	0.4%	$44,398	$46,992	1.5%	0.9%
Development	847	658	-5.6%	658	820	6.2%	-0.4%
Public safety	5,366	6,287	4.3%	6,287	7,432	4.6%	4.8%
Human investment	11,270	11,911	1.4%	11,911	14,076	4.5%	3.1%
Redistributive	13,388	11,418	-3.7%	11,418	12,088	1.5%	-1.2%
Quality of life	$1,019	$1,043	0.6%	$1,043	$1,060	0.4%	0.5%

Bloomberg	FY2002	FY2006	Annual % Change FY02–06
Total expenditures	$46,992	53,999	3.7%
Development	820	812	-0.3%
Public safety	7,432	6,694	-2.5%
Human investment	14,096	15,606	2.7%
Redistributive	11,937	12,145	0.4%
Quality of life	$1,060	$1,132	1.7%

Source: New York City Comptroller's Reports, FY1978–FY2006. CPI: Metropolitan New York. All items; Series Id: CUURA101SA0, CUUSA101SA0, Base Period: 1982–84 = 100. Not seasonally adjusted.

NOTES

CHAPTER ONE

1. Glasberg, *The Power of Collective Purse Strings: The Effect of Bank Hegemony on Corporations and the State.*

2. Inman (1995) defines crisis as a time when the city is unable to raise sufficient revenues to cover the city's expenditures. Also see Wolff, *Fiscal Crises in U.S. Cities: Structural and Non-Structural Causes.*

3. The City University of New York (CUNY) is third in population behind the State University of New York (SUNY) and California State University system.

4. Shalala and Bellamy, A State Saves a City: The New York Case. Symposium on Municipal Finance, 1125.

5. Rockefeller, *Memoirs*, 196.

6. Ibid.

7. Weikart, *Decision Making and the Impact of Those Decisions during NYC's Fiscal Crisis in the Public Schools, 1975–77*, 167.

8. Freudenberg et al., "The Impact of NYC's 1975 Fiscal Crisis on the Tuberculosis, HIV, and Homicide Syndemic," 425.

9. Ibid., 416.

10. Croft, "NYC Park Advocatees' First Annual State of the Parks Address," 2.

11. Lawson, "Owners of Last Resort: The Track Record of New York City's Early Low-Income Housing Cooperatives Created between 1967 and 1975," 61.

12. Schaller, "The Fare Hike Mess," 1.

13. Wallace, "Fire Service Productivity and New York City Fire Crisis: 1968–1979," 433.

14. *New York Times*, "From 1975 to Now, How's New York City Doing," B1.

15. U.S. Bureau of the Census SOCDS Data: Output for New York City.

16. Forsythe, *Memos to the Governor: An Introduction to State Budgeting*, 15.

17. Emergency was dropped from the EFCB in 1978 state legislation.

18. One-shots are nonrecurring revenues.

19. Elkin, *City and Regime in the American Republic*, 8.

CHAPTER TWO

1. Cuomo, "Cuomo Assails Efforts to Thwart New Taxes," B1.

2. Smith, Jean. *John Marshall*, 153.

3. For a detailed account of Shay's Rebellion, see Leonard Richards, *Shay's Rebellion, The American Revolution's Final Battle.*

4. For a detailed amount of the Panic of 1819, read Frederick Jackson Turner, *Rise of the New West*.

5. For a radical interpretation, see Matthew Josephson, *The Robber Barons*, and for a more conservative interpretation of industrial statesmen, see Allan Nevins, *John D. Rockefeller, The Heroic Age of American Enterprise*.

6. Kiewiet, *2003 Constitutional Limitations on Indebtedness: The Case of California*, 380.

7. Zimmerman, *The Private Use of Tax-Exempt Bonds: Controlling Public Subsidy of Private Activity*, 18.

8. Ibid.

9. See Geist, *Under Influence*, 2005. The separation of commercial versus investment banking was in response to banks investing heavily in securities before the Great Depression. These investments led to subsequent bank failures. The solution was to limit commercial banking to home loans and government obligation municipal bonds.

10. Kiewiet, 381.

11. Wesalotemel, *The Fundamentals of Municipal Bonds*, 17, and Lamb and Rappaport, *Municipal Bonds: The Comprehensive Review of Tax-Exempt Securities and Public Finance*, 18.

12. Partnership for New York City, available at http://www.nycp.org/history.html.

13. Preston, "New York to Sell Debt in Week's Biggest Municipal Issue."

14. A commercial bank is what the average citizen thinks of as a bank. Commercial banks are distinguished from investment banks, which are private financial services institutions that help businesses and government raise money in the form of bonds or stocks.

15. Braun et al. "A Political Family Affair? Muni Wives Contribute to Northeast Campaigns," 1.

16. Opp, "Ending Pay-to-Play in the Municipal Securities Business: MSRB Rule G-27 Ten Years Later."

17. Mollenkopf, *The Phoenix in the Ashes: The Rise and Fall of the Koch Coalition in New York City Politics*, 23–43.

18. Sayre and Kaufman, *Governing New York City: Politics in the Metropolis*.

19. Fuchs, *Mayors and Money: Fiscal Policy in New York and Chicago*.

20. Ibid., 39.

21. See Digaetano and Klemanski, Ferman, Stoker, and Stone.

22. Judd, "Everything is always going to hell: Urban Scholars as End-Times Prophets," 23.

23. Stone, "Urban Regimes and the Capacity to Govern," 1993, 17.

24. Stone, "Political Leadership in Urban Politics," 1995, 112.

25. Ferman, *Governing the Ungovernable City: Political Skill, Leadership, and the Modern Mayor*, 2. Also, see Cox, 1992; Eisinger, 1998; and Elkin, 1987.

26. Reichl, *Reconstructing Times Square: Politics and Culture in Urban Development*, 177.

27. Frug, *City Making: Building Communities without Building Walls*, 17.

28. Turner, *Intergovernmental Growth Management*, 85.

29. Peterson, *City Limits*, 15.

30. Mollenkopf, 1992, 14.

31. Logan and Molotch, *Urban Fortunes: The Political Economy of Place.*

32. Vojnovic, "Governance in Houston: Growth Theories and Urban Pressures," 598.

33. Jonas and Wilson, *The City as a Growth Machine: Critical Reflections Two Decades Later,* 7.

34. Domhoff, *Power at the Local Level: Growth Coalition Theory.*

35. Glasberg, 1989, 192.

36. Ranney, *Global decisions, local collisions: Urban life in the new world Order,* 111.

37. Fitch, 1993, xiv.

38. See Castells, *The Information City,* 1989, and Mollenkopf and Castells, "Dual City," 1991.

39. Robinson, *A Theory of Global Capitalism: Production, Class and State in a Transnational World.*

40. Sassen, "Economic Restructuring and the American City," 467.

41. William Sites (2000) sees globalization as transnational market expansion and integration that significantly alters "the nature of places, the relations of power, and the lived experiences of people in most parts of the globe" (123).

42. Cox, *Governance without Government: Order and Change in World Politics,* 23.

43. Judd and Parkinson, *Leadership and Urban Regeneration: Cities in North America and Europe,* 22.

44. Fainstein, *Leadership and Urban Regeneration: Cities in North America and Europe,* 37.

45. Parkinson and Judd, *Regenerating the Cities: The U.K. Crisis and the U.S. Experience.*

46. Sinclair, *The New Masters of Capital.*

47. King and Sinclair, "Private Actors and Public Policy: A Requiem for the Basel Capital Accord," 345–362.

48. Frug, "City Making," 5.

49. Rae, *City Urbanism and Its End,* x.

50. New York State, *The Local Government Handbook.*

51. Sbragia, *Debt Wish: Entrepreneurial Cities, U. S. Federalism and Economic Development,* 82.

52. See pages 173–229.

53. Dillon, *Treatise on the Law of Municipal Corporations of 1872.*

54. Fuchs, *Mayors and Money.*

55. Savitch and Kantor, *Cities in the International Marketplace,* 4.

56. Ibid., 351.

57. See Burch, 1983; Domhoff, 1990; Jenkins and Eckert, 2000; Mintz and Schwartz, 1985.

58. See Stone, 1993, and Mossberger and Stoker, 2001.

59. See Stone,"Rethinking the Policies-Politics Connection," 2005, for a discussion of Peterson's typology.

60. Nevarez, *New Money, Nice Town: How Capital Works in the New Urban Economy.*

CHAPTER THREE

1. Kirby, Quoting U.S. Supreme Court Justice Louis Brandeis.
2. Mann, *LaGuardia Comes to Power 1933*, 17.
3. Jeffers, *The Napoleon of New York: Mayor Fiorello LaGuardia*, 175.
4. Lehman, Letter to Mayor Fiorello H. LaGuardia, 2.
5. Ibid.
6. Jeffers, 230.
7. Glaser and Kahn, "From John Lindsay to Rudy Giuliani: The Decline of the Local Safety Net?," 123.
8. Garrett, *The LaGuardia Years: Machine and Reform Politics in New York City*, 144.
9. Heckscher, *When LaGuardia Was Mayor: New York's Legendary Years*, 80.
10. Barnet and Cavanagh, *Global Dreams: Imperial Corporations and the New World Order*, 369.
11. LaGuardia, *Liberty Magazine*, May 20, 1933.
12. Blumberg, *The New Deal and the Unemployed: The View from New York City*, 48.
13. See Lipietz, *Mirages and Miracles: The Crises of Global Fordism*, and Robinson, "A Theory of Global Capitalism," 2004.
14. Savitch and Kantor, 15.

CHAPTER FOUR

1. Clausen, Bank of America, in *The Money Lenders: Bankers and a World in Turmoil*, Sampson, 136.
2. Tabb, *Economic Governance in the Age of Globalization*, 132.
3. Ibid., 259.
4. There is certainly irony in the fact that Arab countries chose American banks rather than British or French banks to deposit their petrodollars. The choice was made because American missionaries had opened hospitals in some Arab countries and Arab leaders were quite grateful.
5. Sampson, 141.
6. Mizruchi and Davis, "The Globalization of American Banking, 1962–1981," 96.
7. Sampson, 145.
8. Tabb, 113.
9. McMichael, *Development and Social Change: A Global Perspective*, 117.
10. Correra, "Mexico and Latin American Countries, Banks and Fiscal Crisis," 2.
11. Newfield and DuBrul, *The Permanent Government. Who Really Rules New York?*, 34.
12. Brash, "Invoking Fiscal Crisis: Moral Discourse and Politics in New York City," 65.
13. Hubbard, *For Each, the Strength of All: A History of Banking in the State of New York*, 253.

14. The party ended in 1982 when Mexico announced that it was going to default on $60 billion worth of foreign debt. See Hubbard (1995) for a fascinating account of the debt issues in the 1980s.

15. Morris, *Money, Greed, and Risk: Why Financial Crises and Crashes Happen*, 107.

16. Rockefeller, *Memoirs*, 2003, 311; also see Shalala and Bellamy, "A State Saves a City," 1126.

17. Sampson, 137.

18. Feldstein, *The Dow Jones-Irwin Guide to Municipal Bonds*, 201.

19. Chernow, *The House of Morgan: An American Banking Dynasty and the Rise of Modern Finance*, 620.

20. Sampson, 139.

21. Frug, *City Making*, 1999, 17.

22. Bahl, "Fiscal Retrenchment in a Declining State," 278.

23. U.S. Bureau of the Census, 1960 and 1970.

24. Bureau of Economic Analysis: National figures taken from http://bea.gov/national/index.htm#gdp. New York State figures taken from http://www.bea.gov/bea/regional/gsp/.

25. Judd and Swanstrom, *City Politics: The Political Economy of Urban America*, 210.

26. Mauro and Yago, "State Government Targeting in Economic Development: The New York Experience," 67.

27. Newfield and DuBrul, *The Permanent Government*, 25.

28. *Bond Buyer*, "A Conversation with John Mitchell Moral Obligation Bonds, the Industry's Old Days, and More," Centennial Edition, 1.

29. Lefkkowitz at a panel discussion, June 10, 2005, at the Center for Architecture New York City.

30. Netzer, "Innovations in Public Finance," 220.

31. Walsh, *The Public's Business: The Politics and Practices of Government Corporations*, 273.

32. Kramer, *The Days of Wine and Roses Are Over*, 46.

33. Larkin, "New York Debt Past and Present: A Talk with Governor Hugh L. Carey," 2.

34. Ibid.

35. Kramer, 47.

36. Kheel, "Where Is Public Employee Bargaining Heading? Two Experts Give Their View," 3. The New York State Taylor Law prohibits public employees from striking. If a union strikes, the courts can order the union back to work, and if the union leadership fails to obey, they can be jailed for contempt. The Taylor Law has not prevented union workers from striking. The following strikes took place within two years of the passage of the Taylor Law in 1967: teachers' strike in September 1967, sanitation strike in February 1968, and the teachers' strike in fall of 1968.

37. Kramer, 34.

38. Sbragia, *The Municipal Money Chase: The Politics of Local Government Finance*, 24.

39. Bahl, 1979, 277.

156 NOTES TO CHAPTER FIVE

40. Gifford, "New York City and Cosmopolitan Liberalism," 579. Gifford quotes a letter to Senator Daniel P. Moynihan from Charles L. Schultze, Chairman of the Council of Economic Advisors, and Stuart Eizenstate (assistant to the president for domestic affairs and policy), September 22, 1977.

41. Netzer, *Urban Politics New York Style*, 27.

42. New York City Comptroller's Reports, Fiscal Year 1972 to Fiscal Year 2006, Part III—Statistical Information.

43. Bahl, Jump, and Schroeder, *Fiscal Crisis in American Cities: The Federal Response*, 8.

44. Feldstein and Fabozzi, 1987, 110.

45. Committee on Banking, Finance and Urban Affairs, 10.

46. Ibid., 15.

47. *New York Times*, "Questions and Answers on City's Bonds," 39.

48. Roberts, "A Credit Expert Who Rates High at Budget Time," B1.

49. Clairborne, "State May Have to Bail Out New York," A2.

CHAPTER FIVE

1. Smith, *The Wealth of Nations*, V, I, II.

2. New York City Comptroller's Reports, Part III, Statistical Information. Unrestricted federal and state dollars were not separated from federal and state grants in 1974.

3. Bailey, *The Crisis Regime: The MAC, the EFCB, and the Political Impact of the New York City Financial Crisis*, 3.

4. Sampson, *The Money Lenders*, 139.

5. Rockefeller, *Memoirs*, 193.

6. Sampson, 137.

7. Interview with Carol O'Cleireacain, January 29, 2005.

8. Horowitz, Oral History of NYC's Fiscal Crisis at Baruch College School of Public Affairs.

9. Ibid.

10. Gotbaum, *Negotiating in the Real World: Getting the Deal You Want*, 57.

11. Chernow, 1990, 620.

12. Author's class notes, October 1, 1976.

13. Rockefeller, 2003, 294.

14. Arthur Anderson & Co. Report for the Secretary of Treasury regarding New York City financial planning and reporting under the New York City Seasonal Financing Act of 1975, 4.

15. Weikart, *Decision Making*, 18.

16. Bellush and Bellush, "Collective Bargaining, Leadership and the Fiscal Crisis," 19.

17. MAC Presentation 1980, 3.

18. Weikart, *Decision Making*, 74.

19. Ford, *A Time to Heal: The Autobiography of Gerald R. Ford*, 316.

20. Ibid., 318.

21. Bigel, in Dale Horowitz's, Oral History of New York City's Fiscal Crisis.

22. Sampson, *The Money Lenders*, 138.

23. Ford, 319.

24. Rohatyn, Speech of February 26, 2003, 2.

25. Sampson, 138.

26. Committee on Banking, Currency and Housing, 1978, 5.

27. Two journalists, Rosen and Slocum, came upon this information when interviewing former Governor Carey while writing their book, *From Rocky to Pataki*, 1998.

28. Larkin, "New York Debt Past and Present," 2003, 1.

29. Beame, Oral History of New York City's Fiscal Crisis.

30. Subcommittee on Economic Stabilization, *Staff Memorandum on NYC's Progress under the New York City Seasonal Financing Act of 1975*, 11.

31. Mitrisin, *Emergency federal financial assistance to private enterprise: A selective examination of past loan and loan guarantee programs of the federal government*, 74.

32. MAC Presentation 1980, 10.

33. Moynihan, "Routinely Shortchanged," 1.

34. Interview with Carol O'Cleireacain, January 29, 2005.

35. Beame, "Oral History of New York City's Fiscal Crisis."

36. See Kummerfeld (1978) for a detailed description of the legal and fiscal controls put in place "to restore both the city's fiscal health and investor confidence." Also see Glasberg, *The Power of Collective Purse Strings*, 1989.

37. Horowitz, "Oral History of New York City's Fiscal Crisis."

CHAPTER SIX

1. Koch, "Information Bank Abstracts."

2. Proxmire, "Information Bank Abstracts," 211.

3. Message of the Mayor, Office of the Mayor, 1978–2006, 5.

4. Bernstein, *The Politics of Welfare: The New York City Experience*, 138.

5. Schwartz, Oral History, 3–130.

6. See Stanfield, December 15, 1979.

7. Koch, Statement by Koch before the Joint Hearings of the Senate Finance and Assembly Ways and Means Committees.

8. Martin, "Did Tax Reform Kill Segmentation in the Municipal Bond Market," 389.

9. Liebschutz et al., "How State Responses Confound Federal Policy: Reaganomics and the New Federalism in New York," 55.

10. New York City Comptroller's Report for Fiscal Years 1978 to 2006, Part III, Statistical Information.

11. IBO background paper, "Spreadsheet on Tax Cuts" from George Sweeting, Deputy Director. 3.

12. Schmalz, "Assembly Chief Leads Attack on Koch," B1.

13. See Gordon for a short analysis of the planning and building of Battery Park City. Mayor Koch arranged that, in exchange for the building of Battery Park City, Battery Park would provide its surplus funds generated from the sale of bonds to the city for the express purpose of renovating or constructing low- and moderate-income housing. This agreement held only for Mayor Koch in which Battery Park funds were used to renovate 893 apartments for low- and moderate-income families in the Bronx and 664 in Harlem. This agreement has rarely been honored by successive mayors.

14. Dembart, "The Contract Accord: City and Union Both Say They Were Prepared to Settle for Package Transit Workers Sought," 1. Givebacks means labor unions would offer concessions from previously agreed contract provisions.

15. Carey Address to U.S. Representatives Ways and Means Committee.

16. Smothers, "Koch Invites Direct Pressure by Financial Control Board," 2.

17. Coppie, "Annual Budget Review of Financial Control Board," 3.

18. Smothers, 2.

19. Dembart, "Lazard, Stun by Koch, Ends M.A.C. Role," B1.

20. Quindlen, "City Deficit Forecasts Termed Short," 2.

21. IBO Background Paper, "Reviving the New York Stock Transfer Tax: Revenues and Risks," 2.

22. Message to the Mayor, Fiscal Year 2003, 51.

23. New York City Comptroller's Reports, Part III, Statistical Information. Total taxes will not add up since some taxes have been left out.

24. Comptroller's Report for Fiscal Years 1978 to 2006, Part III, Statistical Information. Pension expenditures are included in agency totals in FY1978 so FY1979 is used instead as the base year. Total revenues will not add up since some revenues have been omitted.

25. Haberman, "Key Fiscal Goal Reached by City in Big Note Sale," 1.

26. Goodwin, "City May Get Up to $1 Billion in MAC in Next Five Years," 1.

27. Meislin, "For MAC, Money Talks: Using Surplus Again for Monetary Clout," 1.

28. Citizens Budget Commission's Quarterly, "Collective Bargaining and Budgeting in New York City," 4.

29. Bellush, 1981; Gotbaum quoted in Public Employee Press, December 9, 1977.

30. Smothers, "7% Raise for City Workers Is Unaffordable, Says Koch," B1.

31. Langan, "The Remarkable Drop in Crime in New York City," Appendix Table 2.

32. Barbanel, "Another Dinkins Test: The Bond Market," 6.

33. Mollenkopf, The Phoenix in the Ashes, 1992, 161.

34. Ibid., 142–146.

35. Ibid., 44.

CHAPTER SEVEN

1. New York Times, "The 1993 Campaign, the Race for Mayor, the Candidates in Their Own Words," B6.

2. New York Times, "The 1989 Elections; Excerpts from Speech by Dinkins, a New Link," B7.

3. Ibid.

4. Rich, David Dinkins and New York City Politics, 61.

5. Mitchell, "New York City's Undying Deficit: Slash It, and It Just Grows Back," 1.

6. Lynn, "Mayor Dinkins: An Era Begins, with a Little Fun," B3.

7. Tabb, Economic Governance in the Age of Globalization, 3.

8. New York City Planning Commission, Appendix Tables 5-1 and 5-3.

9. See Clark and Ferguson, *City Money*, 1983; Ehrenhalt, "Economic and Demographic Change," 1993; Fuchs, *Mayors and Money*, 1992.

10. Adler et al., "Do Tax Increases in NYC Cause a Loss of Jobs? A Review of the Evidence," 4.

11. Hanson et al., *Corporate Citizenship and Urban Problem Solving: The Changing Civic Role of Business Leaders in American Cities*, 98.

12. Martin, "Did Tax Reform Kill Segmentation in the Municipal Bond Market."

13. Interview with Carol O'Cleireacain, January 29, 2005.

14. U.S. Department of Commerce, Bureau of Economic Analysis.

15. New York City Office of the Comptroller, 2001, 268.

16. New York State Bureau of Labor Services, 1976 to 2006.

17. Levitan, "Poverty in New York City, 2001: Recession Ends Late Nineties Decline in Poverty Rate," 1.

18. Interview with Allen Proctor, December 18, 2006.

19. NYC Comptroller's Report for Fiscal Years 1978 to 2006, Part III, Statistical Information.

20. Townsend, "Piece by Piece City Slides Back into Big Fiscal Hold," 11.

21. Wynter, "Dinkins' Win: Gladness Tinged with Sadness."

22. *New York Times*, "The Mayor," 1989, 30.

23. Roberts, "Mayor Dinkins: Every Day a Test," B1.

24. Roberts, "A Credit Expert Who Rates High at Budget Time," B1.

25. Purdum, "Credit Agency Urges Mayor," B1.

26. Dinkins, "Dinkins Proposes Increases in Taxes in His First Budget," 2.

27. Roberts, "A Credit Expert Who Rates High at Budget Time," B1.

28. Mouat, "New York's Dinkins Plows Ahead," 8.

29. Finch, "David Dinkins: How's He Doin'?" 182–186.

30. Ibid., 183.

31. Barbanel, "Another Dinkins Test," 1990, 6.

32. *New York Times*, "Mayor Dinkins, Finally on Track," A34.

33. Purdum, "Feinstein Says Use of Control Board Deserves Study, E5.

34. Epstein, "S&P Retains Rating; Warns City," 45.

35. Barsky and Mitchell, "New York's Dinkins Pleases Wall Street but Says 'No' to Many Constituencies," 1.

36. Purdum, "Dinkins' Year: Dreams Delayed by Fiscal Slump," A1.

37. Roberts, Metro Matters, 1991, 6/28.

38. Gottlieb, "Behind Rikers Melee: Tensions Wrought by Strain of Change," B1.

39. Gottlieb, "After the Conflict at Rikers Island, A War of Words," B1.

40. Weikart, "Follow the Money: Mayoral Choice and Expenditure Policy," 230.

41. Bartlett, "The Budget Battles: New York Taxes Battle Middle Class," B4.

42. McKinley, "Dinkins Shifts on Fiscal Plan under Pressure," B1. The state created the Municipal Assistance Corporation during the fiscal crisis to sell bonds for New York City, using city sales tax revenues when the city was shut out of the financial markets. See chapter on 1975 fiscal crisis.

43. Purdum, "The Dinkins' Budget Is a Long Way from the Bottom Line," 44.

44. McKinley, 1991, B1.

45. For a detailed and insight examination of the Crown Heights incident, see Wilbur Rich's book, *David Dinkins and New York City Politics*.

46. For insight into budget surpluses, see Forsythe's article on surplus rolls.

47. Barsky, "Back from the Dead: Having hit bottom, New York City begins a slow turnaround—as it prepares for convention, morale and bond rating are up, crime is down—nice party if no one's killed," 1.

48. Good Jobs New York at http://www.goodjobsny.org/new%20deals%20format/morgan1.htm.

49. Finder, "Political Memo: Dinkins Is Mastering the Art of Being Mayor," A21.

50. Hevesi, "New York City Maintains Its Credit Rating," 1/27.

51. McKinley, "Dinkins Administration Acknowledges Need for Cuts," B3.

52. Feiden, "Criticism from FCB Startles Mayor, May Hurt Campaign," 50.

53. Ibid. Also see "Missed Opportunity: Urban Fiscal Crisis and Financial Control Boards," 1997 January. 110 *Harvard Law Review*, p. 733.

54. See Independent Budget Office's Web site for the number of city positions for the last twenty-six years.

55. Fuerbringer, "Credit Markets; New York City Set to Sell Bonds," D18.

56. Ibid.

57. Levy, "Dinkins Orders Sharp Budget Cuts to Save New York's Bond Rating," 1.

58. Fuerbringer, B1.

59. Belsky, "Woes Mount for City in Coming Bond Sale," 1.

60. Mead, Memo to Budget Policy and Priorities Committee of the CBC from Dean Mead, "The City of New York's January 1998 Financial Plan," 5.

61. The rate is the percentage of every $100 in assessed value that is billed as tax.

62. McKinley, "Dinkins Shifts on Fiscal Plan under Pressure," 1.

63. Independent Budget Office, "Revenue Trends since 1980."

64. Weiss, "Dinkins' Promises Preliminary (New York, New York Mayor David N. Dinkins Proposes Tax Relief for Real Estate Industry at State of the City Address)," 1.

65. The Board of Estimate was a quasi-legislative body composed of the major elected officials in the city—the mayor, comptroller, president of the city council, and the five borough presidents (equivalent to county executives). On the Board of Estimate, the mayor, comptroller, and president of the city council each had two votes, and borough presidents each had one vote, for a total of eleven votes.

66. For a detailed account of the political struggles between the mayor and city council, see J. Phillip Thompson, *Double Trouble: Black Mayors, Black Communities, and the Call for a Deep Democracy*.

67. For a detailed discussion of the program, see Peter Vallone, *Learning to Govern: My Life in New York Politics, from Hell Gate to City Hall*.

68. Dinkins, 1990, A1.

69. Sites, *Remaking New York: Primitive Globalization and the Politics of Urban Community*, 143.

70. New York City Comptroller's Reports for Fiscal Years 1978 to 2006, Part III, Statistical Information.

71. Good Jobs New York. Available at http://www.goodjobsny.org/deals_date. htm.

72. IBO Inside the Budget, "Confronting the Budget Shortfall," 3.

73. Girgenti, Richard, A *Report to the Governor on the Disturbance in Crown Heights*, New York State Division of Criminal Justice Services, 1993.

74. Purdum, "Dinkins' Year: Dreams Delayed by Fiscal Slump," A1.

75. Interview with Allen Proctor.

76. Hicks, "The 1993 Campaign: The Incumbent; Dinkins Focuses on Groups He Sees as Crucial," B3.

77. Rich, *David Dinkins and New York City Politics*, 2007, 196.

CHAPTER EIGHT

1. Blood, "City Feds Say WTC Air's OK; Rule Out Health Risk," A3.

2. Firestone, "Defending Abrasiveness, Giuliani Cites Successes," A1.

3. *New York Times*, "Cold Comfort for the Mayor," Editorial Desk, A34.

4. *New York Times*, "The Mayor's Censorship Office," Editorial Desk, A28.

5. Jordan, "Not All Black and White."

6. Newfield, "The Full Rudy: The Man, the Mayor, the Myth."

7. Quinnipiac Poll, "Race Is Key Factor in New Yorkers' View of Mayor."

8. Giuliani, *Message of the Mayor, 1995 Executive Budget of New York*, 5.

9. U.S. Department of Commerce, Bureau of Economic Analysis. There is a discontinuity in the GDP by state time series as of 1997 so that the data before and after that year are not comparable.

10. New York State Bureau of Labor Services, 1976 to 2006. Also, due to a new estimating methodology implemented in January 2005, substate labor force statistics from January 2000 to the present are not comparable to data from earlier years.

11. Giuliani, Remarks of Mayor Rudolph Giuliani at the Real Estate Board of New York. 2.

12. Berube and Katz, *The State of the English Cities; the State of American Cities*, 29.

13. New York City Comptroller's Reports for Fiscal Years 1978 to 2006, Part III, Statistical Information. Revenues do not add up since some revenues have been omitted.

14. Townsend, "Albany Vote on Police Contracts Helps Turn the City into Road Kill," 9.

15. Interview with Abe Lackman, April 26, 2007.

16. Feiden, "Rudy Kicks Off Revolution; Businesses Enlist to Sell Bold Plan," 1.

17. Independent Budget Office, "Spreadsheet on Tax Cuts."

18. New York City Comptroller's Reports for Fiscal Years 1978 to 2006, Part III, Statistical Information. Taxes do not match total since some taxes have not been included.

19. Myers, "Giuliani Outlines a Budget to Cut Government Size," A1.

20. Roberts, "Giuliani Seeks Funds for New Buyout," B4.

21. Citizens Budget Commission, Statement on the Proposed October Modification of the City of New York's 1995 Budget.

22. Myers, "Giuliani Proposes $800 Million More in Spending Cuts," A1.

23. Mitchell, "The Globalization of American Banking," 1995, A1.

24. Siegel, "City Hit with Cut in Its Bond Rating," A1.

25. Dinkins, "New York City Need Not Have Lost Its Major Credit Rating," 4/14.

26. Siegel, "City Tries to Sell a $31.1B Budget," A1.

27. Siegel, "The Kindest Cuts of All: 31b Won't Hurt, Rudy Says," A1.

28. Liff and Siegel, "Bonds: Rescue or Ruin," A1.

29. Myers, "Mayor Sees More Cuts If Rate Plan Fails," 1/27.

30. Siegel, "McCall Aims at Budget Quick Fixes," A1.

31. Myers, "For Giuliani, Current Budget Woes Overtake Future's," 1/25.

32. Cerullo, Memorandum, "Monthly Report," to Randy M. Mastro, Deputy Mayor for Operations 96-05333, 3.

33. Forsythe, "Fixing the Mess," October 2007, 8. The surplus roll is the cumulative amount of all surpluses from previous years. See Forsythe.

34. New York State Special Deputy Comptroller, "Review of NYC's Financial Plan, Fiscal Years 1998 through 2001."

35. Weikart, "Follow the Money," 229.

36. For a more detailed understanding of Mayor Giuliani and welfare cuts, see this author's paper," The Era of Meanness: Challenging the Barriers to a College Degree."

37. New York City Comptroller's Report 1991, 297.

38. Bodack, "Can NYC Prevent Welfare Recipients from Finishing High School?" 1.

39. Finney, "Welfare Reform and Post-secondary Education: Research and Policy Update," 2.

40. Richardson, "Activists Rush for School. They Champion Law that Benefits Students on Welfare," 3.

41. Ritter, "Tough Lessons in Welfare Reform," 3A.

42. Gittell, From Welfare to Independence: The College Option, a Report to the Ford Foundation, 23.

43. Interview with Allan Proctor, December 18, 2006.

44. Keilin, "Letter to Mayor Rudolph Giuliani."

45. Ibid.

46. Horton, Testimony before the Debt Affordability Hearing, June 3.

47. Vallone, Learning to Govern: My Life in New York Politics, From Hell Gate to City Hall, 210.

48. Interview with author, April 26, 2007.

49. New York Times, "Cold Comfort for the Mayor," A24.

50. Part of the increase was due to the merger of police departments. In Fiscal Year 1994, the Housing Authority and Police Department were merged into the city's police department; in Fiscal Year 1995, the Transit Authority and Police Department were merged.

51. Comptroller's Report for Fiscal Years 1978 to 2006, Part III, Statistical Information. Expenditures do not add up since some expenditures have been omitted.

52. In the arena of education, welfare, and homelessness, Mayor Giuliani was taken to court on countless occasions by advocates who sought to enforce

the law and advocates who won. Examples of these cases are *Callahan v. Giuliani*, *Hanna v. Turner*, *Henrietta v. Giuliani*, *Hernandez v. Barrios-Paoli*, and *Reynolds v. Giuliani*.

53. Townsend, "In Squabbles for Control, Rudy Must Act Like Mayor," 11.

54. Firestone, "Giuliani's "Approval" Rating Below 50% in a Second Poll," B3.

55. Firestone, "Giuliani Faces Dip in Support, New Poll Finds," B2.

56. Levy, "Giuliani Spars with Monitors on the Budget," 1/25.

57. IBO, "IBO's Reestimate of the Mayor's Preliminary Budget for 2002 and Financial Plan through 2005," 3.

58. Buttenweiser and Keilin, "Letter to the Mayor regarding Financial Plan from the Chair of the Board of Trustees and the Chair of the Budget Policy and Priorities Committee."

59. Comptroller's Report for Fiscal Years 1978 to 2006, Part III, Statistical Information. Expenditures do not add up since some expenditures have been omitted.

60. Abrams, *Speaking Freely: Trials of the First Amendment*, 210.

61. Strober and Strober, *Giuliani: Flawed or Flawless, The Oral Biography*, 235.

62. Good Jobs First New York, http://www.goodjobsny.org/deals_date.htm.

63. Ibid.

64. Good Jobs New York, "Good Jobs New York Releases List of Recipients that Include Giuliani Partners, Ernst & Young, Fox News and News America."

65. See Wayne Barrett's articles in the *Village Voice*, as well as his book, *Grand Illusion: The Untold Story of Rudy Giuliani and 9/11*.

66. At the 9/11 Commission Hearings in May 2004 when Giuliani was testifying, members of the audience began yelling, "What about the radios?" See Barrett and Collins, *Grand Illusion*, 2006, 199.

67. Barrett, "Grand Illusion."

68. World Trade Center Disaster Site Litigation, October 17, 2006.

69. Herbert, "The World Trade Center Disaster and the Health of Workers: Five-Year Assessment of a Unique Medical Screening Program," 2.

70. *Daily News*, "Special Report: Abandoned Heroes, Mayor Must Face WTC Crisis," July 23, 2006.

71. Blood, "City Feds Say WTC Air's OK Rule Out Health Risk," 9.

72. Perez-Pena, "Giuliani Will Miss Firefighters' Gathering," A19.

73. Strober and Strober, *Giuliani: Flawed or Flawless*, 2007, 290.

74. New York City Comptroller's Report, Fiscal Year 2007, Number of City Employees—Ten-Year Trend, Statistical Information, 314.

75. Giuliani, *Message of the Mayor, NYC's Mayor's Executive Budget Fiscal Year 2000*, 1.

76. Krauss, "New York's Violent Crime Rate Drops to Lows of 1970s," 1/1.

77. Greenhouse, "The Mayor's Labor Tactics? Think of Giuliani in Reverse," B1.

78. Tierney, "The Holy Terror," 6/60.

79. Messinger, quoted in Strober and Strober, 243.

80. Fuchs, *The Future of New York: 1898 to 1998*.

81. Perez-Pena, "Giuliani Will Miss Firefighters' Gathering," B1.

CHAPTER NINE

1. Bloomberg, State of the City Address.
2. Rattner, "What New York Will Have to Give Up," 25.
3. Rohatyn, "Fiscal Disaster the City Can't Face Alone," 25.
4. U.S. Dept. of Commerce, Bureau of Economic Analysis.
5. Independent Budget Office, "Trends in Revenues."
6. New York City Comptroller's Report for FYs 1978 to 2006. Revenues will not add up since some revenues are not included.
7. Ibid.
8. Bragdon, "From Headache to Migraine: Medicaid Cap Strengthens Need for Remedies in NY," 1.
9. Colangelo, "Mike's Hardly Retiring on Bid for Pension Reform," 58.
10. New York City Comptroller's Reports, FYs 1980 to 2005.
11. Gonzalez, "Pension 'Crisis' Is a Myth," 24.
12. New York State Bureau of Labor Services, 1976 to 2006.
13. Levitan, "Poverty in New York City, 2001: Recession Ends Late Nineties Decline in Poverty Rate," 1.
14. Crain's, "City Fails to Meet Expectations in 2002," 10.
15. Gandel, "Wall Street Slump Risks '70s Replay," 1.
16. Morris, "Wall Street Can't Save New York," 8.
17. Bloomberg, Message of the Mayor, 2.
18. Lipton, "The Mayor's Budget Proposal: Debt; New Bond Issue Is a Step that Pleases No One," B5.
19. Lombardi, "Firm Won't Lower City Bond Rating," 28.
20. Lombardi, "Mike Nixes Plea to Boost Taxes," 14.
21. Bloomberg, State of the City Address, 5.
22. Bartley, "Thinking Things Over: Bloomberg to New York: Drop Dead," A10.
23. Malanga, Business Leadership in Gotham, 1.
24. David, "Taxing Tales: David and Mike," 9.
25. Steinhaurer and Connelly, "In Poll, Pessimism from New Yorkers Rubs Off on Mayor," A1.
26. Pasanen, "Property Tax Reform—NOT." 1.
27. Saul, "Mike: Unions Don't Deserve a Bigger Piece of the Pie," 10.
28. IBO Fiscal Outlook, "Despite Economic Downturn, City Still Faces Budget Shortfalls," 1.
29. Chan, "Taxed: What Makes New York Different," 4/2.
30. IBO Fiscal Brief, "West Side Financing's Complex, a $1.3 Billion Story," 1.
31. Thompson, "Letter to the Mayor from the Comptroller of the City of New York."
32. Sweeting, "Financing Plan for the Proposed Stadium for the Mets (Revised)," 3.
33. Ibid.
34. Sullivan, The Diamond in the Bronx: Yankee Stadium and the Politics of New York.
35. Shiffman, "Atlantic Yards: Staving Off a Scar for Decades," 1.

36. IBO Fiscal Brief, "Atlantic Yards, A Net Fiscal Benefit for the City," 1.

37. Good Jobs New York, "Good Jobs New York Releases List of Recipients that Include Giuliani Parnters, Ernst & Young, Fox News and News America."

38. Damiani, Testimony before the U.S. House of Representatives Committee on Homeland Security Subcommittee.

39. See Good Jobs New York's Web site, http://www.ctj.org/itep/gjny/ and http://www.goodjobsny.org/rec_news.htm

40. Greenhouse and Steinhauer, "City Lays Off 2,000 as Talks Grow Bitter." B1.

41. Saul, "Mike: Unions Don't Deserve a Bigger Piece of the Pie," 6.

42. Andreatta, "Upward of 60,000 Workers Rally at City Hall Demanding Pay Increases," 1.

43. Ibid.

44. Steinhauer, "Building a Name as an Advocate for Public Health," B1.

45. New York City's Comptroller's Report for FYs 1978 to 2006, Part III, Statistical Information. Expenditures will not add up since some expenditures have been omitted.

46. Ibid.

47. Pasanen, "Mixed News in a 'Good News' Budget."

48. Pasanen, "Tax Breaks—Who Wins and Who Loses?"

49. Ibid.

50. Cardwell, "New York to Pay the Poor for Doing the Right Thing," C11.

51. Coalition for the Homeless, State of the Homeless 2007.

52. Coalition for the Homeless, "No Advantage: The Bloomberg Administration's Flawed Approach to Family Homeless," July 20, 2007.

53. Waters and Bach, Closing the Door 2007: The Shape of Subsidized Housing Loss in New York City, 2.

54. Bloomberg, "Mayor Bloomberg Presents PlanNYC: A Greener, Greater New York."

55. Waters and Bach, Closing the Door 2007, 1.

56. NYCLU News, "NYCLU and New York Times Fight Secrecy of NYPD's Unlawful Spying Program," 1.

57. New York City Comptroller's Report for FY 2002 and 2006, Part II-E-Capital.

58. Greenhouse, "The Mayor's Labor Tactics? Think of Giuliani in Reverse," B1.

59. Bloomberg and Schumer, Sustaining New York's and U.S.' Global Financial Services Leadership.

60. Bloomberg, "N.Y. Press Release: Statement by Mayor Bloomberg about Party Affiliation."

CHAPTER TEN

1. Giuliani, Regan lecture, 30 September 1999.

2. Rockefeller, Joseph E. Persico, The Imperial Rockefeller: A Biography of Nelson A. Rockefeller, 164.

3. See Gerald Frug, *City Making* or Lawrence Tribe, *American Constitutional Law*. For the opposite viewpoint, see Sehfter, *Political Crisis, Fiscal Crisis*, and Cannato, *Ungovernable City*.

4. Hackworth, "December. Local Autonomy, Bond-Rating Agencies," 710.

5. Chernow, *The House of Morgan*, 619.

6. Independent Budget Office, "Trends of Revenues Since FY1980."

7. Sampson, *The Money Lenders*, 61.

8. Grimes, *Financial Times*.

9. Steinhauer, "Short on Political Capital, Mayor Invites President to Fund-Raiser at his Home," B3.

10. New York City Comptroller Reports, FY79–FY06.

BIBLIOGRAPHY

Abrams, Floyd. *Speaking Freely: Trials of the First Amendment.* New York: Penguin Group, 2005.

Adler, Moshe, Oliver Cook, and James Parrott. "Do Tax Increases in NYC Cause a Loss of Jobs? A Review of the Evidence." *State Tax Notes.* New York: Fiscal Policy Institute (4 February 2002). http://www.fiscalpolicy.org/research_01.html.

Andreatta, David. "Upward of 60,000 Workers Rally at City Hall Demanding Pay Increases." *New York Sun.* 9 June 2004.

Arthur Anderson & Co. Report for the Secretary of Treasury regarding New York City Financial Planning & Reporting under the New York City Seasonal Financing Act of 1975 (1976). Retrieved from http://newman.baruch.cuny. edu/digital/2003/amfl/mac/pdf_files/Economic_Reports/06-23-76.pdf.

Bahl, Roy. "Fiscal Retrenchment in a Declining State." *National State Journal* 32/2 (June 1979): 277–87.

Bahl, Roy, Bernard Jump, Jr., and Larry Schroeder. "Federal Policy and the Fiscal Outlook for Cities." In Kenneth L. Hubbell, ed., *Fiscal Crisis in American Cities: The Federal Response.* Cambridge, MA: Ballinger, 1979.

Bailey, Robert W. *The Crisis Regime: The MAC, the EFCB, and the Political Impact of the New York City Financial Crisis.* Albany: State University of New York Press, 1984.

Barbanel, Josh. "Another Dinkins Test: The Bond Market." *New York Times.* 2 December 1990.

Barnet, Richard J., and John Cavanagh. *Global Dreams: Imperial Corporations and the New World Order.* New York: Simon & Schuster, 1994.

Barrett, Wayne, and Dan Collins. *Grand Illusion: The Untold Story of Rudy Giuliani and 9/11.* New York: HarperCollins, 2006.

Barsky, Neil. "Back from the Dead: Having hit bottom, New York City begins a slow turnaround—as it prepares for convention, morale and bond rating are up, crime is down—nice party if no one's killed." *Wall Street Journal.* 2 July 1992.

Barsky, Neil, and Constance Mitchell. "New York's Dinkins Pleases Wall Street but Says 'No' to Many Constituencies," *Wall Street Journal.* 14 December 1990.

Bartlett, Sarah. "The Budget Battles: New York Taxes Battle Middle Class." *New York Times.* 2 July 1991.

Bartley, Robert L. "Thinking Things Over: Bloomberg to New York: Drop Dead." *Wall Street Journal.* 19 May 2003.

Beame, Abraham. 2003. Oral History of NYC's Fiscal Crisis. Available at http://www. baruch.cuny.edu/dml/engine.php?action=viewCategoryPage&rootCategory=6.

Bellush, Jewel, and Bernard Bellush. "Collective Bargaining, Leadership and the Fiscal Crisis." Paper delivered at the 1981 Annual Meeting of the American Political Science Association. 3–6 September 1981. New York, NY.

Belsky, Gary. "Woes Mount for City in Coming Bond Sale." *Crain's New York Business.* 3 December 1990.

Bernstein, Blanche. *The Politics of Welfare: The New York City Experience.* Cambridge, MA: Abt Books, 1982.

Berube, Alan, and Bruce Katz. *The State of the English Cities; the State of American Cities.* London: Department for Communities and Local Government, Crown Publications, 2006.

Bigel, Jack. 2003. In Dale Horowitz's, "Oral History of New York City's Fiscal Crisis." http://www.baruch.cuny.edu/dml/engine.php?action=viewCategory Page&rootCategory=6.

Blood, Michael. "City Feds Say WTC Air's OK; Rule Out Health Risk." *Daily News.* 27 October 2001.

———. "N.Y. Press Release: Statement by Mayor Bloomberg about Party Affiliation." June 19, 2007. Available at http://home2.nyc.gov/portal/site/nycgov/ menuitem.c0935b9a57bb4ef3daf2f1c701c789a0/index.jsp?pageID=mayor_ press_release&catID=1194&doc_name=http%3A%2F%2Fhome2.nyc.gov% 2Fhtml%2Fom%2Fhtml%2F2007a%2Fpr205-07.html&cc=unused1978&rc= 1194&ndi=1.

———. "Mayor Bloomberg Presents PlanNYC: A Greener, Greater New York." Press Release April 22, 2007. City of New York. Available at http://www.nyc.gov/portal/site/ nycgov/menuitem.c0935b9a57bb4ef3daf2f1c701c789a0/index.jsp?pageID=mayor_ press_release&catID=1194&doc_name=http%3A%2F%2Fwww.nyc.gov%2Fh tml%2Fom%2Fhtml%2F2007a%2Fpr119-07.html&cc=unused1978&rc=1194 &ndi=1.

———. State of the City Address, 2003. Available at http://www.nyc.gov/ portal/site/nycgov/menuitem.b270a4a1d51bb3017bce0ed101c789a0/index. jsp?pageID=nyc_blue_room&catID=1194&doc_name=http%3A%2F%2Fwww. nyc.gov%2Fhtml%2Fom%2Fhtml%2F2003a%2Fstate_city_2003.html&cc=un used1978&rc=1194&ndi=1.

———. "Message of the Mayor." *NYC's Executive Budget 2003.* New York, 2002.

Bloomberg, Michael R., and Charles E. Schumer. *Sustaining New York's and U.S.' Global Financial Services Leadership.* New York: City of New York.

Blumberg, Barbara. *The New Deal and the Unemployed: The View from New York City.* Cranbury, NJ: Associated University Press, 1979.

Bodack, Sarah F. "Can NYC Prevent Welfare Recipients from Finishing High School?" *Columbia Journal of Law and Social Problems, Inc.* 34 (Winter 2000). http://web. lexis-nexis.com.remote.baruch.cuny.edu/universe/document?_m=dabc8242ded 0f57786075b4db24cbb9d&_docnum=1&wchp=dGLbVtb-zSkVA&_md5=eafa f50a131b7a000d6f983785ba92cd.

Bond Buyer. "A Conversation with John Mitchell Moral Obligation Bonds, the Industry's Old Days, and More. Centennial Edition," 297/28741. 26 September 1991.

Bragdon, Tarren. "From Headache to Migraine? Medicaid Cap Strengthens Need for Remedies in NY." *NY Health Points Policy Briefing, No. 1.* New York: Empire Center for New York State Policy. 15 February 2006.

Brash, Julian. "Invoking Fiscal Crisis: Moral Discourse and Politics in New York City." *Social Text* 76, 21(3):60–83 (2003).

Braun, Martin Z., Michael McDonald, and Ryan McKaig. "A Political Family Affair? Muni Wives Contribute to Northeast Campaigns." *The Bond Buyer*. 21 October 2002.

Burch, Phillip. "The American Establishment." *Research in Political Economy* 6:83–156 (1983).

Buttenwieser, Lawrence, and Eugene J. Keilin. "Letter to the Mayor regarding Financial Plan from the Chair of the Board of Trustees and the Chair of the Budget Policy and Priorities Committee." 1 April 1998. New York: Citizens Budget Commission. http://www.cbcny.org/cbcpubs9399.html.

Cannato, Vincent J. *The Ungovernable City*. New York: Basic Books, 2001.

Cardwell, Diane. "New York to Pay the Poor for Doing the Right Thing." *New York Times*. 30 March 2007.

Carey, Governor Hugh. Address to U.S. Representatives Ways and Means Committee. U.S. Congress, 1975.

Castells, M. *The Information City*. Oxford and Cambridge, MA: Blackwell, 1989.

Cerullo, Alfred C. Memorandum, "Monthly Report," to Randy M. Mastro, Deputy Mayor for Operations 96-05333. November 15, 1996. New York: Municipal Archives.

Chan, Sewell. "Taxed: What Makes New York Different." *New York Times*. 25 February 2007.

Chernow, R. *The House of Morgan: An American Banking Dynasty and the Rise of Modern Finance*. New York: Atlantic Monthly Press, 1990.

Citizens Budget Commission. Statement on the Proposed October Modification of the City of New York's 1995 Budget. New York: Citizens Budget Commission (17 November 1994).

Citizens Budget Commission Quarterly. "Collective Bargaining and Budgeting in New York City," 5(2). New York: Citizens Budget Commission, 1985 Spring.

Clairborne, W. "State May Have to Bail Out New York." *Washington Post*. 22 December 1974.

Clark, Terry, and Lorna Ferguson. *City Money: Political Processes, Fiscal Strain, and Retrenchment*. New York: Columbia University Press, 1983.

Coalition for the Homeless. State of the Homeless 2007: Falling Behind: A Mid-Point Look at the Bloomberg Homeless Plan (2007). Available at http://www.coalitionforthehomeless.org/advocacy/StateoftheHomeless2007.html.

———. "No Advantage: The Bloomberg Administration's Flawed Approach to Family Homelessness." Briefing Paper. 20 July 2007. http://www.coalitionforthe homeless.org/advocacy/No_Advantage.html.

Colangelo, Lisa. "Mike's Hardly Retiring on Bid for Pension Reform." *New York Daily News*. 24 January 2007.

Committee on Banking, Currency, and Housing. *Report on the Intergovernmental Emergency Assistance Act*. 6 November 1975. U.S. House of Representatives, Report 91 632.

Committee on Banking, Finance, and Urban Affairs, House of Representatives. August 1977. *Transactions in Securities of the City of New York*. Washington, DC: Government Printing Office.

Coppie, Comer S. "Annual Budget Review of Financial Control Board," in Ken Auletta's papers. New York Public Library Rare Books and Manuscripts Office, Box 18.2 (11 June 1979).

Correra, E. Mexico and Latin American Countries. Banks and fiscal crisis (2002). Retrieved from http://www.cfeps.org/events/pk2004/confpapers/correa.pdf.

Cox, K. R. "Introduction: Globalization and Its Politics in Question." In K. R. Cox, ed., Governance without Government: Order and Change in World Politics. Cambridge: Cambridge University Press, 1997.

———. "The Local and Global in the New Urban Politics: A Critical View." Environmental and Planning D 11:433–48 (1992).

Crain's New York Business. "City Fails to Meet Expectations in 2002." 7 July 2003.

Croft, Gregory. "NYC Park Advocatees' First Annual State of the Parks Address." 15 June 2006. Available at http://nycparkadvocates.org/stateofparks.

Cuomo, Mario. "Cuomo Assails Efforts to Thwart New Taxes." New York Times. 11 April 1983.

Daily News. "Special Report: Abandoned Heroes, Mayor Must Face WTC Crisis." Available at http://www.nycpba.org/wtc/media/nydn060723.html (23 July 2006).

Damiani, Bettina. Testimony before the U. S. House of Representatives Committee on Homeland Security Subcommittee on Management, Integration, and Oversight (2006). Available at http://www.ctj.org/itep/gjny/testimony_congress_submitted.htm (July 13).

David, Greg. "Taxing Tales: David and Mike." Crain's New York Business. 25 November 2002.

Dembart, Lee. "The Contract Accord: City and Union Both Say They Were Prepared to Settle for Package Transit Workers Sought." New York Times. 6 June 1978.

———. "Lazard, Stun by Koch, Ends M.A.C. Role." New York Times. 8 March 1979.

Digaetano, A., and J. S. Klemanski. "Urban Regime Capacity: A Comparison of Birmington, England, and Detroit, Michigan." Journal of Urban Affairs 15(4): 267–84 (1993).

Dillon, John Forrest. Treatise on the Law of Municipal Corporations of 1872. New York: James Cockcroft, 1872.

Dinkins, David. "New York City Need Not Have Lost Its Major Credit Rating." Editorial, New York Times. 23 July 1995.

———. "Dinkins Proposes Increases in Taxes in His First Budget." New York Times. 25 May 1990.

———. "Excerpts of the Victory Speeches of Dinkins and Koch." New York Times. 14 September 1989.

Domhoff, G. William. The Power Elite and the State. Hawthrone, NY: Aldine de Gruyter, 1990.

———. Power at the Local Level: Growth Coalition Theory. Available at: http://sociology.ucsc.edu/whorulesamerica/power/local.html (April 2005).

Ehrenhalt, S. M. "Economic and Demographic Change: The Case of New York City." Monthly Labor Review. 116: 40–50 (February 1993).

Eisinger, P. K. The Rise of the Entrepreneurial State: State and Local Economic Development Policy in the United States. Madison: University of Wisconsin Press, 1998.

Elkin, S. L. *City and Regime in the American Republic*. Chicago: University of Chicago Press, 1987.

Epstein, V. "S&P Retains Rating; Warns City." *Crain's New York Business*. 11 February 1991.

Fainstein, S. "The Changing World Economy and Urban Restructuring." In Dennis Judd and M.. Parkinson, *Leadership and urban regeneration: Cities in North America and Europe*. London: Sage Publications, 1990.

Feiden, Douglas. "Rudy Kicks off Revolution; Businesses Enlist to Sell Bold Plan." *Crain's New York Business*. 9–12 February 1994.

———. "Criticism from FCB Startles Mayor, May Hurt Campaign."*Crain's New York Business*. 31 May 1993.

Feldstein, Sylvan G., and Frank Fabozzi. *The Dow Jones-Irwin Guide to Municipal Bonds*. Homewood, IL: Dow Jones-Irwin, 1987.

Ferman, Barbara. *Governing the Ungovernable City: Political Skill, Leadership, and the Modern Mayor*. Philadelphia: Temple University Press, 1985.

———. *Challenging the Growth Machine: Neighborhood Politics in Chicago and Pittsburgh*. Kansas City: University Press of Kansas, 1996.

Ferretti, Fred. *The Year the Big Apple Went Bust: The Intimate Blow-by-Blow Account of New York's Financial Follies*. New York: G. P. Putnam's Sons, 1976.

Finch, Peter. "David Dinkins: How's He Doin?" *Business Week*. 18 June 1990.

Finder, Alan. "Political Memo: Dinkins Is Mastering the Art of Being Mayor." *New York Times*. 5 July 1992.

Finney, J. "Welfare Reform and Post-secondary Education: Research and Policy Update." *IWPR Welfare Reform Network News* 2:1 (1998).

Firestone, David. "Giuliani Faces Dip in Support, New Poll Finds." *New York Times*. 5 December 1995.

———. "Giuliani's "Approval" Rating Below 50% in a Second Poll." *New York Times*. 18 April 1995.

———. "Defending Abrasiveness, Giuliani Cites Successes." *New York Times*. 25 June 1995.

Fitch, Robert. *The Assassination of New York*. New York: Vesco, 1993.

Ford, Gerald. R. *A Time to Heal: The Autobiography of Gerald R. Ford*. New York: Harper & Row, 1979.

Forsythe, Dall W. *Memos to the Governor: An Introduction to State Budgeting*. Washington, DC: Georgetown University Press, 1997.

———. "Fixing the Mess: Financial Management after the New York City Fiscal Crisis." Paper delivered at Annual Conference of the ABFM Conference. Available at http://wagner.nyu.edu/faculty/publications/publications.php?fac=405.

Freudenberg, Nicholas, Marianne Fahs, Sandro Galea, and Andrew Greenberg. "The Impact of NYC's 1975 Fiscal Crisis on the Tuberculosis, HIV, and Homicide Syndemic." *American Journal of Public Health*, 96(3):423–34 (2006).

Frug, Gerald. *City Making: Building Communities without Building Walls*. Princeton, NJ: Princeton University Press, 1999.

Fuchs, Ester. "The Future of New York: 1898, 1998." *Fordham Urban Law Journal*, 27 (October 1999). Available at LexisNexis™ Academic.

———. *Mayors and Money: Fiscal Policy in New York and Chicago*. Chicago: University of Chicago Press, 1992.

Fuerbringer, J. "Credit Markets; New York City Set to Sell Bonds." *New York Times.* 20 July 1993.

Gandel, S. "Wall Street Slump Risks '70s Replay." *Crain's New York Business.* 29 July 2002.

Garrett, C. *The LaGuardia Years: Machine and Reform Politics in New York City.* New Brunswick, NJ: Rugters University Press, 1961.

Geist, C. R. *Under Influence: How the Wall Street Elite Put the Financial System at Risk.* New York: John Wiley & Son, 2005.

Gifford, Bernard R. "New York City and Cosmopolitan Liberalism." *Political Science Quarterly* 93/4: 559–84 (Winter 1978–9).

Gittell, Marilyn. *From Welfare to Independence: The College Option, a Report to the Ford Foundation.* New York: Howard Samuels State Management and Policy Center, City University of New York, 1990.

Giuliani, Rudolph. *New York City's Financial Plan.* New York: City of New York (31 January 1996).

———. *Message of the Mayor, NYC's Mayor's Executive Budget Fiscal Year 2000.* New York: City of New York (22 April 1999).

———. Regan lecture. Retrieved from http://www.ci.nyc.ys./html/om/html/99b/reganlibrary.html (30 September 1999).

———. *Message of the Mayor, 1995 Executive Budget of New York.* New York: City of New York, 1994.

———. Remarks of Mayor Rudolph Giuliani at the Real Estate Board of New York. New York: Municipal Archives (June 1995).

Glasberg, David. S. *The Power of Collective Purse Strings: The Effect of Bank Hegemony on Corporations and the State.* Berkeley: University of California, 1989.

Glaser, E. L., and M. E. Kahn. "From John Lindsay to Rudy Giuliani: The Decline of the Local Safety Net?" *FRBNY Economic Policy Review* (1999), 117–31.

Gonzalez, Juan. "Pension 'Crisis' Is a Myth." *New York Times.* 12 January 2006.

Good Jobs First New York. *Report on New York City's Biggest Retention Deals.* Available at http://www.ctj.org/itep/gjny/deals_date.htm.

Good Jobs New York. "Good Jobs New York Releases List of Recipients That Include Giuliani Partners, Ernst & Young, Fox News and News America." Available at http://www.goodjobsny.org/zea_pr.htm.

Goodwin, Michael. "City May Get Up to $1 Billion in MAC in Next Five Years." *New York Times.* 30 October 1983.

Gordon, David L. *Battery Park City: Politics and Planning on the New York Waterfront.* United Kingdom: Gordon and Breach, 1997.

Gotbaum, Victor. *Negotiating in the Real World: Getting the Deal You Want.* New York: Simon & Schuster, 1999.

Gottlieb, Martin. "Behind Rikers Melee: Tensions Wrought by Strain of Change." *New York Times.* 20 August 1990.

———. "After the Conflict at Rikers Island, A War of Words." *New York Times.* 27 August 1990.

Greenhouse, Steven. "The Mayor's Labor Tactics? Think of Giuliani in Reverse." *New York Times.* 29 April 2003.

Greenhouse, Steven, and Jennifer Steinhauer. "City Lays Off 2,000 as Talks Grow Bitter." *New York Times.* 17 May 2003.

Grimes, Christopher. "Ranked Outsider." *Financial Times*. 6 January 2007. http://www.ft.com/cms/s/0f7feae0-9d2b-11db-8ec6-0000779e2340.html.

Haberman, Clyde. "Key Fiscal Goal Reached by City in Big Note Sale." *New York Times*. 18 February 1981.

———. "On Bonds Offered by City Now Favorable." *New York Times*. 6 March 1981.

Hackworth, Jason. "December. Local Autonomy, Bond-Rating Agencies and Neolibreal Urbanism in the United States." *International Journal of Urban and Regional Research*, 26.4 (2002):707–25.

Hanson, Royce, Hal Wolman, David Connolly, and Katherine Pearson. *Corporate Citizenship and Urban Problem Solving: The Changing Civic Role of Business Leaders in American Cities*. Washington, DC: Brookings Institution Metropolitan Policy Program (Summer 2006).

Heckscher, August. *When LaGuardia Was Mayor: New York's Legendary Years*. New York: W. W. Norton, 1978.

Herbert, Robin, et al. "The World Trade Center Disaster and the Health of Workers: Five-Year Assessment of a Unique Medical Screening Program." 2006. Available at http://www.wtcexams.org.

Hevesi, Alan. G. *Comprehensive Annual Financial Report of the Comptroller for the Fiscal Year ended June 30, 2001*. New York: Office of the City Comptroller.

Hevesi, Dennis. "New York City Maintains Its Credit Rating." *New York Times*. 2 May 1992.

Hicks, Jonathan. "The 1993 Campaign: The Incumbent; Dinkins Focuses on Groups He Sees as Crucial." *New York Times*. 2 November 1993.

Horowitz, Dale. Senior Managing Director. Salomon Brothers. Oral History of New York City's Fiscal Crisis, Baruch College, City University of New York, 2003. Available at http://www.baruch.cuny.edu/dml/engine.php?action=viewCategoryPage&rootCategory=6.

Horton, Raymond D. Testimony before the Debt Affordability Hearing. Available at http://www.cbcny.org/testim698.html (3 June 1998).

Hubbard, J. T. W. *For Each, the Strength of All: A History of Banking in the State of New York*. New York: New York University Press, 1995.

IBO Background Paper. "Reviving the New York Stock Transfer Tax: Revenues and Risks." New York: Independent Budget Office (November 2003).

IBO Fiscal Brief. "West Side Financing's Complex, a $1.3 Billion Story." New York: Independent Budget Office (August 2004).

———. "Atlantic Yards: A Net Fiscal Benefit for the City?" New York: Independent Budget Office (September 2005).

IBO Fiscal Outlook. "Despite Economic Downturn, City Still Faces Budget Shortfalls." New York: Independent Budget Office (December 2003).

IBO Inside the Budget. "Confronting the Budget Shortfall: How Bad Are the Gaps," #94. New York: Independent Budget Office (7 January 2002).

IBO Memorandum, "Financing Plan for the Proposed Stadium for the Mets (revised)," from George Sweeting to council Member David I. Weprin. New York: Independent Budget Office (21 April 2006).

Independent Budget Office. "Trends in Revenues." New York: Independent Budget Office. Available at www.ibo.nyc.ny.us.

————. "Spreadsheet on Tax Cuts" from George Sweeting, Deputy Director. New York: Independent Budget Office (February 7, 2007).

————. "IBO's Re-estimate of the Mayor's Preliminary Budget for 2002 and Financial Plan through 2005." New York: Independent Budget Office (2001).

Inman, R. P. "How to Have a Fiscal Crisis: Lessons from Philadelphia." *American Economic Review, Papers & Proceedings*, 85(2): 378–83 (1995).

Jeffers, H. Paul. *The Napoleon of New York: Mayor Fiorello LaGuardia.* New York: John Wiley & Sons, 2002.

Jenkins, Craig, and Craig M. Eckert. "The Right Turn in Economic Policy: Business Elites and the New Conservative Economics." *Sociological Forum*, 15(2), 307–38 (2000).

Jonas, Andrew, and David Wilson. "Introduction." In A. Jonas and D. Wilson, eds., *The City as a Growth Machine: Critical Reflections Two Decades Later.* Albany: State University of New York Press, 1999.

Jordan, Howard. "Not All Black and White." *Gotham Gazette.* Available at http://www.gothamgazette.com/commentary/85.jordan.shtml.

Josephson, Matthew. *Robber Barons.* New York: Harcourt, 1962.

Judd, Dennis R. "Everything is always going to hell: Urban Scholars as End-Times Prophets." *Urban Affairs Review*, 41(2): 119–31 (2005).

Judd, Dennis R., and M. Parkinson, eds. *Leadership and Urban Regeneration: Cities in North America and Europe.* London: Sage Publications, 1990.

Judd, Dennis R., and Todd Swanstrom. *City Politics: The Political Economy of Urban America*, 5th ed. New York: Pearson Education, 2006.

Keilin, Eugene J. "Letter to Mayor Rudolph Giuliani." 11 April 1999. New York: Citizens Budget Commission.

Kheel, Theodore. "Where Is Public Employee Bargaining Heading? Two Experts Give their View." *New York Teacher.* 19 January 1975.

Kiewiet, D. Roderick. *Constitutional Limitations on Indebtedness: The Case of California*, 2003. Available at http://igs.berkeley.edu/library/htConstReform2003-KIEWIETtext.pdf.

King, Michael R., and Timothy J. Sinclair. "Private Actors and Public Policy: A Requiem for the New Basel Capital Accord," *International Political Science Review*, 24(3): 345–62 (2003).

Kirby, Alec. Quoting U.S. Supreme Court Justice Louis Brandeis. Available at http://www.uwstout.edu/faculty/kirbya/.

Koch, Ed. Statement before the Joint Hearings of the Senate Finance and Assembly Ways and Means Committee. In Ken Auletta's Papers at the Rare Book and Manuscripts Office of the New York Public Library, Box 9.11 (9 February 1983).

————. Information Bank Abstracts. *New York Times.* 1 February 1978. Retrieved from http://web.lexis-nexis.com.remote.baruch.cuny.edu/universe/document?_m=26211962f73d9c407f45fa1129c97508&_docnum=2&wchp=dGLbVtb-zSkVb&_md5=6c2180ef7e110b96680d731be86391ad (June 7).

————. *Message of the Mayor.* New York: Office of the Mayor, 1978.

Kramer, Daniel C. *The Days of Wine and Roses Are Over.* New York: University Press of America, 1997.

Krauss, C. "New York's Violent Crime Rate Drops to Lows of 1970s." *New York Times.* 31 December 1995.

Kummerfeld, Donald. D. "Improving the Process for Local Spending Decisions: The New York City Experience." *National Tax Journal*, XXIX (1978).

LaGuardia, Fiorello. Quote from *Liberty Magazine*. 20 May 1933.

Lamb, Robert, and Stephen Rappaport. *Municipal Bonds: The Comprehensive Review of Tax-Exempt Securities and Public Finance*. New York: McGraw-Hill, 1980.

Langan, Patrick A. "The Remarkable Drop in Crime in New York City." Washington, DC: Bureau of Justice Statistics. Paper prepared for the International Conference on Crime, Rome. 3–5 December 2003.

Larkin, G. "New York Debt Past and Present: A Talk with Governor Hugh L. Carey." *The Bond Buyer*. 2 December 2003.

Lasswell, Harold D. *Who Gets What, When, How?* New York: Whittlesey, 1936.

Lawson, Ronald. "Owners of Last Resort: The Track Record of New York City's Early Low-Income Housing Cooperatives Created between 1967 and 1975." *Review of Radical Political Economics*, 30(4): 60–97 (1998).

Lefkkowitz, Stephen. Former UDC Chief Legal Counsel, at a panel discussion, "Origins: How UDC Began." 10 June 2005. Center for Architecture, New York City.

Lehman, Governor Herbert H. Letter to Mayor Fiorello H. LaGuardia. 5 January 1934. New York: Municipal Archives.

Levitan, Mark. "Poverty in New York, 2002: One-Fifth of the City Lives Below the Federal Poverty Line." New York: Community Service Society. 30 September 2003.

———. "Poverty in New York City, 2001: Recession Ends Late Nineties Decline in Poverty Rate." New York: Community Service Society. 26 September 2002.

Levy, Clifford. "Giuliani Spars with Monitors on the Budget." *New York Times*. 10 August 1996.

———. "Dinkins Orders Sharp Budget Cuts to Save New York's Bond Rating." *New York Times*. 3 July 1993.

Liebschutz, Sarah F., Irene Lurie, and Richard W. Small. "How State Responses Confound Federal Policy: Reaganomics and the New Federalism in New York." *Publius*, 13(2): 51–63, The State of American Federalism (Spring 1983).

Liff, Bob. "5-Yr. Pact Gets City, Union Nod." *Daily News*. 18 November 1995.

Liff, Bob, and J. Siegel. "Bonds: Rescue or Ruin." *New York Times*. 13 January 1996.

Lipietz, Alain. *Mirages and Miracles: The Crises of Global Fordism*. London: Verso, 1987.

Lipton, E. "The Mayor's Budget Proposal: Debt; New Bond Issue Is a Step That Pleases No One." *New York Times*. 14 February 2002.

Logan, John R., and Harvey L. Molotch. "The City as Growth Machine." In S. S. Fainstein and S. Campbell, eds., *Readings in Urban Theory*. Oxford: Blackwell, 2002.

———. *Urban Fortunes: The Political Economy of Place*. Berkeley,: University of California Press, 1987.

Lombardi, F. "Firm Won't Lower City Bond Rating." *Daily News*. 13 March 2002.

———. "Mike Nixes Plea to Boost Taxes." *New York Times*. 1 March 2002.

Lynn, Frank. Mayor Dinkins: An Era Begins, with a Little Fun. *New York Times*. 2 January 1990.

MAC Presentation to the Honorable G. William Miller, Secretary of the Treasury. 1980. New York: Municipal Assistance Corporation for the City of New York. Retrieved from http://newman.baruch.cuny.edu/digital/2003/amfl/mac/pdf_files/ Economic_Reports/09-10-80.pdf (September 10).

Malanga, S. *Business Leadership in Gotham*. Retrieved from http://www.city-journal. org/html/eon_4_11_03sm.html (Summer 2004).

Mann, Arthur. *LaGuardia Comes to Power 1933*. Chicago: University of Chicago Press, 1965.

Martin, Matthew R. "Did Tax Reform Kill Segmentation in the Municipal Bond Market?" *Public Administration Review*, 54/4 (July/August 1994): 387–90.

Mauro, Frank, and Glenn Yago. "State Government Targeting in Economic Development: The New York Experience." *Publius*, 19(2):63–82 (1989).

Mayor's Executive Budget 1995. *Message of the mayor*. New York: City of New York.

McKinley, James C., Jr. "Control Board Assails Dinkins 4-Year Fiscal Plan." *New York Times*. 19 December 1991.

———. "Dinkins Shifts on Fiscal Plan under Pressure." *New York Times*. 14 November 1991.

———. "Dinkins Administration Acknowledges Need for Cuts." *New York Times*. 26 May 1993.

McMichael, Philip. *Development and Social Change: A Global Perspective*. Thousand Oaks, CA: Pine Forge Press, 1996.

Mead, Dean M. Memo to Budget Policy and Priorities Committee of the CBC from Dean Mead, "The City of New York's January 1998 Financial Plan." New York: Citizens Budget Commission (24 March 1998).

Meislin, Richard J. "For MAC, Money Talks: Using Surplus Again for Monetary Clout." *New York Times*. 30 July 1987.

Messinger, Ruth. 2007. Quoted in Strober and Strober, *Giuliani, Flawed or Flawless? The Oral Biography*. New York: John Wiley & Sons, 2007.

Mintz, Beth, and Michael Schwartz. *The Power Structure of American Business*. Chicago: University of Chicago Press, 1985.

Mitchell, A. "New York City's Undying Deficit: Slash It, and It Just Grows Back." *New York Times*. 17 January 1995.

Mitrisin, J. *Emergency Federal Financial Assistance to Private Enterprise: A Selective Examination of Past Loan and Loan Guarantee Programs of the Federal Government*. Washington, DC: Economics Division, Congressional Research Service, United States Library of Congress. 28 November 1974.

Mizruchi, M. S., and G. F. Davis. "The Globalization of American Banking, 1962– 1981." In Frank Dobbin, ed., *The Sociology of the Economy*. New York: Russell Sage, 2004.

Mollenkopf, John. *The Phoenix in the Ashes: The Rise and Fall of the Koch Coalition in New York City Politics*. Princeton, NJ: Princeton University Press, 1992.

Mollenkopf, John, and Manuel Castells, eds. *Dual City: Restructuring New York*. New York: Sage, 1991.

Morris, C. R. *Money, Greed, and Risk: Why Financial Crises and Crashes Happen*. New York: Random House, 1999.

———. "Wall Street Can't Save New York." *Wall Street Journal*. 8 July 1993.

Mossberger Karen, and Gerry Stoker. "The Evolution of Urban Regime Change: The Challenge of Conceptualization." *Urban Affairs Review*, 36 (2001), 6:810–35.

Mouat, Lucia. "New York's Dinkins Plows Ahead." *Christian Science Monitor*. 10 April 1990.

Moynihan, Daniel. P. Introduction: "Routinely Shortchanged." *Fortune*. 28 April 1997. www.ksg.harvard.edu/taubmancenter/pdfs/fisc/intro_96.pdf.

————. Letter to the President, 4 January 1978.

Myers, S. L. "For Giuliani, Current Budget Woes Overtake Future's." *New York Times*. 28 January 1996.

————. "Mayor Sees More Cuts If Rate Plan Fails." *New York Times*. 13 January 1996.

————. "Giuliani Outlines a Budget to Cut Government Size." *New York Times*. 3 February 1994.

————. "Giuliani Proposes $800 Million More in Spending Cuts." *New York Times*. 26 October 1994.

Netzer, Dick. "The Economy and the Governing of the City." In Jewel Bellush and Dick Netzer, eds., *Urban Politics New York Style*. Armonk, NY: M.E. Sharpe, 1990.

————. "Innovations in Public Finance." In Gerald Benjamin and T. Normal Hurd, eds., *Rockefeller in Retrospect: The Governor's New York Legacy*. Albany, NY: The Nelson A. Rockefeller Institute of Government, 1984.

Nevarez, L. *New Money, Nice Town: How Capital Works in the New Urban Economy*. New York: Routledge, 2003.

Nevins, Allan. *Study in Power: John D. Rockefeller, Industrialist and Philanthropist*, 2 vols. New York: Scribner's, 1953.

New York City Office of the Comptroller. *Annual Comprehensive Financial Reports*. Fiscal Years 1972 to 2006. New York: Office of the Comptroller.

New York City Planning Commission. Appendix Table 5-1 and 5-3. http://www.nyc. ov/html/dcp/html/census/nny_appendix.shtml.

New York State. *The Local Government Handbook*, 5th ed. Department of State. New York: New York State, 2000.

New York State Bureau of Labor Services. 1976 to 2006. Total Employed, Local Area Unemployment Statistics Program, not seasonally adjusted. http://www. labor.state.ny.us/workforceindustrydata/laus_pr. asp?reg=nys&geog=21093561 New%20York%20City.

New York State Special Deputy Comptroller. "Review of NYC's Financial Plan, Fiscal Years 1998 through 2001," 2 July 1997. New York: NYS Special Deputy Comptroller.

New York Times. "The Mayor's Censorship Office." Editorial Desk. 24 February 1995.

————. "Cold Comfort for the Mayor." Editorial Desk. 27 April 1995.

————. "The 1993 Campaign: The Race for Mayor, the Candidates in Their Own Words." 1 November 1993.

————. "Mayor Dinkins, Finally on Track." Editorial. 9 November 1990.

————. The 1989 Elections; Excerpts from Speech by Dinkins, a New Link. 8 November 1989.

————. "The Mayor." Editorial. 8 November 1989.

————. "From 1975 to Now, How's New York City Doing." 10 April 1983.

————. "Questions and Answers on City's Bonds." 14 December 1974.

Newfield, Jack. "The Full Rudy: The Man, the Mayor, the Myth, the Nation." 17 June 2002. Available at http://www.thenation.com/doc/20020617/newfield.

Newfield, Jack, and Paul DuBrul. *The Permanent Government. Who Really Rules New York?* New York: Pilgrim Press, 1981.

NYCLU News. "NYCLU and *New York Times* Fight Secrecy of NYPD's Unlawful Spying Program." New York Civil Liberties Union, Spring 2007.

Office of the Mayor. 1979–2006. *New York City Mayor's Executive Budgets, Fiscal Years 1979–2006.* New York: Office of the Mayor.

Opp, Kevin. "Ending Pay-to-Play in the Municipal Securities Business: MSRB Rule G-27 Ten Years Later." *Colorado Law Review.* 243 (2005). Available at http://web.lexisnexis.com.remote.baruch.cuny.edu/universe/document?_m=722fcdf5 1110225c6df00cea19cc0491&_docnum=28&wchp=dGLbVlzzSkVA&_md5= ac1113f0262c7c4efcb8f100997effd5.

Parkinson, Michael, and Dennis Judd. "Urban Revitalization in America and the U.K.—the Politics of Uneven Development." In M. Parkinson, B. Foley, and D. Judd, eds., *Regenerating the Cities: The U.K. Crisis and the U.S. Experience.* Manchester, England: Manchester University Press, 1988.

Partnership of New York City. Available at http://www.nycp.org/history.html.

Pasanen, Glenn. "Property Tax Reform—NOT." 2007 January. Available at http://www.gothamgazette.com/article/finance/20070111/8/2076.

————. "Mixed News in a 'Good News' Budget." 2007 October. Available at http://www.gothamgazette.com/article/finance/20070712/8/2227.

————. "Tax Breaks—Who Wins and Who Loses," 2008 February. Available at http://www.gothamgazette.com/print/2426.

Perez-Pena, Richard. "Giuliani Will Miss Firefighters' Gathering." *New York Times.* 14 March 2007.

Persico, Joseph E. *The Imperial Rockefeller: A Biography of Nelson A. Rockefeller.* New York: Simon & Schuster, 1982.

Peterson, P. *City Limits.* Chicago: University of Chicago Press, 1981.

Preston, Darrell. New York to Sell Debt in Week's Biggest Municipal Issue. 2 February 2006. Available at http://www.bloomberg.com/apps/news?pid=newsarchive& sid=aa2lkgnW1v0U.

Proxmire, William. "Information Abstract Banks." *New York Times.* 7 June 1978.

Purdum, Todd. "The Dinkins Budget Is a Long Way from the Bottom Line." *New York Times.* 20 January 1991.

————. "Feinstein Says Use of Control Board Deserves Study." *New York Times.* 8 December 1991.

————. "Dinkins's Year: Dreams Delayed by Fiscal Slump." *New York Times.* 26 December 1990.

————. Credit Agency Urges Mayor to Ready More Budget Cuts. *New York Times.* 14 November 1990.

Quindlen, Anna. "City Deficit Forecasts Termed Short." *New York Times.* 10 December 1979.

Quinnipiac Poll. "Race Is Key Factor in New Yorkers' View of Mayor." 2 August 2000. Available at http://www.quinnipiac.edu/x1302.xml?ReleaseID=634.

Rae, Douglas W. *City Urbanism and Its End*. New Haven: Yale University Press, 2003.

Ranney, David. *Global Decisions, Local Collisions: Urban Life in the New World Order*. Philadelphia: Temple University Press, 2003

Rattner, Steve. "What New York Will Have to Give Up." *New York Times*. 28 November 2001.

Reich, Alexander. J. *Reconstructing Times Square: Politics and Culture in Urban Development*. Lawrence: University Press of Kansas, 1999.

Rich, Wilbur. *David Dinkins and New York City Politics*. Albany: State University of New York Press, 2007.

Richards, Leonard. *Shay's Rebellion: The American Revolutions Final Battle*. Philadelphia: University of Pennsylvania Press, 2003.

Richardson, C. "Activists Rush for School. They Champion Law that Benefits Students on Welfare." *Daily News*. 6 November 2000.

Ritter, John. "Tough Lessons in Welfare Reform." *USA Today*. 17 February 1997.

Roach. S. "The Dilemmas of Fiscal Policy Making in New York City: 1978–1996." Baruch College Honors Theses, 2000. Available at http://newman.baruch.cuny.edu/digital/2000/honors/roach_1996/roach_1996.htm#table_1.

Roberts, Sam."Giuliani Seeks Funds for New Buyout." *New York Times*. 30 September 1994.

———. "Metro Matters; Focus of Scrutiny: How Dinkins Outdraws Cuomo." *New York Times*. 11 March 1991.

———. "Mayor Dinkins: Every Day a Test." *New York Times*. 7 April 1991.

———. "A Credit Expert Who Rates High at Budget Time." *New York Times*. 20 December 1990.

Robinson, William I. *A Theory of Global Capitalism: Production, Class and State in a Transnational World*. Baltimore, MD: John Hopkins University Press, 2004.

Rockefeller, David. *Memoirs*. New York: Random House, 2003.

Rockefeller, Nelson. Quoted in Joseph E. Persico. 1982. *The Imperial Rockefeller: A Biography of Nelson A. Rockefeller*. New York: Simon & Schuster, 1982.

Rohatyn, Felix. M. Moran Weston II Distinguished Lecture in Urban and Public Policy. Given at Columbia University, School of International and Public Affairs, New York. 26 February 2003.

———. "Fiscal Disaster the City Can't Face Alone." *New York Times*. 9 October 2001.

Rosen, Hy, and Peter Slocum. *From Rocky to Pataki: Character and Caricatures in New York Politics*. New York: Syracuse University Press, 1998

Rosenthal, E. "Mayor's Stalled Plans Leave Public Hospitals in Trauma." *New York Times*. 24 May 1996.

Rubin, Irene. *Class, Tax, and Power: Municipal Budgeting in the United States*. Chatham, NJ: Chatham House, 1998.

Sampson, A. *The Money Lenders: Bankers and a World in Turmoil*. New York: Viking, 1982.

Sassen, Saskia. "Economic Restructuring and the American City." *Annual Review Sociology*, 16 (1990): 465–90.

Saul, Michael, "Mike: Unions Don't Deserve a Bigger Piece of the Pie." *Daily News*. 10 January 2004.

Savas, E. S. *Privatization in the City: Successes, Failures and Lessons*. Washington, DC: CQ Press, 2005.

Savitch, H. V., and Paul Kantor. *Cities in the International marketplace: The Political Economy of Urban Development in North America and Western Europe*. Princeton: Princeton University Press. 2002.

Sayre, Wallace S., and Herbert Kaufman. *Governing New York City: Politics in the Metropolis*. New York: W. W. Norton, 1965.

Sbragia, Alberta M. *The Municipal Money Chase: The Politics of Local Government Finance*. Boulder, CO: Westview Press, 1983.

———. *Debt Wish: Entrepreneurial Cities, U.S. Federalism, and Economic Development*. Pittsburgh: University of Pittsburgh Press, 1996.

Schaller, Bruce. The Fare Hike Mess. *Gotham Gazette*. 28 April 2003. http://www.gothamgazette.com/article//20030428/200/361.

Schmalz, Jeffrey. "Assembly Chief Leads Attack on Koch." *New York Times*. 11 February 1988.

Schwartz, Allen G. Oral History (2000), Columbia Oral History Project, Box 3-130.

Schwartz, Richard. Ensuring the Success of the Agency Advisory Group Program (March 1994), Box, 02/07/001, Folder 0004. New York: Municipal Library Archives.

Shalala, Donna. Quotation from classroom lecture. New York: Teachers College, Columbia University, 21 October 1976.

Shalala, Donna, and Carol Bellamy. "A State Saves a City: The New York Case. Symposium on Municipal Finance." *Duke Law Journal*, 6 (1976): 1119–32.

Shefter, Martin. *Political Crisis, Fiscal Crisis: The Collapse and Revival of New York City*. New York: Columbia University Press, 1992.

Shiffman, Ron. "Atlantic Yards: Staving Off a Scar for Decades. *Develop—Don't Destroy Brooklyn*." Position Papers (3 June 2006). Available at http://dddb.net/php/reading/shiffman.php.

Siegel, J. "City Tries to Sell a $31.1B Budget." *New York Times*. 15 June 1995.

———. "City Hit with Cut in Its Bond Rating." *New York Times*. 11 July 1995.

———. "McCall Aims at Budget Quick Fixes." *New York Times*. 26 December 1995.

———. "The Kindest Cuts of All: 31b Won't Hurt, Rudy Says." *New York Times*. 1 February 1996.

Sinclair, Timothy J. *The New Masters of Capital: American Bond Rating Agencies and the Politics of Creditworthiness*. Ithaca, NY: Cornell University Press, 2005.

Sites, W. *Remaking New York: Primitive Globalization and the Politics of Urban Community*. Minneapolis: University of Minnesota Press, 2003

———. "Primitive Globalization? State and Locale in Neoliberal Global Engagement." *Sociological Theory* 18(1) (2000): 121–24.

Smith, Adam. *Wealth of Nations*, Book IV–V, chapter I, part II. London: Penguin, 1776.

Smith, Jean. E. *John Marshall: Definer of a Nation*. New York: Henry Holt, 1996.

Smothers, Ronald. "Koch Invites Direct Pressure by Financial Control Board." *New York Times*. 16 October 1979.

———. "7% Raise for City Workers Is Unaffordable, Says Koch." *New York Times*. 13 December 1979.

Stanfield, Rochelle L. "Federal Aid Comes Out of the Closet in the Mountains and Desert West." *National Journal*, 2098–2110 (15 December 1979). In A. M.

Sbragia, *The Municipal Money Chase: The Politics of Local Government Finance.* Boulder, CO: Westview Press, 1983.

Steinhauer, Jennifer. "Building a Name as an Advocate for Public Health." *New York Times.* 4 May 2004.

———. "Short on Political Capital, Mayor Invites President to Fund-Raiser at his Home." *New York Times.* 24 January 2002.

Steinhauer, J., and M. Connelly. "In Poll, Pessimism from New Yorkers Rubs Off on Mayor." *New York Times.* 13 June 2003.

Stoker, G. "Regime Theory and Urban Politics." In David Judge, Gerry Stoker, & Harold Wolman, eds., *Theories of Urban Politics.* Thousand Oaks, CA: Sage, 1995.

Stone, Clarence N. "Rethinking the Policy—Politics Connection." *Policy Studies,* 26(3/4) (2005), 241–60.

———. Reviewed Work: *Cities in the International Marketplace: The Political Economy of Urban Development in North America and Western Europe* by H. V. Savitch; Paul Kantor. *The Journal of Politics,* 66 (November 2004), 4:1323–24.

———. "Political Leadership in Urban Politics." In David Judge, Gerry Stoker, and Harold Wolman, eds.,*Theories of Urban Politics.* London: Sage, 1995.

———. "Urban Regimes and the Capacity to Govern: A Political Economy Approach." *Journal of Urban Affairs,*15 (1993), 1: 1–28.

———. *Regime Politics: Governing Atlanta, 1946–1988.* Lawrence: University Press of Kansas, 1989.

———. "Systemic Power in Community Decision Making." *American Political Science Review,* 74 (December 1980), 978–90.

Strober, Deborah Hart, and Gerald Strober. *Giuliani: Flawed or Flawless, The Oral Biography.* New York: John Wiley & Sons, 2007.

Subcommittee on Economic Stabilization. *Staff Memorandum on NYC's Progress under the NYC Seasonal Financing Act of 1975* (P.L. 94–143). Committee on Banking, Currency and Housing. Washington, DC: U.S. House of Representatives. 20 July 1976.

Sullivan, Neil J. *The Diamond in the Bronx: Yankee Stadium and the Politics of New York.* New York: Oxford University Press, 2001.

Sweeting, George. Revised Letter to Council Member David Weprin and the City Council Finance Committee Member Hiram Monserrate (21 April 2006). Available at http://www.ibo.nyc.ny.us/.

Tabb, William. K. *Economic Governance in the Age of Globalization.* New York: Columbia University Press, 2004

Thompson, J. Phillip, III. *Double Trouble: Black Mayors, Black Communities, and the Call for a Deep Democracy.* Oxford: Oxford University Press, 2006.

Thompson, William. "Letter to the Mayor from the Comptroller of the City of New York." 20 October 2004. New York, NY.

Tiebout, C. "A Pure Theory of Local Expenditures." *Journal of Political Economy* 64:416–424 (1956).

Tierney, John. "The Holy Terror." *New York Times.* 3 December 1995.

Townsend, Alair A. "Albany Vote on Police Contracts Helps Turn the City into Road Kill." *Crain's New York Business.* 19 February 1996.

———. "In Squabbles for Control, Rudy Must Act Like Mayor." *Crains New York Business.* 7–13 March 1994.

———. "Piece by Piece city slides back into Big Fiscal Hold." 25 January 1993. *Crain's New York Business.*

Tribe, Lawrence. *American Constitutional Law,* Volume 1, 3rd ed. Eagan, MN: West, 2000.

Turner, Frederick Jackson. *Rise of the New West, 1819–1829.* New York: Harper & Brothers, 1906.

Turner, Robyne S. "Intergovernmental Growth Management: A Partnership Framework for State-Local Relations." *Publicus,* 20C32: 79–96, 1990.

U.S. Bureau of the Census. 1960 and 1970. Table S2. Median Family Income by State and Population by State and Counties. Washington, DC: Census Bureau.

———. SOCDS Data: Output for New York, NY. Available http://socds.huduser. org/Census/incpov.odb?msacitylist=5600.0*3600051000*1.0&metro=msa.

U.S. Department of Commerce. Bureau of Economic Analysis. Available at http://www.bea.gov/regional/index.htm#gsp.

Vallone, Peter. *Learning to Govern: My Life in New York Politics, From Hell Gate to City Hall.* New York: Chaucer Press, 2005.

Vojnovic, I. "Governance in Houston: Growth Theories and Urban Pressures." *Journal of Urban Affairs,* 25 (2003), 589–624.

Wallace, Roderick. "Fire Service Productivity and New York City Fire Crisis: 1968–1979." *Human Ecology,* 9(4) (1981): 433–64.

Wall Street Journal. "Dinkins team says no to stock tax." 12 September 1990.

Walsh, Annmarie Hauck. *The Public's Business: The Politics and Practices of Government Corporations.* Cambridge: MIT Press, 1978.

Waters, Tom, and Victor Bach. *Closing the Door 2007: The Shape of Subsidized Housing Loss in New York City. New York: Community Service Society, 2007.*

Weikart, Lynne. "Follow the Money: Mayoral Choice and Expenditure Policy." *American Review of Public Administration,* 33(2), 209–32 (2003).

———. *Decision Making and the Impact of Those Decisions during NYC's Fiscal Crisis in the Public Schools, 1975–77.* Dissertation. New York: Columbia University, 1983.

Weiss, Lois. "Dinkins' Promises Preliminary (New York, New York Mayor David N. Dinkins Proposes Tax Relief for Real Estate Industry at State of the City Address)." 13 January 1993. New York: Real Estate Weekly.

Wesalotemel, J. *The Fundamentals of Municipal Bonds,* 5th ed. The Bond Market Association. New York: John Wiley & Sons, 2001.

Wolff, Guntram. B. *Fiscal Crises in U.S. Cities: Structural and Non-Structural Causes.* Bonn: Center for European Integrative Studies. August 2004. Available at www.zei.de/download/zei_wp/B04-28.pdf.

World Trade Center Disaster Site Litigation, #21 MC 100(AKH), 03 Civ.00007 et al. 17 October 2006. 456 F. Supp.2d 520.

Wynter, Leon E. "Dinkins' Win: Gladness Tinged with Sadness." *Wall Street Journal.* 9 November 1989. Available at http://global.factiva.com.remote.baruch.cuny. edu/ha/default.aspx.

Zimmerman, Dennis. *The Private Use of Tax-Exempt Bonds: Controlling Public Subsidy of Private Activity.* Washington, DC: Urban Institute Press, 1991.

Zimmerman, Joseph F. "The Development of Local Discretionary Authority in New York." *Publius: The Journal of Federalism* 13 Winter, 89–103 (1983).

INDEX

Abate, Catherine M., 70
Adams, Floyd, 106
African Americans, 106; and Mayor
Bloomberg, 114, 120, 133, 140; and
Mayor Dinkins, 63, 70, 75, 85; and
Mayor Giuliani, 88, 133; and Mayor
Koch, 50, 88; population, 4
Agency Advisory Group Program, 94
Alder, Coleman & Company, 42
Alequin, Rafael Martinez, 131
Allen & Company, 65
Altman, Roger C., 69
American Airlines, 44
American Federation of State, County,
and Municipal Employees, 41, 44
American Revolutions: first, 1; second,
1, 135; third, 1, 135, 136
Anders, Alan, 114
Andersen, Arthur, 106
Arabs, 30, 45, 154n. 4
Arrick, Martin, 105
Arthur Young & Company, 42
Assassination of New York, The, 17
Atlantic Yards, 124
Attica Prison, 9

Badillo, Herman, 91
Bahl, Roy, 35
Bailey, Robert, 40
Bank Act of 1933, 8–9
Bank Holdings Act, 11
Bank of America, 45, 124, 134
Bank of New York, 124
bankruptcy, 41, 45, 46, 137
banks: Arab use of American, 154n.
4; commercial, 4, 8–9, 11, 50–51,
152nn. 9, 14; and elected officials,

136–37; globalization of, 26, 30–31,
37, 45, 46; and Great Depression,
8; investment, 4, 11, 152n. 9; jobs
in, 64; and MAC bonds, 43; and
Mayor Beame, 40–42, 47; and 1975
fiscal crisis, 30–31; and public policy
decisions, 143; state, 9
Barry, Francis, 42
Baruch College, School of Public
Affairs, 97
Baruch, Bernard, 140
Battery Park City Authority, 33, 53,
108, 157n. 13
Beacon program, 82
Beame, Abe, 4; and the banking
community, 40–42, 136; on David
Dinkins, 64; and David Rockefeller,
40–41; and EFCB, 43–44; and FEA,
43–44; and federal loans, 44–47; and
financial elites, 139; and "gang of
four," 42; and Governor Carey, 43–
44; and labor unions, 41–42, 44, 51,
139; layoffs, 2, 43, 46; and MAC,
42–44, 47; and MAC bonds, 42–44;
and 1975 fiscal crisis, 39–48; and
President Ford, 45–46; and revenues,
39–40, 40 table 5.1; and sanitation
workers, 45; and taxes, 15
Bear Stearns, 12, 108, 119, 134
Bendix Corporation, 53
benefits, 128
Bensonhurst murder, 63
Bernstein, Blanche, 50
Bigel, Jack, 41
"Black Monday," 65
block grants, 50
Bloomberg L. P., 108, 113

183